# HERBS & SPICES
## Cookbook

# HERBS & SPICES
## Cookbook

## Margaret Roberts

SOUTHERN
BOOK PUBLISHERS

ISBN 1 86812 483 5

First edition, first impression 1988
Second edition, first impression 1993

Published by
Southern Book Publishers (Pty) Ltd
PO Box 3103, Halfway House 1685

Illustrations by Rita Weber
Photographs by Andrzej Sawa
Phototypesetting by Book Productions, Pretoria
Printed and bound by National Book Printers,
Goodwood, Cape

*For gardeners, for cooks, for the health-conscious —*
*for all who want a wholesome way of eating*

# Acknowledgements

RECIPE FOR AN UNUSUAL COOKERY BOOK

### Ingredients

2 good cooks: *Maureen Engelbrecht*, assistant, demonstrator, versatile organiser, untiring supporter at the Herbal Centre; winner of several baking and cookery awards; and *Joey Patterson*, B.Sc. Home Economics, lecturer and experienced teacher, who willingly shared her knowledge and put all her energy into the preparation of the dishes for this book.

1 botanical artist, *Rita Weber*, with talent and enthusiasm, who worked quickly and happily and who grew to love herbs.

2 editors: *Sally Antrobus*, General Books Editor, who guided and planned; and *Catherine Murray*, my copy editor, whose eye to detail, and whose long hours of tidying up and reorganising bulky manuscripts have shaped and trimmed the mixture to a palatable whole.

1 remarkable friend, who was willing to constantly drive long distances for ingredients and utensils, and who helped and supported, encouraged and cared for all of us.

1 typist, *Rosemary Miller*, whose patience and hard work were very much appreciated.

1 publishing house, incorporating a team of friendly, supportive people like *Madeline Munnik*, the Publishing Services Controller, who was able to tie up loose ends.

1 discerning Publishing Director, *Basil van Rooyen*, who had faith in the finished dish.

1 competent and experienced designer and layout artist, *Peter Sauthoff*, who served it all to perfection.

10 kg energy

1 or 2 cups interest

A small team of willing helpers – studio kitchen and garden staff at the Herbal Centre who ran, cleaned and washed up, fetched and carried and were still able to smile graciously.

1 prolific herb garden

Seasoning: good humour

## *Method*

Mix together in a large demonstration kitchen the cooks, the baskets of herbs and spices and the other ingredients. Add the constant help and support of the good friend. Blend well. Add the cup or two of interest, the 10 kg of energy, and season with laughter.

Fold in the editors and stir in the rest of the team at the publishing house. When nicely mixed and almost done, give it to the designer for the final arrangement of ingredients.

Pour into a large publishing house, and bake in a moderate to hot oven until well done.

Decorate with the excellent line drawings and photographs and sprinkle with my deepest gratitude.

Serve in a tasteful cover, and distribute all over the country!

# Preface

This is not just another cookery book. Not just another collection of recipes, not just another fad diet, and not just another look at boring ways of serving boring dishes. This book is different.

When Jonathan Ball invited me to his office to discuss this book, his injunction was 'I don't want just another cookery book – this one must show why herbs and spices are important in the diet.' Those words gave me all the encouragement I needed. I immediately set to work, dredging up the recipes I have used and enjoyed in the 24 years of living on a farm and cooking for my family, using ingredients that were readily available, fresh, organically grown, seasonal and inexpensive.

Many people ask me how my interest in herbs began, and if I think back I realise that it all started with my interest in healing and the medicinal and nutritional uses of natural ingredients – something I was thrust into by my eldest child's allergies and illnesses.

Living on a farm in my early years of child rearing with doctors many miles away, I was forced to use my medical training as a physiotherapist to the full. My sick little boy was in and out of hospital, one course of antibiotics after another was pumped into him and one specialist after another was visited. I slept anxiously listening for croupy coughs, and woke anxiously fearing the day and the struggle it would bring to look after him. There was no one to turn to for help or guidance.

I read avidly all I could lay my hands on about health and right eating, but in those days books on the subject were few. I watched over all my children anxiously and worried desperately as the winters took their toll. The bitter winds that swept across the valley filled me with dread as colds turned into pneumonia. Then, when my children's health was at its worst, my work as a physiotherapist at the hospital gave me the chance to talk to doctors, and I discovered the basic truth, 'You are what you eat'. With the guidance of a most deep-thinking paediatrician, I set about cultivating organically – no sprays, no fertilizers – a vegetable garden from which we lived.

I threw out every tinned, preserved, refined, fast-food ingredient from my pantry. I replaced sugar with honey from the farm; white rice with brown. I had our own home-grown wheat milled at a nearby mill; I baked my own bread; made my own butter, yoghurt and cream cheese from the milk from our Friesland herd. I eased meat out of our diets (although we were cattle farmers!) and I never allowed instant foods, carbonated drinks, condiments or junk foods into my kitchen again.

I was thought to be quite odd, and my cooking extraordinary! But, strangely enough, the endless visitors to the farm began to enjoy my coarsely ground mealie meal – made from farm mealies – with honey and yoghurt for breakfast. They raved about my brown health loaves, and spread my home-made butter and fruit purées – made with fruit from the garden – with relish. My thick vegetable soups and wholewheat scones were food for the gods, they said. And the flavouring! Where were the ketchup, the bottled sauce, the instant powdered dressing and thickener for the succulent gravies? I would explain that those glorious tastes came from my little patch of herbs. And one by one I taught them how to make herb salts, herb butters, herb sauces and vinegars, and showed them how to get every ounce of goodness out of raw, fresh fruit and vegetables, and even garden weeds. I began to see Peter growing tall and strong and all the children getting glowing skins, clear eyes, perfect teeth and shining hair. As I watched them develop into beautiful, healthy adults, I knew I'd won! My herbs, my organically grown vegetables, my stand for health and self-sufficiency – we'd won!

So, as you turn these pages and come with me down my kitchen garden path, fill your basket with a snip of thyme, pick a bunch of chives, pull out a few radishes, a sprig of mint, a leaf or two of basil and let me show you how to combine your garden-fresh pickings into healthy, delicious and satisfying meals.

Because I am not satisfied with reaching just a few friends, to help them to get a new perspective on healthy eating, I recently developed the only health cookery school not only in South Africa, but in the southern hemisphere. Students come here for day workshops, lectures and demonstrations on how to cook for specific ailments. In this way my circle of healthy friends extends wider and wider, and my quest for healthy eating reaches into many lives. With the help of this book, my greatest dream – of a healthy South Africa – may even become reality. At very least, my hope is that you, the reader, will develop a new lifestyle in which health will be the order of the day. *Bon appetite!*

# Contents

## THE COOK'S NOTES

## THE COOK'S GARDEN

## NATURE'S MEDICINES

# Useful Information

Quantities given in this book are in the form of cups, tablespoons and teaspoons, and the approximate equivalents for these in millilitres are given below. Solid weights are given in kilograms and grams with larger liquid quantities in litres. Most cooks have become acquainted with these, but the conversion tables below give their approximate imperial equivalents.

## Equivalent Measures (approximate)

| | | | | | | |
|---|---|---|---|---|---|---|
| $\frac{1}{8}$ t | = | 0,5 ml | | $\frac{1}{2}$ c | = | 125 ml |
| $\frac{1}{4}$ t | = | 1 ml | | $\frac{3}{4}$ c | = | 187 ml |
| $\frac{1}{2}$ t | = | 2,5 ml | | 1 c | = | 250 ml |
| 1 t | = | 5 ml | | $1\frac{1}{2}$ c | = | 375 ml |
| $1\frac{1}{2}$ t | = | 7,5 ml | | $\frac{2}{5}$ c | = | 100 ml |
| $\frac{1}{2}$ T | = | 6 ml | | $\frac{4}{5}$ c | = | 200 ml |
| 1 T | = | 12,5 ml | | $1\frac{1}{4}$ c | = | 312 ml |
| $\frac{1}{4}$ c | = | 62 ml | | $2\frac{1}{2}$ c | = | 625 ml |

## Metric / Imperial Equivalent Measures

| Metric | Imperial |
|---|---|
| **Capacity** | |
| 150 ml | $\frac{1}{4}$ pint |
| 300 ml | $\frac{1}{2}$ pint |
| 600 ml | 1 pint |
| $\frac{1}{2}$ litre | 0,88 pints |
| 1 litre | $1\frac{3}{4}$ pints |
| | |
| **Weight** | |
| 25 g | 1 oz |
| 50 g | 2 oz |
| 100 g | 4 oz |
| 225 g | 8 oz |
| 350 g | 12 oz |
| 450 g | 1 lb |
| 1 kg | $2\frac{1}{4}$ lb |

**Length**

| | |
|---|---|
| 2,5 cm | 1 in |
| 15 cm | 6 in |
| 30,5 cm | 12 in |
| 1 m | 3 ft 3 in |

# Oven Temperatures

| | °C | °F | Gas Mark |
|---|---|---|---|
| Very slow | 120 | 250 | ½ |
| Slow | 150 | 300 | 1 |
| Moderately slow | 160 | 325 | 2 |
| Moderate | 180 | 350 | 3 |
| Moderately hot | 190 | 375 | 4 |
| Hot | 200 – 220 | 400 – 425 | 5 – 6 |
| Very hot | 230 – 260 | 450 – 500 | 7 – 9 |

# Abbreviations

| | |
|---|---|
| l | litre |
| ml | millilitre |
| kg | kilogram |
| g | gram |
| cm | centimetre |
| mm | millimetre |
| c | cup, containing 250 ml |
| T | tablespoon, containing 12,5 ml |
| t | teaspoon, containing 5 ml |
| a pinch | less than ⅛ t |

All measurements are taken level.

# Herbs
# and
# Spices

# Allspice

Pimento, Jamaica Pepper, Clove Pepper
*Pimenta officinalis*

The allspice tree is native to the Caribbean Islands and Central America and, although the tree can grow in other parts of the world, it does not bear fruit except in these unique environments. So every packet of allspice you buy has come a long way!

The evergreen allspice tree grows to between 7,5 and 9 metres in height and the fruit is harvested from midsummer on, when it is mature but still green in colour. It is only after drying that the pea-sized berries turn the familiar dark reddish-brown.

The name *allspice* comes from the combination of aroma and flavour of the seeds – an exquisite blend of cloves, nutmeg and cinnamon.

A mixed pickling spice is available commercially which contains allspice berries with a mixture of other seeds and spices, so do not let this confuse you when buying.

The pimento should also not be confused with *pimiento*, which is a type of capsicum or sweet pepper. Allspice trees are cultivated on a large scale in Jamaica and this is why allspice is often known as Jamaica pepper.

Ground allspice berries are a delicious flavouring in cakes, steamed and cream puddings and stewed fruit. Sprinkle lightly over brinjals, hubbard squash, courgettes, beetroot and sweet potatoes. Add a pinch of allspice to the gravy of a pot roast.

A delicious summer drink can be made by boiling two cups of pearl barley in two litres of water. Add six allspice berries and simmer gently for one hour. Stand until cool, then strain. Add lemon juice to taste and sweeten if necessary with brown sugar or honey.

Allspice aids digestion and crushed allspice added to tea helps to relieve stomach disorders.

# Crushed Mixed Spice

How infinitely satisfying it is to have your own blend of mixed spice! I save small attractive bottles throughout the year and fill these with my own blend. Corked and tied with a narrow gingham ribbon they make a beautiful and welcome Christmas present for anyone interested in cooking. Remember to cork them well to keep them airtight.

Allspice is important in this mixed spice recipe. The same blend can be made of ready-ground ingredients and a little added to bread or biscuit dough is unforgettable:

10 teaspoons coriander seed
 2 teaspoons allspice
 4 teaspoons cinnamon

 1 teaspoon nutmeg
 1 teaspoon ginger
 1/2 teaspoon cloves

Crush each ingredient separately in a mortar or put through the coffee grinder, then measure out and blend well.

# Uncrushed Mixed Spice

10 tablespoons coriander seeds
 3 tablespoons allspice berries
 6 tablespoons cinnamon pieces
 6 whole nutmegs, roughly crushed

 2 pieces ginger, approx. 6 cm in length, roughly chopped
10 cloves

Small quantities of this blend can be tied into muslin squares and used in pickling and chutney recipes.

# Pickling Sauce

This recipe can be used not only for onions, but also for small cucumbers, beetroot, kohlrabi and celery stalks. Large quantities are used in this recipe as the keeping quality of this pickling sauce is excellent and if one is going to go to the trouble of preparing the vegetables it seems a shame not to make a good quantity, for this is sure to become a family favourite!

½ bag small onions (or ½ bag cucumbers, celery stalks, cauliflower bracts, green beans, etc. for a mixed pickle)
2 litre bottles dark vinegar
12 – 14 cups brown sugar

4 heaped tablespoons rough pickling spice (this can be tied in small bags but I find bottled pickles look attractive with the odd bits of seed and bark)

Pour boiling water over the onions to make them easy to peel. Soak the vegetables in well-salted water for 4 – 6 hours. Drain in a sieve.

In the meantime, boil up the vinegar, sugar and spices and keep the pot boiling. Add to this 3 – 4 cups of the drained, prepared vegetables and boil for 1 – 2 minutes. Remove from the spicy sauce and pack into bottles. Keep covered. When all the vegetables have been cooked and put in bottles, pour over the boiling sauce, seal the bottles immediately and label and date each bottle.

I always find there is a little of the sauce over and I keep this bottled for salad dressing and to add to fish dishes. Its sweet and sour flavour enhances so many dishes and you will enjoy experimenting with the combinations.

As in most dishes, variations on the above recipe are possible, and if you keep more or less to this ratio you will find it a pleasing blend with no one ingredient predominating.

# Angelica

*Angelica archangelica*

This handsome biennial is a lovely focal point in the garden, yet few realise that this plant is the green crystallised cake decoration we have all grown up with. I remember the thrill of seeing a sturdy wooden box of angelica from France being opened in a quaint little dried fruit shop in Cape Town. The thick waxed paper was carefully unfolded to reveal the stiff green shiny stalks in their powdery sugar packaging – mouth-watering! The length amazed me: 20 cm seems enormous when only slivers are used in confectionery. It was only when I grew my own angelica that I saw the lush beauty and thickness of the stems. It does best in semi-shade and only grows from fresh seed.

There are many recipes for crystallising angelica stems and the one given below is an ancient English recipe which is a good base to begin with. A piece of root ginger can be added to the syrup to give a different flavour once you have mastered the art.

Angelica features prominently in legends of the past and particularly in the folklore of Lapland, Iceland and Russia. Interestingly, it has always been prized for the sensation of warmth it creates when eaten – and perhaps that is why it is so treasured in those cold countries. Angelica also had a place in pagan rites and then later in Christian festivals.

Its benign qualities and its wonderful medicinal properties – its protection against infection and its assistance in soothing digestion and improving circulation and respiration – have made it a valuable herb through the centuries. Today it is used in homoeopathy and in tea form as a quick home remedy for the ailments already mentioned.

Chopped young leaves have a fresh, mild taste in salads and fresh stalks added to milk puddings, custards and stewed fruit give flavour and goodness and aid digestion. They also take the tartness from rhubarb and apples. An old remedy for flatulence is to slowly chew a bit of stalk until the condition is relieved.

To give a subtle and elusive flavour to dry white wine, steep a stalk and leaf or two in the bottle just before serving. Angelica has been used for many centuries in the flavouring of wines, vermouth and some liqueurs such as chartreuse. Remember that the earliest liqueurs were prepared in monasteries as medicines. The monks valued this plant 'from the angels' and used every part of it – roots, stems, leaves and seeds – for medicine.

I urge you to grow and enjoy this unusual herb. At last we can buy angelica seedlings in South Africa; many nurseries are importing the seed.

Angelica combines well with the mints, ginger, cinnamon and vanilla, but its subtle flavour perhaps makes it most suited to use on its own.

## Crystallised Angelica

angelica stems
boiling water
2 tablespoons salt

500 ml water
700 g sugar
castor sugar

Cut angelica stems into mangeable pieces – I find 5 cm easy. Place them in a bowl and cover with boiling water to which you have added the salt. Leave to soak for 24 hours. Then peel the skin from the stalks and boil briskly in a syrup made from the water and sugar for one hour. Remove from the syrup and drain. The next day again boil the pieces of angelica in the same syrup for an hour and leave to cool in the syrup. By now the stems should be transparent but still green. Drain and leave to dry. Roll in castor sugar and store in an airtight tin lined with wax paper or in a well-sealed glass jar. Use chopped on desserts and cakes.

## Angelica Ice-cream                                                   Serves 6

4 eggs
juice of 1 large lemon
1 cup sweetened condensed milk

2 cups heavy cream, stiffly whipped
4 tablespoons chopped cystallised
   angelica

Separate the eggs and whip the whites stiffly. Beat the lemon juice into the condensed milk to thicken it. Beat the egg yolks and add to the condensed milk and lemon juice. Whip well. Fold in the beaten egg whites, the whipped cream and the chopped angelica. Pour into a freezer-proof bowl or into ice trays and freeze. Serve with a decoration of chopped pecan nuts or almonds, cherries and a few pieces of angelica.

# Anise

*Pimpinella anisum*

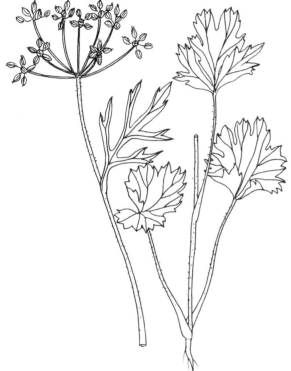

Anise is an annual herbaceous plant that grows to about 30 cm in height. It originated in the region east of the Mediterranean but now grows abundantly in Turkey, Spain, Bulgaria, Syria and the United States of America.

The anise fruit, called 'aniseed', is tiny, oval and brown, with the very typical flavour and fragrance of liquorice. This seed gives the well-known anisette liqueur its characteristic flavour.

The Romans discovered that the seeds of anise aided digestion after large banquets and so the spice was one of the ingredients baked into a special cake which was served at the end of the meal. This is said to be the origin of our special-occasion spicy fruit cakes.

Anise grows easily in light, well-drained soil in full sun and needs to be sown in spring after all danger of frost is past. The leathery, flat, white flower heads bloom in midsummer. If one can get the seeds to germinate, anise is well worth having in the garden; but the seedlings need protection and as they are so fragile and soft they should be sown where they are to establish. Water them regularly in the summer and never allow them to dry out. Do not sow the seed too deeply – I find they do best sown in shallow drills 12 mm deep and 30 cm apart. Harvest the heads before the seeds drop. Leave them in the sun in cardboard boxes until they dry out completely, then clean them and pack into airtight bottles.

For culinary uses aniseed can be stored for many years, but for propagating sow fresh seed from the previous season. Aniseed is a breath-sweetener when chewed and is used commercially for flavouring cough syrups and lozenges.

A little powdered aniseed added to stews helps digestion, and a little added to food is excellent for young children who find digestion difficult. Aniseed tea, made by adding a little honey and 1 teaspoon of seed to a large cup of water and boiled for

15 minutes, will also soothe a fretful child and aid sleep and indigestion.

Aniseed, whole or ground, can be added to many foods such as breads, cakes, biscuits, stewed or baked apples and pears, pasta and vegetables that are difficult to digest like cabbage, onions, cucumbers, carrots, turnips and beetroot. It gives an elusive flavour to rich stews, cheese dishes and savoury tarts. Do not combine aniseed with other herbs and spices as the flavours do not mingle well, but anise leaves give a piquant taste to salads and soups and these can be freely combined with other herbs.

There is another anise called 'star anise' which is the seed from a tree, *Illicium anisatum*, that is indigenous to China. The oil from these seeds is similar to that of the annual anise and has the same medicinal properties.

Experiment with the quantities of anise that you find most pleasing; a general rule is half a teaspoon of ground aniseed to a dish that serves six. It has a strong flavour, so start sparingly. I find crushed seeds give more flavour than the bought ground spice and this is easily done using a pestle and mortar.

The aniseed biscuit recipe below is a wonderful after-dinner 'sweet' and, served with a herb tea like mint or rosemary, is a pleasing end to a heavy meal and will aid the digestive processes beautifully.

## Aniseed Biscuits — Makes about 18 medium-sized biscuits

250 g butter
1 cup brown sugar
3 cups well-sifted brown flour

3 teaspoons baking powder
6 teaspoons crushed aniseed

Melt butter in a saucepan, stir in sugar and flour and lastly the baking powder. Mix well, then turn mixture into a shallow baking dish that has been well buttered. Press down well, taking care to press down the corners too, smooth with a wooden spoon and then sprinkle with the crushed aniseed and press this into the mixture.

Bake at 180 °C (350 °F) for about 30 minutes or until pale brown, cut into squares, leave to cool in the pan and then dust with castor sugar. Store in an airtight tin.

# Basil

*Ocimum basilicum*

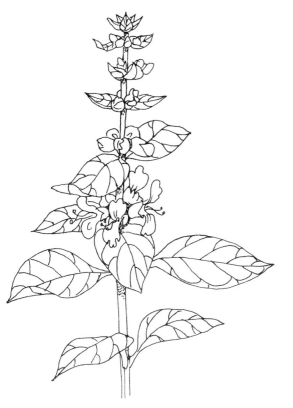

Basil originated in India, where it is regarded as a sacred herb and is still grown for decoration in the temples. Its clove-like, unique fragrance has drawn much attention through the ages. It was well known and loved in ancient Greece and Rome and there are many legends that surround it. The wise men of ancient times derived its name from Basilisk, a mythical serpent-like creature whose venom was so potent it could kill with a look. Basil was an antidote! It was also used in ancient times to draw out the poison from insect bites and stings and even today basil is important in counteracting much that is unwholesome in modern food. It aids digestion and helps eliminate chemical preservatives taken into the body in our food.

Basil is an annual and is frost-tender. If it is sown in spring it will take the whole summer to develop and by the first frosts seeds can be gathered. The dried matured branches with their seed husks can be used as an attractive addition to dried flower arrangements.

There are several varieties of basil. The dark purple *Ocimum basilicum purpureum* is beautiful and unusual in the garden.

Bunches of fresh basil hung in the kitchen or a pot of basil on the kitchen windowsill are wonderful fly deterrents and a ready source of fresh leaves for cooking.

If you are drying basil for winter kitchen use, the fullest flavour is just before the plant comes into flower. Cut the leafy stalks, hang in bunches to dry in a cool airy shed or place on sheets of newspaper, then strip and store the cumbled leaves in an airtight jar.

In Italy dried basil is crumbled so finely it can be pushed through a sieve. In this fine, dust-like form it is used abundantly in pasta dishes, giving a unique clove-like flavour and aiding digestion at the same time.

The uses of basil are varied and wide. It has an affinity with tomatoes and therefore all tomato-based dishes are particularly delicious with a touch of basil. It also combines well with celery, parsley and mint but does not happily blend with other herbs as it has too strong a flavour. Add basil to brinjals, courgettes and marrow or squash dishes, spinach, cucumber, peas and lentils. Chopped into cream cheese with a squeeze of lemon juice, it makes a delicious dip or sandwich spread. Use basil sparingly in salads as its strong flavour tends to swamp everything else.

My favourite way of storing basil is to pack a crock or jar with alternating layers of fresh basil leaves and coarse salt, corked and kept in a cool place. Whenever a few leaves are needed just shake off the salt, wash the leaves and use them immediately.

## Basic Pasta Sauce                                   Serves 6 – 8

This simple blend can be used as a base with which to experiment according to your own taste and in combination with cheese dishes, omelettes, egg soufflés, meat dishes, fish – like kingklip or hake – and all sorts of pasta. It makes a delicious sauce to have with mealiepap at a braaivleis!

4 *large onions, finely chopped*
4 *tablespoons olive oil (or sunflower or*
   *maize oil)*
10 *ripe tomatoes skinned by plunging*
   *into boiling water*
4 *tablespoons basil vinegar*
1 *teaspoon sea salt*

1 *cup sultanas, soaked in hot water*
   *for an hour*
*freshly ground black pepper*
½ – 1 *cup brown sugar\**
*a dash of sweet or semi-sweet sherry*
3 *level tablespoons cornflour*
4 *tablespoons fresh chopped basil or*
   2 *tablespoons dried basil*

\* depending on taste – I start with ½ cup and taste as I go along, as some tomatoes are less acid than others.

Choose a fairly deep pot. Fry the onions in the oil until lightly browned. Add all the other ingredients except the basil. Cook on medium heat until soft, then add the cornflour (blended with a little cold water) to thicken it. Add the chopped fresh basil in the last 2 minutes of cooking.

# Basil Vinegar

Basil vinegar is wonderful in salad dressing and very easy to make. Use it in soups and stews.

2 litres white grape vinegar
6 sprigs basil

1 red chilli

Push the sprigs of basil (remember – the fresher the herb the stronger the flavour) into the vinegar with the chilli and leave in the sun for 10 days. During this time you can replace the sprigs with fresh ones. When the flavour is to your liking, strain and bottle into pretty bottles, label and use with relish. I aways put a fresh sprig of leaves into the bottle as it looks good on the kitchen shelf.

# Basil Vegetable Tart                                     Serves 6

This is a wonderful standby and I find the quantities should really be doubled as it is such a firm favourite.

## Pastry

4 tablespoons soft butter
3 cups sifted brown flour

1 teaspoon sea salt
3 tablespoons iced water

Rub the butter into the flour and salt until it resembles breadcrumbs. Add water gradually to make a fairly soft dough. Press this into a pie dish 25,5 cm in diameter, prick with a fork and trim the edges. Bake at 350 °F (180 °C) for 20 minutes, or until lightly browned.

## Filling

2 onions, chopped and fried in a little oil
10 Swiss chard spinach leaves, chopped,
    including stalks
4 cups courgette slices
2 cups chopped celery stalks
3 eggs

salt
black pepper
1 cup milk
3 tablespoons chopped fresh basil
1 cup grated cheese

Cook the vegetables until soft and add to the fried onions. Whisk the eggs, salt, pepper and milk and pour over the vegetables. Mix well. Finally add the chopped basil. Sprinkle with the grated cheese and bake at 350 °F (180 °C) for 30 minutes or until firm. Decorate with fresh basil. Serve hot or cold.

# Pesto Sauce

This classic Genoese sauce can be used on all types of pasta and it can be added to soups and stews too for an unusual taste. It is best to use fresh basil, but if it is winter and there is no basil available, use the salt-stored leaves from your crock.

*large bunch fresh basil –*
*to give 4 cups leaves*
*2 – 3 cloves garlic*
*little salt*

*4  tablespoons walnuts or pine nuts*
*4  tablespoons grated Parmesan cheese*
*5 – 6 tablespoons olive oil*

Strip the leaves from the fresh basil and using a large pestle and mortar pound the leaves with the garlic. Add a little salt and the walnuts or pine nuts, pounding well all the time. Add the grated Parmesan cheese and pound to a smooth paste, gradually incorporating the olive oil.

Try this on baked potatoes and with hard-boiled eggs.

Use fresh basil when you make pesto

Pound the basil and garlic in a pestle and mortar

# Bay

*Laurus nobilis*

Bay is a favourite herb tree and makes beautiful pot or tub specimens – always a pleasing shape and evergreen. The dark glossy leaves are aromatic and filled with flavour, making bay a must for every cook.

Native to the shores of the Mediterranean, the bay laurel is grown all over the world both as a herb and as a decorative shrub. It can be used for topiary work and always looks handsome. In frost-free climates it grows enormous: up to 9 metres. However, even a small tree will keep you supplied with leaves for a long time.

Bay goes back a long way in history. In ancient Italy and Greece it was used to make the wreath that crowned the victorious on the battlefield and in the sports arena, it was used in pagan rites, and in the places of learning poet laureate was the trophy. It was also used in early medicine: the oil extracted from the leaves and berries was applied to sprains and bruises; it was used to aid flatulence, hysteria and the aches and pains of rheumatism; and the powdered berries were said to improve the appetite. Bay found its place in cookery not only as a flavouring, but also to work on the digestive tract in eliminating wind, gripes and heartburn. It is interesting to note how many herbs in our diet perform this dual function.

The bay leaf is essential in bouquet garni and below is a basic recipe for this famous combination of herbs. It can of course be varied and you can experiment for yourself, but this is the traditional combination.

Bay is delicious with fish dishes, meat dishes (liver, pork and mutton) and combines beautifully with many other herbs. Surprisingly, it gives an unusually delicious taste to milk puddings.

15

Dried powdered bay leaves can be added direct to soup or stew. Try one teaspoon to a medium-sized pot of stew for a pungent, delicious taste. Remove leaves before serving as bay can become bitter if left in the dish too long.

## Bouquet Garni

1 sprig each thyme, marjoram
  and parsley

1 bay leaf
2 peppercorns

Tie these in a muslin square and use in soups, stews and casseroles. Remove after cooking.

## Bean and Lentil Casserole                                    Serves 8

4 cups dried haricot beans
  (soaked overnight)
3 cups brown lentils (soaked overnight)
4 bay leaves or 2 teaspoons dried
  powdered leaves
2 large onions, chopped
4 tablespoons maize oil
4 large tomatoes, skinned and sliced

4 leeks, thinly diced
2 carrots, thinly diced
2 stalks celery, thinly diced
2 tablespoons cornflour
1 cup tarragon vinegar
1 cup brown sugar
½ cup seedless raisins
salt and pepper to taste

Boil the beans with the bay leaves until tender. Add the lentils later as the beans take longer to cook. Fry the onions in oil until golden. Add tomatoes, leeks, carrots and celery and fry. Drain the beans and lentils and add to the fried vegetables. Stir the cornflour into the vinegar and pour into the pot. Add sugar, raisins and seasoning. Place in a casserole, sprinkle with breadcrumbs, dot with butter and bake at 180 °C (350 °F) for 30–45 minutes. Serve with a green salad and crusty bread.

## Rich Rice Pudding                                           Serves 6

3 cups cooked brown rice
3 cups milk
3 eggs, well-beaten
1 cup brown sugar

ground cinnamon
½ cup sunflower seeds
3 bay leaves

Mix well all the ingredients except the bay leaves and pour into a baking dish. Push the bay leaves deep into the pudding and spinkle with cinnamon. Bake at 180 °C (350 °F) for ½ to ¾ hour or until set. Serve with whipped cream.

# Bergamot

Bergamot is one of the prettiest, most showy herbs. It comes in a range of glowing colours – red, cerise, pink, a deep magenta and a rare white. The leaves and flowers are beautiful in pot-pourris and it is a very worthwhile perennial in the garden as it gives so much for so little care.

Bergamot is related to the mint family and, like mint, gives of its best if it has afternoon shade and a fair amount of water.

It is native to North America where it is known as 'oswego' and is lavishly used as a cure-all tea by the Oswego Indians. Try a cup of bergamot tea to soothe a sore throat and a cold.

Do not confuse this bergamot with oil of bergamot, though their fragrance is similar. Oil of bergamot comes from the bergamot orange, *Citrus bergamia*, which gives Earl Grey tea its distinctive flavour.

Use bergamot leaves – the young fresh ones – in fruit salads and in summer drinks and jellies. Combine with apples as a side dish when serving pork.

Dried bergamot sprinkled on veal is a delicious treat. Rub the leaves through a coarse sieve to give a fine texture as the midrib can be tough and stringy.

For a really different taste combine freshly chopped bergamot with cabbage dishes, boil a sprig in the water of cooking rice, and for a braaivleis try cooking samp (stamped mealies) with a sprig or two of bergamot. If the samp is cooked slowly so as not to dry it out it makes an enjoyable dish served with a tomato gravy.

Chop bergamot with mint, mix with white sugar and a touch of iced water to a crumbly consistency and serve with spanspek, green melons or watermelon.

# Apple Jelly **Serves 6**

4  sour green apples
1  cup water
2  tablespoons chopped bergamot

2  cloves
brown sugar

Peel and core the apples, slice and boil in the water to which the chopped bergamot and cloves have been added. Boil until the apples are soft. Rub through a sieve, add a little brown sugar and serve with roast pork.

# Bergamot Salad **Serves 6**

 1  butter lettuce, washed and torn into
    small pieces
10  bergamot flowers, petals only

½  chopped cucumber
4  tablespoons cream cheese curds
2  tablespoons chopped fresh mint

Toss together.

### Dressing

½  cup lemon juice
½  cup honey

½  cup bergamot tea
½  cup oil

Shake in a screw-top bottle to blend.

# Bergamot Tea **Serves 2**

2  cups boiling water
1 – 3 sprigs bergamot the length of your
    index finger

This tea tastes like Earl Grey tea. Pour water over the roughly chopped leaves and stems and boil for 10 minutes. Leave to steep for an hour. Drink, warmed with honey, after dinner or as a cure for throat infections or flatulence, nausea and stomach ache. Draw off the water and use in salad dressings.

18

# Bergamot Jelly

4 cups bergamot tea (warmed)
1 cup honey
1 cup red wine or port

4 rounded teaspoons gelatine dissolved
  in a little hot water
1/2 cup lemon juice

Dissolve the honey in the warm tea. Add the wine, the dissolved gelatine and the lemon juice. Pour into individual glasses and set in the fridge. Serve with whipped cream and a sprinkling of freshly chopped bergamot leaves. Top with a cherry.

Bergamot jelly is tasty and healthy

# Borage

*Borago officinalis*

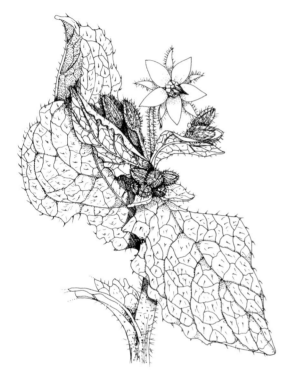

Like many other herbs, borage has its place in history. The crusaders took it on their journeys to give them courage, as it was believed to bring 'gladness and cheer'.

Borage is important in the diet, particularly for people under stress and for convalescents. Each hairy leaf is packed with minerals, vitamins and a wonderfully beneficial saline mucilage. Borage is the only herb that stimulates the adrenal cortex of the kidneys to produce their own cortizone, so it is essential for those with kidney problems. It reduces fevers, soothes insect stings and bites, swellings and bruises, and as a bed-time drink gives one a peaceful night.

The bland cucumber-like taste of young borage leaves makes it combine well with many other herbs. It should really only be used fresh as it loses all its flavour when dried. Use the glorious blue borage flowers lavishly in fruit salads, fruit cup and fruit cocktails. Infuse them in fruit drinks an hour before serving so that the fresh cucumber-like flavour can penetrate.

Chop young borage leaves finely, almost mincing them, and combine with chopped celery and green mustard leaves in a salad; or mix with cream cheese for sandwiches; or chop the older leaves for soup and stews.

Always try to have a borage plant or two in the garden for a continuous supply of leaves and flowers, as its nutritional value is so high that it should be included daily in your diet.

# Borage Fruit Cup

10 grenadillas
1 litre grenadilla juice
1 cup borage flowers

little sugar or honey to sweeten
1 litre ginger ale
1 litre ginger beer

Blend and serve in a punch bowl with the borage flowers floating on top.
   This also freezes well and can be used to make ice lollies for children. To do this, insert a sucker stick into the ice cube sections just before it freezes solid.

# Bed-time Borage Health Tea

4 borage leaves, roughly chopped
1 cup boiling water

honey to taste

Pour the boiling water over the leaves and allow to steep for five minutes. Strain and add a little honey. Sip just before going to sleep. This is a wonderful tea to bring down fevers and ease stressful situations.

# Borage Fritters

This dish is a great favourite with everyone and, served with stews, curry or just a green salad and cheese, it is a wonderfully nutritious meal in itself.

several young borage leaves (approx. 12)
sunflower oil

### Batter

1 cup flour (I use sifted brown flour)
1/2 – 3/4 cup milk
1 beaten egg

sea salt and pepper
1/2 teaspoon grated nutmeg

Combine and beat the ingredients well, adding a little more milk if necessary to make a fairly liquid batter. Dip each leaf into the batter and fry in deep, hot oil until golden brown. Fry only four or five at a time so that they do not stick together. Drain, and serve immediately while they are still hot and crisp.

# Herb Health Soup

This is my winter standby and is so packed with goodness and flavour that it can form the base of all your winter menus. You can vary it to give it your own individual stamp, but here is the basic recipe using ingredients that are all easily available.

1   *cup butter beans*
1   *cup haricot beans*
1   *cup pearl barley*
1   *cup brown lentils*
1   *cup split peas*
4   *cups chopped onions*
1   *handful chives*
10  *celery stalks and leaves, chopped*
4   *cups chopped leeks*
*maize or sunflower oil*
4   *tomatoes, skinned and chopped*

4   *cups borage leaves, roughly chopped*
2   *cups grated carrots*
4   *teaspoons marmite*
*salt and pepper*
4   *tablespoons debittered Brewers yeast*
*comfrey leaves*
*sow's thistle* (Sonchus olearceus)
*fat hen* (Chenopodium album)
*chickweed* (Stellaria media)
½   *cup parsley*

Soak beans, barley, lentils and peas overnight. In a large pot (not aluminium) fry onions, chopped chives, celery and leeks in ½ – ¾ cup maize or sunflower oil until golden brown. Add all the other ingredients and top up with water – about 2 – 3 litres, depending on how thick you like the soup. Simmer slowly for about an hour. Just before the cooking time is up, add a handful or two of chopped comfrey leaves, sow's thistle, fat hen and chickweed and parsley. The addition of the weeds, comfrey and parsley adds greatly to the nutritional value of the soup and is surprisingly delicious.

I make a huge pot of this soup twice a week and keep some in the fridge for unexpected visitors. Served with a herb or mealie bread it makes a perfect meal. Vary with vegetables and weeds in season.

# Calendula

Marigold
*Calendula officinalis*

Used as a herb in cooking, calendula always surprises. It is one of the most useful of all herbs for its valuable medicinal properties, its yield of brilliant yellow dye, its versatility in cooking and its beneficial cosmetic constituents.

It was respected and used with reverence in ancient Greece and before that was known in Indian and Arabic cultures. It is indigenous to the Mediterranean region but is distributed throughout the world as a garden plant.

Usually annual, its brilliant orange and yellow flowers draw the eye, particularly in spring plantings. As it dries well and the plant benefits from being picked, you could have enough dried petals to last the year from only half a dozen plants.

Medicinally calendula is a tonic herb excellent for conjunctivitis, toning the circulatory system, healing wounds, treating skin ailments and it is an antiseptic. The petals can be used to colour butter and eggs and substitute the most expensive spice in the world, saffron. They give a rich, golden colour to soups, stews, cakes and puddings and, because of the lack of flavour in both the leaves and petals, it is a herb that combines readily with many other stronger flavoured herbs. Young leaves can be chopped into salads and the bright petals are delicious in omelettes, cheese and egg dishes and added to poultry and stuffing.

For those with circulatory problems, skin rashes, eczema and dry flaky skin, calendulas in the diet for a few weeks will make all the difference.

# Potato and Calendula Soufflé

500 g potatoes, peeled and diced
1 bay leaf
1½ cups milk
4 tablespoons butter
2 tablespoons fresh calendula petals,
    chopped **or**
1 tablespoon dried powdered calendula
    petals

salt and pepper
2 eggs, well beaten
grated cheese
crumbled cornflakes

Cook the potatoes and bay leaf in boiling salted water until tender. Drain and sieve or mash well. Heat the milk, butter, petals, salt and pepper and fold this into the potatoes; then mix in the beaten eggs. Butter an oven-proof dish, fill with the potato mixture, cover with a thick layer of grated cheese (about 2 cups), sprinkle with crumbled cornflakes (about half a cup), dot with butter and brown for 15 minutes at 350 °F/180 °C. Serve hot with a salad.

# Calendula Mealiemeal Pancakes

Serves 6

This is a wonderful standby as these Mexican-type 'tortillas' can be made ahead of time and, with a variety of 'fillings' or sauces, make an easy, nutritious supper dish that no one ever gets tired of.

1½ cups water
1 teaspoon salt
3 tablespoons butter
1 cup mealiemeal (coarse ground if
    possible)

2 tablespoons fresh calendula petals,
    finely chopped **or**
1 tablespoon dried calendula petals,
    finely ground
1¼ cups wholewheat flour
little paprika

Bring water to boil, add salt and half the butter, stir in mealiemeal and calendula petals, turn heat to low, cover and cook for about 5 – 7 minutes. Stir in remaining butter and set aside to cool. Stir flour into the cooked mealiemeal and knead to a pliable consistency, adding a little milk or water if necessary. Pinch off balls the size of a golf ball and flatten between the hands to make a flat pancake; or roll out, dusting with flour to keep it from sticking. Fry in a lightly greased pan for about 1½ minutes on each side. Have a clean cloth ready and stack the pancakes in the cloth, keeping covered. Should you need to reheat them, just warm them through quickly on each side before serving.

# Tomato Sauce

This is an old-fashioned, rich tomato sauce that far surpasses any shop-bought variety. I recommend a selection of herbs to flavour it but the combinations are left to you. The rich colour and fullness of the sauce are enhanced with calendula petals but these can be omitted.

The best time to make this sauce is when tomatoes are plentiful in the garden. It freezes well and keeps well in the refrigerator.

*1,36 kg or more fully ripe tomatoes*
*salt*
*sugar*
*ginger*
*pepper*
*2 teaspoons minced fresh sweet basil or*
  *1 teaspoon dried*

*2 teaspoons minced fresh thyme or*
  *1 teaspoon dried*
*2 tablespoons minced fresh calendula*
  *petals or 1 teaspoon dried*
*2 tablespoons Worcestershire sauce*

Place the tomatoes in an earthernware or oven-proof casserole or pot. Do not peel or slice and add nothing whatsoever. Cover and bake at 180 °C/350 °F for about an hour or until the tomatoes are soft. Press through a sieve. Heat the resulting purée in a pot, and for every 0,45 kg of tomatoes, add *1 teaspoon salt, 1 tablespoon sugar, ½ teaspoon ginger*, and *pepper to taste*. Then add the minced fresh or dried sweet basil, the minced fresh or dried thyme, the minced fresh or dried calendula petals, and the Worcestershire sauce.

Briefly bring to the boil, cool and bottle or place in containers for freezing. Use in soups and stews as a condiment and over pastas and savoury tarts.

Calendula petals can be used fresh or dried in pancakes

# Caper

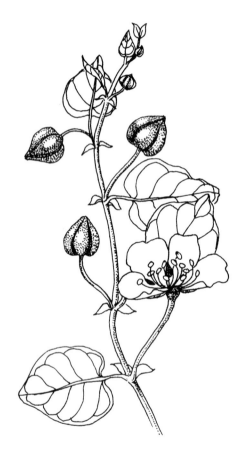

The caper shrub is indigenous to the Mediterranean region and grows freely in North Africa to the Sahara Desert and in the Caucasus region. It is a perennial, thorny shrub that needs the warmth and sunshine of tropical and sub-tropical zones but can be cultivated in South Africa's warmer areas. Surprisingly, the cultivated plant is often spineless.

The unopened flower buds of the caper bush, pickled in wine vinegar, have been used as a condiment for 2 000 years. Dioscorides suggested a medicinal use for them – to aid the digestion of 'ripe' meat – but it was not widely used for anything other than culinary purposes.

Capric acid develops in the buds during pickling and it is this that gives the characteristic piquant flavour of so many sauces and savoury dishes that call for this special ingredient.

If capers are not available, an excellent substitute can be made by pickling green nasturtium seeds. Two alternative recipes for this appear on pages 115 amd 116.

If you are lucky enough to be able to grow your own caper bush, a recipe for caper pickle is given below.

Use capers in tartar sauce, herb butter, vinaigrette dressings, Liptauer cheese and as a garnish with fish, meat, hors-d'oeuvres and a little, finely chopped, in salad dressings.

# Caper Pickle

Pick a quantity of unopened flower buds and leave them overnight spread on a tray. Next morning pack them into a glass jar and pour over them the spicy vinegar dressing below. Seal and store for 4 – 6 weeks before using.

## Spicy Vinegar Sauce

1 litre good white vinegar
4 bay leaves
1 tablespoon coriander seeds

2 teaspoons peppercorns
1 nutmeg, roughly broken

Add the bay leaves, coriander seeds, peppercorns and nutmeg to the vinegar. Boil briskly for 10 minutes, keeping the pot covered. This vinegar keeps for several months.

## Hard-boiled Egg Salad                 Serves 6

6 eggs
1 lettuce
1 cucumber, thinly sliced

1 pineapple, chopped
fresh parsley sprigs
fresh tarragon sprigs

Boil the eggs for 10 – 15 minutes. Pour off boiling water and cover with cold water. Make a rich mayonnaise while the eggs are cooling:

### Mayonnaise

1 tin sweetened condensed milk
1½ cups tarragon vinegar
¾ cup maize or sunflower oil
1 teaspoon salt

½ teaspoon black pepper
2 tablespoons drained capers
1 tablespoon freshly chopped tarragon

Whisk together the condensed milk, vinegar, oil, salt and pepper. Add the drained capers and tarragon and blend. (This keeps well for up to a month in the fridge.)

On a bed of lettuce leaves place the sliced hard-boiled eggs, thinly sliced cucumber and the chopped pineapple, alternating the layers. Pour the mayonnaise over this and decorate with fresh sprays of parsley and tarragon. Serve immediately with crusty brown bread.

# Lemon Dressing for Grilled Fish **Serves 6**

1  *cup lemon juice*
2  *tablespoons brown sugar*
½  *cup olive oil*

1  *cup finely chopped gherkins*
½  *cup capers*
*a little salt and pepper*

Blend well. This can be served warm or cold. Pour over the fish just before serving, or serve separately at the table.

I find a quick and easy way to blend a dressing is to place all the ingredients in a screw-top jar and to shake well.

A vinegar sauce made with coriander, bay leaves, peppercorns and nutmeg will keep for several months

# Caraway

*Carum carvi*

Caraway is a biennial herb belonging to the carrot family and its fern-like leaves and lace-like flower heads press beautifully.

It is indigenous to Europe and has been introduced to North Africa, parts of Asia and India. It has medicinal and therapeutic uses and was respected and favoured in biblical times. The ancient Arabs called the seeds *karawiya*. This precious herb has been used for 5 000 years – seeds of caraway have been found at Mesolithic sites among the remains of food – and is still popular today. Its popularity stems from the fact that it is a magical cure for flatulent indigestion and lack of appetite, and it is used for treating diarrhoea. It is safe to use as a treatment for tummy upsets in children.

Caraway grows easily from seeds sown in spring but they should be sown straight into the ground in the position where they are to grow as they do not transplant easily.

The whole plant can be used, from the young leaves in a salad to the roots boiled as a vegetable and served with butter, a squeeze of lemon juice and salt and pepper. The seeds are probably the best-known flavouring and, because of their aid to digestion, are often served with cheese after a meal.

Try adding crushed seeds to butter, and serve this in individual little dishes with biscuits and cheese at the end of a meal; or mix crushed caraway seeds into cream cheese or cottage cheese with a little salt; or make a caraway tea for the end of the meal by crushing 1 teaspoon of seeds per cup of boiling water, pour the water over the seeds, add a sprig of mint (any mint will do as all mint flavours combine well with caraway), steep, then strain and drink sweetened perhaps with a little honey. Alternatively, tie the seeds in a muslin bag, 1 teaspoon per cup, place the bag in a teapot with a sprig of mint and serve as you would an after-dinner tea.

With its distinct liquorice flavour, caraway combines beautifully with several

29

vegetables – particularly courgettes, cabbage, beetroot, cauliflower, chicory, potatoes, broad beans and butter beans. Use powdered caraway in pork dishes (half a teaspoon per 4 servings), meatloaf, beef stews and with grilled liver and onions. Try a little in home-baked bread but use very sparingly as in bread its taste is accentuated.

## Basic Whole Grain Bread

This is a blueprint even for beginners and many variations can be made using this recipe as the perfect base. If you follow the recipe carefully it will never flop and you will become so efficient in the art of bread-making that you will never want to eat shop-bought bread again! I make this recipe two or three times a week so that I always have a freshly baked loaf on hand.

To this basic recipe you might like to add 2 teaspoons of crushed caraway seeds, 1 cup of raisins or ½ cup of chopped or minced fresh herbs like the young leaves of caraway, thyme, oregano, dill, basil, lovage, anise or sage.

For two loaves:

2½ cups warm water
1 heaped tablespoon brown sugar
1 tablespoon active dry yeast (always keep the tin in the fridge)

6 cups wholewheat flour
1 tablespoon salt (or less depending on taste)

Pour the warm (not hot) water into a large bowl, add sugar and stir. Sprinkle the yeast on top of the water. In a few minutes the yeast will bubble up to the top of the bowl. Stir in 3 cups of the flour a little at a time, and beat well until the dough becomes smooth and stretchy. Add the salt and the rest of the flour cup by cup, mixing and kneading well until it leaves the sides of the bowl clean. Turn out onto a floured board and knead well. As the dough gets harder to knead, sprinkle the remaining flour onto the board (I find it easier to work directly on the scrubbed table top) and knead the dough on top of it. Knead, push and fold until the dough is springy and soft.

Return the dough to the bowl and cover snugly with a clean cloth, leaving space for the dough to double in bulk. Place in a warm spot. (I have a table outside the kitchen window in the sun and I leave the bowl there.) On a warm day it takes about half an hour to rise. On a rainy or wintry day, place the bowl in front of the fire or in the warming drawer of the stove, well covered, and check that the heat is not too intense.

Grease two loaf tins. Divide the risen dough in half, press into the tins and cover to let it rise a second time until the loaves have doubled in bulk. Preheat the oven to 375 °F/190 °C towards the end of this rising period. By now the bread should just be rounded above the rim of the tin.

Bake for 40 minutes. When you remove it from the pan and tap the sides and bottom it should sound hollow and the colour should be a rich golden brown.

# Savoury Beetroot and Caraway Jelly Serves 6 plus

6 *beetroots*
2 *onions, chopped*
4 *tablespoons chives, chopped*
¾ *cup red wine*
2 *teaspoons salt*

3 *tablespoons lemon juice*
2 *tablespoons honey*
2 *teaspoons caraway seeds*
6 *tablespoons gelatine*
*few fresh caraway leaves*

Cook the beetroots and save the water in which they were cooked. Peel and slice, and arrange the sliced beetroots, the chopped onions and chives in a dish. Take 1½ cups of the water in which the beetroot was cooked, the wine, salt, lemon juice, honey and caraway seed, blend and bring to the boil. Take a little of the hot liquid and melt the gelatine in it. Mix into the whole, pour over the beetroot and onions, cool and set in the fridge. Decorate with fresh caraway leaves. This is a delicious summer salad and keeps well in the fridge.

Caraway seeds are a wonderful addition to a basic whole grain bread

# Cardamom

*Elettaria cardamomum*

This perennial bush grows 1,75 – 3,5 metres high and it is grown commercially in India, where it is indigenous, Sri Lanka and Guatemala. The most expensive spice in the world is saffron and cardamom comes a close second as every seed pod must be clipped from the bush by hand.

The dried, bleached pods are three sided, 5 mm – 1 cm long and contain tiny black seeds which have the warm, delightful, pungent and highly aromatic flavour that gourmet cooks value so highly.

The Vikings were among the first to discover cardamom on their travels over a thousand years ago and they took it back to Scandinavia. Even today true Danish pastries have a faint aroma of cardamom.

Cardamom's medicinal uses are well known. It is a carminative herb, employed in flatulent dyspepsia, it allays griping caused by purgatives and it is often used to flavour other medications. It has a limited use in cosmetics and scented waters and is perhaps best known as a flavouring combination in commercially packaged pickling spices and mixed spices. Cardamom is best loved in coffee (add a dash to after-dinner coffee for a really delicious fragrant taste and to aid digestion after a heavy meal) and is equally tasty in mulled wines.

Cardamom is often included in cake, biscuit and pastry recipes. Added to curry powders and beverages it combines with cinnamon, mint, hyssop, mace and bay. It enhances the flavour of brown rice, peas, celery, egg dishes such as curried eggs, apple dishes, fresh melon and meat curries, such as mutton and pork. But do not combine it with cloves, nutmeg, bergamot, ginger, oregano, chives and mustard, as its elusive, fragrant taste is swamped by these.

Add a little cardamom to fruit cake mixtures, sweet pastry, pancake batter and biscuit dough. Substitute it for cinnamon and nutmeg in recipes and you will enjoy a whole new range of flavours.

# Kichadi                                                           Serves 6

This is a favourite savoury dish served for all meals in India, rather like pilaf, and makes a good luncheon dish.

2  onions, chopped
1  green pepper, chopped
small piece of cinnamon stick
seeds from 3 cardamom pods
dash of turmeric powder
2  teaspoons ground fenugreek seeds

4  tablespoons olive oil
2  cups brown rice
6  cups water
2  teaspoons salt
1  cup split peas

Sauté chopped onions, green pepper and spices in the oil in a large heavy-bottomed pot until the vegetables are soft. Add the rice and stir for about 5 minutes, add water and salt and bring to the boil. Cover and cook on low heat for 20 minutes. Sauté the split peas in 2 tablespoons of oil and then add to the cooking rice and cook for another 30 minutes.

With a green salad, this makes a substantial meal. As a variation add a diced raw tomato at the end of the cooking time or substitute lentils or haricot beans for the peas.

# Cardamom Apple Crisp                                       Serves 8 plus

8  crisp, green apples
juice of 1 lemon
1/2  teaspoon cardamom seeds, crushed
2  tablespoons wholewheat flour

3/4  cup raisins or sultanas
1 1/2  cup apple juice or 1/4 – 1/2 cup
   sugar mixed in 1 1/2 cups water

## Topping

1  cup large flake oats
1/3  cup wheat germ
1/2  cup wholewheat flour
1/2  teaspoon salt

2  teaspoons cinnamon
1/2  cup brown sugar
1/2  cup soft butter

Preheat the oven to 375 °F/190 °C. Grease a large baking dish, approximately 25 x 33 cm. Peel and slice the apples and arrange in the baking dish. Mix together the lemon juice, cardamom, flour, raisins and apple juice or water/sugar mixture and pour over the apples. Mix the topping in a bowl and press down on top of the apples.

Bake for 25 minutes or until apples are soft and topping is golden brown. Serve with cream.

33

# Cardamom Cake

*fresh breadcrumbs*
*340 g wholewheat flour*
*5 teaspoons baking powder*
*110 g soft butter*

*200 g brown sugar*
*3 teaspoons ground cardamom seeds*
*90 ml milk*
*140 ml cream*

## *Topping*

*25 g flaked almonds*
*25 g brown sugar*

*2 teaspoons cinnamon*

Grease a 900 g loaf tin and line with fresh breadcrumbs. Mix flour and baking powder and rub in butter until it resembles fine breadcrumbs. Mix in sugar and cardamom. Add milk and cream until the mixture is a stiff dough. Spread into the tin and sprinkle the topping over it evenly. Dot with butter.

Bake at 400 °F/200 °C for approximately 1 hour.

# Mulled Wine

*1 bottle good red wine*
*2 teaspoons cardamom seeds*
*twist of fresh lemon peel*

*2 tablespoons brown sugar*
*1 small sprig rosemary*

Warm the wine in an enamel pot on low heat. Add cardamom seeds, lemon peel (I pare thinly the peel of a whole lemon and use it all as I love the lemon taste), brown sugar and rosemary.

Allow to simmer slowly for half an hour in a covered pot. Strain through muslin and serve in warmed earthenware mugs in front of the fire on a cold frosty night. It is a wonderful nightcap and aids digestion beautifully.

# Cassia

Cassia and cinnamon were commonly confused in early writings, possibly because they belong to the same family. Known as *kwei* in the Chinese herbals, cassia reached Europe from China via Arabian and Phoenician traders and was used as an inferior substitute for cinnamon, as it is today.

Cassia is an attractive evergreen tree and grows 7 – 9 metres high. It is native to China and is cultivated there and in Burma as a commercial crop. The usable part is the bark and this contains medicinal properties that have been used since 2700 BC. It is carminative, astringent, aromatic and a stimulant and can be used as a powder or infusion for flatulence, nausea and dyspepsia. It is effective either alone or combined with other drugs for the treatment of diarrhoea. It can substitute cinnamon but has a sweeter, more subtle flavour and is easily differentiated by its coarser, thicker bark.

It is thought that the cinnamon mentioned in the Bible is probably cassia. The sages of ancient times regarded this tree as the tree of life – whoever ate of it would have life and peace eternal – and it is believed that this tree grew in the garden of Eden.

Being a 'sweet spice', cassia's fragrant taste blends best with fruits, cakes and biscuits. It combines well with nutmeg, cloves, sesame, ginger, myrtle, bergamot, melissa (lemon balm) and angelica.

A stick of bark cooked with brown rice gives an aromatic lift to the blandness of the rice. In milk puddings either a piece of bark cooked in the batter or a sprinkling of powdered cassia does much to enhance the flavour.

A hot cocoa drink with a dash of powdered cassia sprinkled on top of it is a treat at night before retiring.

Sprinkle cassia over pancakes, fritters – like banana or pumpkin – milk tart, rice and sago puddings, custards, stewed apples, rhubarb, apricots and peaches (it is glorious over fresh sliced peaches with a little brown sugar and cream). Try sprinkling a little over sauerkraut and on cheese cakes.

# Banana Cheese Cake

### Crumb Crust

¾ cup wholewheat breadcrumbs
¼ cup dried skim milk powder
¾ teaspoon cassia
¼ cup large flake oats

¼ cup wheat germ
½ cup melted butter
1 tablespoon honey

### Filling

2 medium ripe bananas
2 eggs
1 cup plain yoghurt
1 cup cottage cheese
juice of ½ lemon

1 teaspoon vanilla
½ cup wholewheat flour, sifted
¼ teaspoon salt
3 – 6 tablespoons honey

Preheat the oven to 350 °F/180 °C. Mix together the crumb crust ingredients (perhaps you should double up before you begin!) and press into a 22 cm pie plate.

Slice the bananas. Blend the eggs, yoghurt, cottage cheese, lemon and vanilla in a blender and, when well whisked, add the flour and salt. Add the honey a little at a time while blending at low speed. Finally add the bananas. Pour the filling into the crust and bake for 20 – 30 minutes. Remove from the oven and dust with ground cassia.

For an even lighter pudding, grease the pie plate and simply sprinkle in 4 tablespoons of wheat germ, then add the filling. This is quick and easy and equally delicious.

# Sweet and Sour Cabbage

2 onions, chopped
2 tablespoons butter
2 green apples, peeled and grated
1 red cabbage, finely shredded (about
    8 cups)
¾ cup stock or water

2 tablespoons wholewheat flour
salt and pepper
6 tablespoons brown sugar
6 tablespoons apple cider vinegar
2 teaspoons ground cassia

Sauté the chopped onion in the butter until soft. Add the grated apple, shredded cabbage and almost all the stock. Simmer for 5 minutes. In a screw-top jar shake the wholewheat flour, salt, sugar, vinegar and cassia and a tablespoon or two of the stock. Stir into the cabbage and cook for another 10 minutes or until the cabbage is just tender. Serve with your favourite potato dish.

# Cabbage Cooked with Milk and Cassia

*cabbage, finely shredded*  
*milk*  
*2 teaspoons cassia per pot*  
*butter*

*salt*  
*pepper*  
*lemon juice*  
*parsley*

Simmer the finely shredded cabbage in milk with cassia for 10 minutes. Drain, toss in butter, add salt and pepper and a squeeze of lemon juice, and serve with a little chopped parsley. You will be surprised how many cabbage loathers you will convert into cabbage lovers – and as cabbage is cheap, healthy and easy to come by we should include it in our diets more often!

Convert your family to cabbage by cooking it in cassia and milk

# Cayenne

Tabasco Pepper, Chilli Pepper
*Capsicum frutescens*

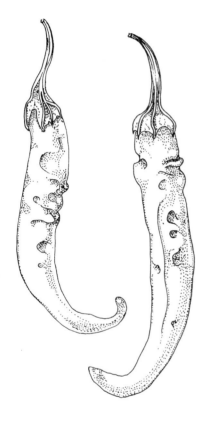

Capsicum is a variety of herbaceous plant. There are many varieties, annual and perennial, and the name covers a range of fruit which we know as chillis, peppers and cayennes. Chillis are the smallest and hottest of the capsicum family. In tropical countries they are used fresh while in Europe and the colder climates they are used dried and ground.

All species of capsicum are American in origin. In 1494 a physician to the fleet of Columbus on a voyage to the West Indies discovered the use of chillis by native tribes.

The medicinal uses of capsicum are interesting – as a stimulant, an aid to digestion and as a treatment for diarrhoea. However, its main uses are in the form of a condiment made from the hot varieties and as a nutritive vegetable in the form of sweet peppers.

A light sprinkling of cayenne over savoury food relieves heartburn and indigestion immediately and it can replace pepper in everyday cookery for this purpose. Cayenne is still included in many Pharmacopoeias. It originally came from Cayenne in French Guinea and is the hottest of all the spices. It grows wild in South America and India and is cultivated as a crop elsewhere. It is antiseptic and rubefacient and, like the other capsicums, is beneficial in digestion; it also has the effect of easing colic, flatulence and improves the peripheral circulation. It can also be employed as a liniment for neuralgia and rheumatism and, being antiseptic, a weak solution is beneficial as a throat gargle. However, large doses are an extreme irritant to the gastro-intestinal tract so it should be used with caution and in moderation for this purpose.

Cayenne may be used in all savoury dishes. It combines well with most savoury herbs but should be used sparingly as it can completely override other flavours. I find cayenne particularly delicious in omelettes, soufflés and with grilled fish.

# Vegetable Relish

This crisp and tasty relish is delicious with curries and egg dishes and gives a lift to uninteresting salads.

2  cups shredded cabbage, tightly packed
½  cup grated carrot, tightly packed
½  cup finely chopped onion
½  cup finely chopped green pepper

6  tablespoons vinegar
1 – 2 teaspoons salt
cayenne pepper to taste

Combine all the vegetables. Mix the vinegar, salt and cayenne and pour over the vegetables. Stir all together and refrigerate, tightly covered, overnight.

# Stuffed Peppers

Green peppers are very easily grown in the vegetable garden and, added to salads or stuffed, they are hard to beat as a flavouring asset. I save some of the biggest green peppers and allow them to turn their brilliant red on the bush. Pick them while they are rich and succulent, before they start to dry out. Cut off the stalk end, remove the seeds and stuff with different fillings. Use *rice, green mealies* or *green peas* as a base and combine with the ingredients below. For 6 green peppers you will need 3 cups of rice or peas or green mealies.

1  finely chopped onion, fried in oil
2  peeled chopped tomatoes
¼  cup diced celery stalks and leaves

1  teaspoon powdered ginger
3  teaspoons salt
cayenne to taste

Combine with the rice or green peas or mealies and stuff the peppers. Place in a baking dish and bake for 30 minutes at 350 °F/180 °C. Any extra filling can be placed around the peppers on the serving dish.

# Celery

Celeriac, Turnip Root Celery
*Apium Graveolens* Var. *Rapaceum*

Celery is a well-loved herb that enhances so many dishes. The celery we eat today was developed and cultivated by Italian gardeners on the banks of the River Po in the seventeenth century, before which wild celery was used. The Romans loved its meaty, savoury taste.

The whole plant can be used – leaves, chopped stems, and even the root – and is a beneficial addition to salads. It gives winter soups a delicious flavour and is equally good in stews and sauces.

Celery may be used to treat excess weight, rheumatism and nervousness, and is an excellent tonic and stimulant. The seeds, made into a tea, are a very effective diuretic which is also delicious. As celery grows easily in the garden, it is possible to have it always at hand.

Celeriac has a similar taste to celery but the leaves are coarser and it has a fleshy root, which is delicious grated in salads and soups. Both celery and celeriac combine well with most vegetables and all the savoury herbs except bergamot, anise and caraway. Try combinations of watercress, nasturtium, sage, lovage, the mints and mustard and create a variety of glorious salads with celery as the base.

# Celery Stalks

Cooked celery stalks make a wonderful side dish. Chop *2 blanched celery heads* into thumb-length pieces. Boil in salted water until tender. Drain. Serve with either of the sauces below.

### Butter and Tarragon Sauce

4  tablespoons butter
2  tablespoons chopped chives
2  tablespoons chopped tarragon

salt and pepper
juice of ½ – 1 lemon

Melt the butter and sauté the tarragon and chives in it. Add the salt, pepper and lemon juice and pour over the celery stalks.

### Basic White Sauce

2  tablespoons butter
2  tablespoons wholewheat flour
1  cup milk

½  teaspoon salt
herbs or spices to taste

Use a heavy-bottomed pot to prevent scorching. Melt the butter, stir in the flour and cook for 3 minutes over low to medium heat, stirring constantly. Add the milk slowly, stirring constantly, and bring to the boil. Adjust seasonings, add herbs and spices and pour over celery stalks. Sprinkle with grated cheese.

# Celery Soup                                      Serves 8 – 10

This is a wonderful basic soup and can be varied by adding many different vegetables and herbs. It is useful for slimmers too!

2  cups chopped onions
1  cup chopped parsley
2  cups grated carrots
4  tablespoons oil (sunflower or maize)
4  cups chopped celery stalks and leaves

1  cup chopped borage, fennel combined
1  cup grated celeriac root and a
    few leaves
10  cups water
celery salt and pepper

Sauté the onion, parsley and carrots in the oil until soft. Add the other chopped vegetables and herbs, celery salt, pepper and the water. Simmer for 15 minutes. Pour into the liquidiser and blend. Serve hot with freshly baked bread and cottage cheese. It is a meal in itself!

# Celeriac and Potato Salad

10 new potatoes
1 celeriac root
1 cup chives, chopped

## Dressing

2 teaspoons salt
¼ teaspoon pepper
1 dessertspoon brown sugar

2 tablespoons olive oil
2 tablespoons cream
1 cup plain yoghurt

Boil the new potatoes in their jackets, cool, peel and slice. Arrange a layer in a glass dish. Peel and grate the celeriac root and sprinkle some over the potatoes with some of the chopped chives. Pour over this half the mixed dressing. Arrange another layer of potatoes, chives and celeriac and top with the rest of the dressing. Decorate with fresh celery leaves and a dusting of allspice.

Celery soup makes a good meal for slimmers

# Chervil

*Anthriscus cerefolium*

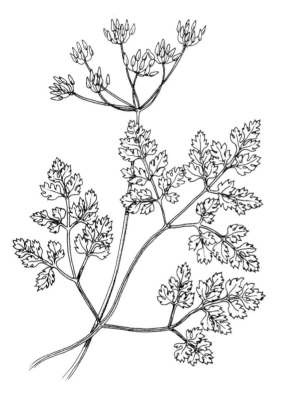

Chervil belongs to the carrot family. Like aniseed and parsley, its flavour is elusive, rather spicy and delicate. Its medicinal values made it a much sought-after herb in Roman times. It is a blood cleanser and effective rheumatic and kidney treatment. Today it is mainly used in cookery and its wonderful medicinal properties have been largely forgotten.

Chervil is sometimes biennial but I plant it as a shade-loving annual and pick the outer leaves as one would pick parsley to encourage growth.

Chervil is used in *fines herbes* mixtures and is a wonderful garnish. It can be used in white sauces, it combines well with cheeses, cottage and cream cheese, scrambled eggs, omelettes, salads and sandwich fillings and it goes well with fish and poultry.

# Chervil Soup Serves 6

Chervil soup is perhaps the best-known chervil dish. It is a nourishing, healing soup for aches and pains and excellent for those suffering from stress, tensions and stomach ulcers.

*500 g fresh potatoes, peeled and diced*
*2 onions, chopped*
*4 – 6 cups chicken stock*
*salt and pepper to taste*

*6 tablespoons chopped chervil*
*6 tablespoons plain yoghurt*
*chervil for garnishing*

Simmer the potatoes and onion in the stock for about an hour in a saucepan with a well-fitting lid. Purée in a blender and return to the saucepan. Add salt (I use vegetable salt) and pepper and fold in the chervil. Bring to the boil and serve immediately with a tablespoon of yoghurt and a few sprigs of fresh chervil floating in each bowl.

## Quick Chervil Sauce

Pour this over baked potatoes, fish dishes or use as a savoury pancake topping.

*3 tablespoons butter*
*salt and freshly ground black pepper*

*4 – 6 tablespoons fresh chervil,*
  *well chopped*

Melt the butter and add the salt, pepper and chervil.

Chopped chervil added to soup makes it ideal for those suffering from tension

Chervil sauce is an easy way to include chervil in the diet

# Chervil Quiche

## Pie Crust

1½  cups wholewheat flour
½  cup wheat germ
1  teaspoon salt

10  tablespoons soft butter
4 – 6 tablespoons cold water

Stir together the flour, wheat germ and salt. Rub in the butter and then work in enough water to hold the dough together. For the best results refrigerate the ball of dough in a plastic bag for an hour, or leave overnight in the fridge. Then roll out and line a large pie plate or 2 smaller ones. Bake at 400 °F/200 °C for 10 – 12 minutes and fill.

## Filling

3  eggs, well beaten
2  cups milk
salt and pepper
1  cup grated cheddar cheese

1  cup chopped chervil
pinch nutmeg
1  tablespoon butter
extra 3 – 4 tablespoons grated cheese

Whisk together the eggs, milk, salt and pepper. Spread the cheese evenly over the bottom of the pie crust and on top of that the chopped chervil. Pour the milk mixture over it, sprinkle with a little nutmeg and the 3 – 4 tablespoons of grated cheese. Dot with butter and bake for 30 minutes at 350 °F/180 °C – or until set. If the middle is not quite firm do not worry! Quiche needs to stand for 10 minutes before serving and it will firm up in that time. Garnish with chervil.

Asparagus (1 – 1½ cups) can be added to this, or thinly sliced courgettes, or cooked onions. If you keep to 1 – 1½ cups of well drained and lightly cooked vegetables, you can make a variety of delicious quiches that are always a great favourite.

# Chicory

*Chichorium intybus*

Chicory is an ancient herb which was much used and respected by Arabian, Egyptian and Roman physicians. It has been found growing wild for many centuries throughout Europe and was used, as it is today, for treating liver and gall bladder complaints. Chicory is familiar to all of us as the roasted ground root which often substitutes coffee or is added to it.

Chicory is classed as a vegetable when it is cultivated for blanching, a process which reduces the extreme bitterness of the plant. It is important to use chicory as soon as possible as it perishes rapidly. Here is a method to blanche your own.

About 4 – 6 months after planting chicory seedlings, dig out several plants, cut off the foliage, and stand the roots close together in a deep box or pot. Cover with a light, sandy soil about 15 cm deep above the top of the plants, press down lightly and keep the plants moist, but do not overwater. Store the box or pot in a cool dark shed. As they grow, the new young leaves become elongated and blanched, and the plant should resemble a pale elongated lettuce. If they are exposed to light the leaves will turn green and become excessively bitter, so keep the boxes in a dark place. As soon as the white leaves appear above the soil the plants are ready for lifting.

This vegetable makes a delicious casserole. I find that any bitterness in the leaves can be removed by boiling them lightly first, and quickly throwing off the water. Should you want to use the green unblanched plant, use only the young leaves. These can be added sparingly to salads and their flavour is enhanced by adding thyme, oregano, marjoram, garlic or onions. The blue flowers of wild chicory can also be added to salads, though, like the leaves, their bitterness can be unpleasant and they too should be used sparingly.

# Chicory Casserole

2  large onions, chopped
butter
4  chicory heads, sliced and lightly boiled
salt and pepper
lemon juice

1  cup grated cheese
2  eggs, beaten
1  tablespoon cornflour
2  cups milk
2  teaspoons thyme or oregano

Fry the onions in a little butter. Arrange a bed of chicory in a buttered casserole dish. Sprinkle with salt and pepper and a squeeze of lemon juice. Add a layer of onions. Cover with another layer of chicory. Add the grated cheese as a top layer and pour over this the whisked eggs, cornflour, milk, salt and pepper and the thyme and oregano. Dot with butter and bake for ¾ to 1 hour at 150 °C/300 °F. Serve hot, decorated with chopped parsley and chives.

# Chicory Coffee Substitute

Chicory root protects the liver against excessive coffee drinking, particularly of the instant variety, so why not consider making your own coffee substitute.

Grow the varieties Magdeburg, Brunswick or Witloof. Interestingly, all of these contain vitamins B, C, K and P, as well as a wealth of mineral salts. This makes chicory a diuretic and a tonic – but, like all herbs, it should be used in moderation as excessive and continued use can impair the function of the retina of the eye.

Mince a quantity of well-washed roots. Spread on baking trays and place in a low oven overnight. Grind down further in a coffee grinder and store in airtight bottles. This can be added to coffee or used on its own, according to your taste.

# Chives

*Allium schoenoprasum*

Chives were first cultivated in the Middle Ages. Until then they were the only member of the onion group found wild in Europe and North America. There are several varieties of chives, including the large, flat-leafed variety known as Chinese chives, *Allium tuberosum*, and a garlic-flavoured variety which has recently become popular.

Chives are a wonderful flavouring to so many dishes. They are good for digestion and help keep the body disease-free, warding off bronchial diseases, colds and flu.

Chives are one of the ingredients in the classic blend of delicately flavoured herbs known as *fines herbes*, which consists of equal quantities of finely chopped chives, tarragon, chervil and parsley. This blend can be added to sauces, soups, casseroles, vegetables, fish and chicken dishes.

One can dry chives but, as the fresh ones are so prolific, it really is a joy to have a clump at the kitchen door ready for picking. Although they die down in winter, it is only for a short period and for those few weeks a few leaves can be dried and stored in airtight jars.

Chives combine well with many herbs and sprinkled on egg salads or cream cheese they are glorious. Add them to cheese dishes, stews and soups in the last five minutes of cooking time to allow their flavour to be at its best.

# Rice and Courgette Pie

675 g crisp young courgettes
2 cups cooked brown rice
juice of 1 lemon
1 cup chopped chives
½ cup chopped parsley
1 teaspoon salt

pepper to taste
2 tablespoons oil
1 cup grated cheddar cheese
1 cup cottage cheese
crushed cornflakes

Slice the courgettes and boil in salted water until just soft. Mix rice with lemon juice, chives, parsley, salt and pepper. Grease a pie dish with the oil and place a layer of rice mixture, a sprinkling of cheese, a layer of courgettes, the cottage cheese and top with a cup of crushed cornflakes and a little grated cheese. Dot with butter and bake at 180 °C/350 °F for 15 – 20 minutes. This is delicious with a rich beef stew or a bobotie.

## Boiled Mealies and Chives

This is surely the only way to eat mealies! As the evening draws in, have a pot of water boiling on the stove. Go into the garden, pick the mealies and peel off the husks as you run in from the garden and toss the mealies into the pot. Boil briskly for 6 – 10 minutes. Serve immediately – dripping with butter into which chopped chives have been mixed. This is the best way to eat them for the sugar in mealies turns to starch within minutes of their being picked, so it must be done on the run!

## Mealie and Green Pepper Pie
Serves 6

As the season advances and the mealies become slightly harder to chew, slice them off the cob and make this tasty pie.

1 cup green pepper, thinly sliced and
    chopped
1 cup chopped chives
3 tablespoons butter
6 cups cooked mealies, cut off the cob

1 cup grated cheese
salt and pepper
2 eggs, whisked
2 tablespoons cornflour
3 cups milk

Fry the pepper and chives lightly in the butter. Add the mealies and sauté briefly. Place in a greased pie dish, cover with grated cheese, season and pour over it the whisked eggs, cornflour and milk. Dot with butter and bake at 180 °C/350 °F for 20 – 30 minutes or until lightly browned and set. Sprinkle with fresh chopped chives and serve.

# Chive Vinegar

*1 bottle white grape vinegar*
*chives*

Pack the bottle of white grape vinegar with chives and place it in the sun for 10 days. Every 3 days replace the chives with fresh ones. I use the chive flower heads as the bottle looks so pretty on the kitchen dresser and the pink flowers give a pink tinge to the vinegar. Use in salad dressings.

Chive vinegar makes your salad-dressing extra special

# Cinnamon

*Cinnamomum zeylanicum*

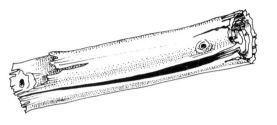

The cinnamon tree is similar to the cassia tree. It is native to Sri Lanka and Malabar but cultivated in the West Indies and several other Eastern countries. It is the bark of the young shoots that is harvested and this is thinner and finer with a sweeter, more delicate flavour than cassia bark. Whereas cassia can be used in savoury dishes and to spice meat and poultry, cinnamon is at its fragrant best in creams, chocolates and cakes.

Cinnamon's uses are many and it has been in use since the ancient Egyptians used it to embalm mummies. It is mentioned in the Old Testament in the same context as myrrh, olibanum, gold and silver. Chinese traders rediscovered it in the thirteenth century and it was documented in 1275.

Cinnamon is antiseptic, deodorant, stimulant and digestive and half a teaspoon made into a tea with half a cup of boiling water is an excellent mouth wash and treatment for diarrhoea, colds and flu.

Both whole and ground cinnamon are ingredients in pot-pourri blends. Try a cinnamon stick in the sugar bowl to give a subtle flavour to after-dinner coffee or a hot chocolate drink. Use this precious spice with thought and care, for it is one of nature's most glorious tastes.

Cinnamon can be combined with other herbs and spices but its special flavour and fragrance tend to be swamped by stronger spices and herbs. To savour it fully, cinnamon should be used alone in milk puddings, custards, mousses, ice-creams, cakes – particularly chocolate cake – biscuits and creams. A little can be added to stews, pickles and vegetable dishes like squash and pumpkin, but as there are so many other herbs to enhance those dishes, I would rather reserve its use for sweet dishes.

# Cinnamon Cheese Dessert **Serves 4**

This is a quick cheese cake type of dessert that is healthy and nutritious and, served with fresh fruit slices like bananas, peaches and green melon, is an instant favourite.

2  cups cottage cheese
2  eggs, well beaten
1  tablespoon melted butter
pinch salt
3  tablespoons brown sugar or
   2 tablespoons honey

juice of 1 lemon
1  teaspoon grated lemon rind
1 – 2 teaspoons ground cinnamon

Whip all the ingredients, except the lemon juice, rind and cinnamon, together in a blender. When well blended, add the lemon juice and rind and half of the cinnamon. Spoon into glass dishes, sprinkle with the remainder of the cinnamon and serve with fruit. This is also an excellent dessert for slimmers.

## Cinnamon Pancakes

All South Africans love *pannekoek* and pancakes on a rainy day are a traditional treat.

Because I use only unrefined products for health, I use brown flour in all my recipes, but white flour may be used if preferred.

2½  cups wholewheat flour
2  teaspoons baking powder
1  tablespoon brown sugar
1  teaspoon salt

2  large eggs
2½ – 3 cups fresh milk
4 tablespoons maize oil

Stir dry ingredients with a fork. Whisk eggs and milk and mix into dry ingredients. Pour a little of the oil into a pan, place on medium heat and pour 2 tablespoons of batter into it, tilting the pan to spread it evenly. When it bubbles turn over or toss the pancake and cook the other side.

Have a large plate standing on a pot of boiling water on the stove next to you. Put the pancakes on this, sprinkle with brown sugar and ground cinnamon and a squeeze of lemon juice. Cover to keep hot while you make the other pancakes.

# South African *Boere Pannekoek*

Here is the South African *boere pannekoek* recipe that is a favourite at every *boeredag*, fête and every school sports day. Perhaps they taste best made in a tent on on a gas burner!

2  cups white flour
2  eggs
little salt

1 – 1½ cups water
sugar
cinnamon

Mix enough water into the mixture to make a fairly thin batter, add salt and beat. Add the well-beaten eggs, mix well and pour a little into a well-greased pan. Turn or toss when the batter bubbles. Roll in sugar and cinnamon. The secret is to have the pan hot and to work quickly.

# Cinnamon Chocolate Cake

This is the most delicious chocolate cake I know and it has been my children's favourite birthday cake since they were tiny. It is moist and rich and not too sweet, and it never fails!

1  cup soft butter
1¾  cups brown sugar
4  egg yolks
5  tablespoons cocoa
2  teaspoons cinnamon

½  teaspoon salt
2½  cups sifted brown flour
4  teaspoons baking powder
1  cup sour milk*
7  stiffly beaten egg whites

* To make sour milk mix 1 cup of milk with 2 tablespoons vinegar.

Cream butter and sugar, then add egg yolks one at a time, beating well. Add the cocoa which has been blended with a little water, and the cinnamon and salt, and then add the flour and baking powder alternately with the sour milk. Fold in the stiffly beaten egg whites.

Line two deep 23 cm pans with greased paper, divide the dough, pour into the pans and bake for about 40 minutes at 180 °C (350 °F). Cool for 15 minutes in the tins, then remove to wire cooling racks.

### Filling

⅔  cup butter
1  cup unsweetened evaporated milk
1  cup brown sugar
3  egg yolks, well beaten

1  teaspoon vanilla essence
2½  cups coconut
½  cup chopped pecan nuts or almonds

Mix together the butter, milk, sugar and egg yolks and cook over a low heat until it thickens, stirring all the time; be careful not to let it burn. Cool slightly, then add vanilla, coconut and nuts. Use as a filling and a topping. Dust with cinnamon.

# Cloves

*Syzygium aromaticum*

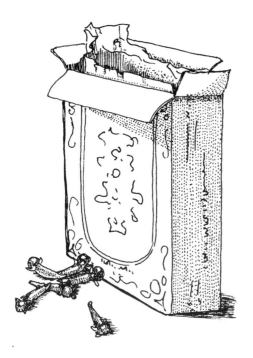

Clove trees are native to the five islands comprising the Moluccas proper and were first discovered by the Chinese. The dried, unopened flower buds are mentioned in the writings of Chinese physicians before 266 BC and a custom of the Han Dynasty (266 BC – AD 220) was to retain a clove in the mouth while addressing the emperor. Pliny the Elder also wrote of the wonders of this rare spice and by the fourth century cloves were widely used throughout Europe. The trading of cloves caused much rivalry between some European countries and as a result the French began cultivating the beautiful, evergreen clove trees in Mauritius.

Cloves are antispasmodic, counter-irritant and carminative. They are used in flatulent colic, for the treatment of toothache, neuralgia and rheumatism. Five cloves in a cup of boiling water make a wonder brew for eye infections (use as a wash) and as a gargle for sore throats. Oil of cloves is a well-known dental application, but prolonged use can cause irritation to the gums as it has rubefacient qualities.

Cloves may be used in combination with other spices in mulled wines, liqueurs, cakes, puddings and curries and they act as a preservative in pickles. Cloves, whole and ground, are used as a fixative in pot-pourris.

# Clove Brandy Aperitif or Liqueur

This is an amazing after dinner liqueur as it is excellent for the digestion and it has a fragrance that lingers. It is also a medicinal brandy that stimulates the digestive juices – a tablespoon before meals is the recommended dose.

2  cups clove-scented carnation petals  
1  litre brandy  
2  thumb-length twists of orange peel  

12  cloves  
3  tablespoons brown sugar  

Snip the bitter white 'heels' off the carnation petals. Pour the brandy over the petals, add the orange peel and cloves and shake well. Add the sugar and shake again. Store for a fortnight, shaking up each day. Strain through muslin and bottle.

# Fish Marinade

This basic marinade is an easy way to make an uninteresting fish dish more exciting. I make several bottles and keep them on the kitchen shelf for quickly marinating fish, pork or chicken breasts. If you place the fish or meat in the marinade overnight (in the refrigerator in hot weather) it penetrates deeply, giving a delicious flavour and acting as a preservative. A large fish can be marinated for five days!

1  litre white vinegar  
10  cloves  
6  peppercorns  
2  teaspoons fresh thyme or 1 teaspoon  
   dried  

$\frac{1}{2}$  teaspoon ground cloves  
2  teaspoons salt  
$\frac{1}{2}$  teaspoon cayenne  
1  tablespoon brown sugar  
1  bay leaf  

Push all the ingredients into the vinegar bottle and shake. For a strong flavour prepare the marinade 2 weeks before using and stand in the sun for a day or two. The bay leaf and thyme then release their flavours into the vinegar and the result is delicious.

# Spiced Pears

Apples can be used instead of pears and this is an old time favourite. I use an un-glazed clay dish with a lid to bake in as this keeps in all the succulent juices and flavours, but a pyrex dish with a lid is perfect too.

6 *pears*
2 *teaspoons butter*
2 *teaspoons brown sugar*

*ground and whole cloves*
*1 cup sunflower seeds*

Peel the pears, cut off the stalks and core. Pack the cavity with the butter, brown sugar and a pinch of ground cloves per pear. Stud with cloves – 2 or 3 into each pear. Place in a baking dish. Dot with more butter, a sprinkling of brown sugar and the sunflower seeds. Cover and bake at 150 °C (300 °F) for about an hour or until the fruit is soft.

Serve with cream or 'junket' (also known as milk cheese).

## Junket or Milk Cheese
*Serves 4*

1 *litre milk*
2 *teaspoons liquid rennet or 2 crushed*
  *rennet tablets*

4 *tablespoons sugar*
*ground cloves*

Warm the milk to body temperature. Remove from heat and stir in the rennet mixed with a little warmed milk. Add the sugar and stir well. Sprinkle with a little ground cloves and set in the refrigerator.

To make the cheese leave out the sugar and cloves. Once it has set pour through butter muslin and leave to drain overnight suspended over a deep bowl. The whey that drips into the bowl is a nourishing drink excellent for invalids (stir in a little honey if you like it sweet). The soft curds are delicious with fruit. Raw or unpasteur-ised milk gives a better result.

# Van der Hum Liqueur

This is a favourite South African liqueur and is delicious after a heavy meal.

3  bottles good brandy (750 ml each)
1  small bottle rum (325 ml)
20  cloves
1  crushed nutmeg
4  sticks cinnamon
6  cardamom seeds

1  small piece fresh ginger root
    (walnut-sized)
½  cup fresh orange blossom
peel of 6 naartjies cut into thin strips
4  cups brown sugar
3  cups water

Fill a crock, jar or small cask with the brandy and rum. Tie the spices which have been bruised in a muslin bag, add the naartjie peel, orange blossoms and shake up every day for 4 weeks. At the end of this time make a syrup of the sugar and water. Boil for 20 minutes in a covered pot, then cool. Strain the brandy mixture and discard the spices, peel and blossom. Mix the brandy mixture and syrup well and stand for another 4 weeks, shaking occasionally. Cork well.

Cloves give my spiced pears their distinctive flavour

57

# Comfrey

*Symphytum officinale*

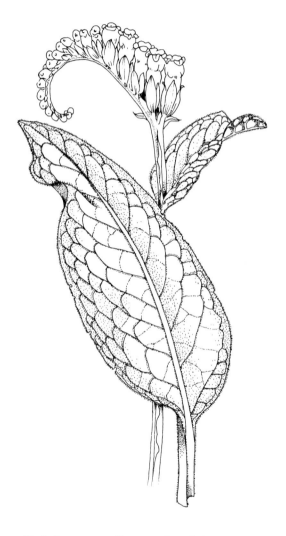

Comfrey is native to Europe and Asia and has been introduced and naturalised elsewhere. One of nature's most amazing healing plants, it is used throughout the world as an ulcer cure, bone knit aid, for pleurisy and bronchitis, in the treatment of wounds, bruises, skin ulcers, rheumatism, neuralgia, arthritis, varicose veins and as a general health tonic.

A tablespoon of chopped comfrey to a cup of boiling water is a soothing tonic drink and is wonderful for treating stomach ulcers. Sweeten with honey if desired.

Young leaves can be coated in a standard batter and fried in oil and, with salt and pepper, this makes a delicious vegetable dish. Comfrey is related to borage and has the same unobtrusive flavour, so it can be used in many dishes to enhance stronger-flavoured herbs.

If you have indulged in too much wining and dining comfrey root tea will give soothing relief to gout! Boil 3 tablespoons of chopped, well-washed root in 4 cups of water for 20 minutes. Stand to steep further, then strain and bottle and store in the refrigerator. Drink one small wineglassful 3 times a day.

Use comfrey lavishly in soup and stews. Chop it finely or purée it in spinach dishes, add it to meat dishes and use it as an ingredient in a slimming health drink. Comfrey is an endless asset – no garden should be without it.

# Slimming Health Drink

This is nourishing enough to use as a cleansing diet and can be drunk throughout the day.

6 carrots, scraped
2 carrot leaves
10 comfrey leaves
4 fennel stalks and leaves

4 apples, peeled and cored
1 pineapple, peeled and sliced
6 celery stalks and leaves
1 cup parsley

Push all the ingredients through a juice extractor and pour into glasses. Drink immediately. Make this fresh several times a day.

# Comfrey Gaspacho

Serves 6 – 8

This is a delicious soup served cold on a hot day. It is ideal for a luncheon as it is light, amazingly healthy and slimming.

10 ripe tomatoes, skinned and sliced
2 cucumbers, peeled and diced
10 chopped green onions
6 tablespoons chopped chives
4 tablespoons lemon juice
10 young green comfrey leaves, chopped

2 seeded, chopped green peppers
4 tablespoons chopped celery
2 tablespoons chopped parsley
salt and pepper
3 – 4 cups chicken stock
2 – 4 tablespoons brown sugar

Put all the ingredients except the chopped chives and parsley through a liquidiser. Serve in a glass punch bowl with the chopped chives and parsley sprinkled over it. Keep well chilled until served. Hook lemon wedges around the rim of the bowl.

# Mutton and Comfrey

2  kg best end mutton
4  large onions, chopped
2  garlic cloves, peeled and chopped
½  cup sunflower cooking oil
6  carrots, scraped and diced
6  potatoes, peeled and halved
4  tomatoes, skinned
3  tablespoons cornflour mixed with
    3 tablespoons debittered yeast

juice of 3 lemons
salt and pepper
about 4 cups water
10  chopped comfrey leaves
4  cups chopped celery leaves and stalks
1 cup chopped parsley

Fry the diced mutton in the oil with the onions and garlic until browned. Add all the other ingedients except the cornflour and debittered yeast which, mixed with a little water, must be added at the end of the cooking time to thicken the stew. Simmer gently on low heat in a solid-bottomed, well-lidded pot until tender. More water may need to be added – I usually find an hour's cooking time is about right. Serve with a green salad and fresh bread. This is perfect for a winter evening.

The vegetables in the comfrey slimming drink make it nourishing enough to use as a cleansing diet

# Coriander

*Coriandrum sativum*

Coriander is an easy-to-grow annual. It is indigenous to Europe but once introduced to an area it quickly seeds itself and becomes part of the flora. It has been cultivated for over 3 000 years and is mentioned in numerous medieval medical texts, by the ancient Greeks, by early Sanskrit authors who called it *kustumburu*, and by the ancient Egyptians on their papyrus scrolls. Its name is derived from the Greek word *koris*, which means 'bedbug', since the plant has a similar smell!

Chewing a seed of coriander will stimulate the gastric juices and warmed, bruised seeds applied to a painful rheumatic area will alleviate pain, but it is predominantly used to ease and prevent griping caused by other medication. It is probably the most widely used herb in the world, and the whole plant is aromatic and delicious. The root can be cooked as a vegetable; the leaf can be used in salads; and the seeds can be used in baking, confectionery, liqueur manufacture and can be added to pot-pourri as a fixative.

Coriander is a pretty, decorative annual to grow. It will flourish beautifully in full sun and well-drained soil and even a few plants produce a bountiful harvest of seeds at the end of summer.

It has a milder flavour than other spices, so it can be used in a larger proportion. It combines well with other herbs and spices and is delicious in soups, stews, fish, meat and curry dishes, sausage stuffings, lentil and bean bakes, milk puddings, custards and cakes and biscuits. What a range!

Leaves and stalks can be chopped and added to soups and stews and ground seeds are good in meat loaves, pasta dishes and cheese and vegetarian dishes.

As a condiment, however, I find coriander at its best.

61

# Coriander Chutney

juice of 3 lemons
2 cups coriander leaves
1 tablespoon minced fresh ginger
4 – 6 finely chopped spring onions,
    including the green tops

little salt
1 teaspoon ground coriander

Put the lemon juice into the blender and add the finely chopped coriander leaves a little at a time until a paste is formed. Combine ginger, spring onions, salt and ground coriander and add slowly until well blended.

This is delicious served with meat and cheese dishes, or with vegetarian dishes, and gives a lift to uninteresting dishes. It can be kept a short time in the fridge, but I find it is far nicer to make it fresh each time.

## South African Pickled Fish

Any firm-fleshed fish can be used here but Kabeljou or Cape salmon (geelbek) are best.

4 kg fish (uncooked)
2 tablespoons sea salt
3 lemons
6 bay leaves
6 large onions, sliced and chopped
1 – 2 red chillis
2 tablespoons curry powder

1 teaspoon turmeric
4 tablespoons sugar
salt to taste
10 peppercorns or 3 teaspoons lemon
    pepper
6 cups vinegar
2 tablespoons coriander seeds

Debone and slice the fish. Sprinkle with salt and stand until it is room temperature. Then steam the fish or grill with a little oil. Fry the onions lightly.

Boil up all the other ingredients and, while still hot, place a layer of fish in the casserole and over it a layer of onions. Pour over the sauce, follow with another layer of fish, more onions and cover with sauce. Allow to cool. Cover securely and for the most delicious results allow it to stand for 24 hours before serving. Keep it in the fridge if the weather is hot.

# *Boerepampoen* Fritters

*Boerepampoen* is the huge flat white pumpkin grown in the mealielands and it stores well, so these fritters can be made for a winter supper.

3 – 4 *cups mashed, cooked* boere-
    pampoen
1 *cup brown flour, sifted with*
    3 *teaspoons baking powder*
3 *well-beaten eggs*

½ *teaspoon salt*
2 *teaspoons ground coriander*
½ *cup milk (or less)*
2 *tablespoons brown sugar*

Mix and beat the above ingredients to make a soft batter. Heat a pan with a cup of sunflower or maize oil in it. Place spoonfuls of pumpkin batter into it – do not allow them to touch – and turn as the underside browns. Drain on crumpled brown paper, dredge with cinnamon sugar and a squeeze of lemon juice.

Make cinnamon sugar by adding 2 – 4 teaspoons of ground cinnamon to 1 cup of sugar. Shake in a jar.

*Boerepampoen* fritters
make a wonderful win-
ter supper

# Cumin

Like coriander, cumin is an annual herb. It is the ripe seed head that is the most important part of this plant and these are intensely pungent with a curry-like taste and fragrance.

Cumin is indigenous to the upper regions of the Nile, and has spread to the Mediterranean region and India. It is cultivated on the North African coast, in the Middle East, Malta and China, and the seeds – *fructus cumini* – were widely used in the Middle Ages. Cumin was used in the time of the prophet Isiah, and Dioscorides mentions cumin in his early medical writings.

Medicinally cumin is used in the treatment of diarrhoea and dyspepsia, and its most common culinary uses range from curries to liqueurs, with cumin oil as an important ingredient in the perfume industry. It is interesting to know that cumin is chiefly employed in veterinary medicine.

Because of its pungent taste, cumin must be used sparingly. It combines well with hot spices and is part of the curry combinations. With meat, poultry and game cumin is at its best and it enhances egg dishes, breads and pickles. Take care when combining cumin with other herbs as it tends to overpower. A pinch of seed is usually sufficient in a dish.

# Baked Cumin Tomatoes

**Serves 6**

6 *large tomatoes*
3 *tablespoons finely chopped onions*
1 *tablespoon freshly chopped basil*
1 *cup coarse wholewheat breadcrumbs*

2 *tablespoons soft butter*
*salt and pepper*
½ *teaspoon cumin seed, crushed*
1 *beaten egg*

Cut the tomatoes in half and hollow out a little of the pulp, enough to make a shallow nest for the stuffing. Combine the other ingredients and place in the tomato halves. Dot with butter and bake at 240 °C/400 °F for about 10 minutes or until the tomatoes are soft and the stuffing browned. Serve as a side dish with fish or meatloaf.

# Mulligatawny Soup

**Serves 10**

This is a rich, tasty soup that has many variations. I find this one the most satisfying and it is a wonderful start to a winter meal as it is warming and cheering and very nutritious. It can be served with separate bowls of cooked rice as part of the main course, or you may like to add the rice to the soup just as it is served.

½ *chicken*
2 *large onions, finely chopped*
2 *bay leaves*
1 *teaspoon ground cumin seed*
½ *teaspoon ground coriander seed*
½ *teaspoon turmeric*
½ *teaspoon ground cardamom seeds*
3 *cloves*
10 *ground peppercorns*
8 *tablespoons red lentils*

4 *tablespoons brown rice*
2 *garlic cloves, peeled and finely chopped*
½ *teaspoon paprika*
4 *tablespoons butter*
1 *tablespoon sifted flour*
*juice of 1 lemon*
*juice of 1 orange*
1 *cup coconut milk**
*salt to taste (about 2 teaspoons)*

* If you have no fresh coconuts available, make the milk by soaking 2 tablespoons of desiccated coconut in a cup of boiling water for about half an hour. Then squeeze the milky fluid through a cloth. This is not an essential ingredient but it does give that extra touch of blandness that the hot spices need.

Cut up and bone the chicken and boil in 1,5 litres of water. Add half the onion, bay leaves, spices and lentils and simmer covered until tender. Meanwhile cook the rice separately. Fry the remaining onion, garlic and paprika in the butter and add to this the flour. Stir well and add to this paste the lemon and orange juice and the coconut milk. Pour into the soup and bring to the boil. Add salt to taste. Cook for 5 minutes and finally add the rice. Serve piping hot.

# Curry

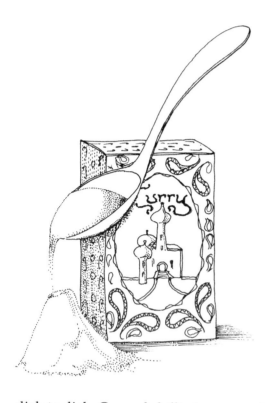

The most important influence on South African cooking probably came with the importing of Malay slaves to the Cape in the seventeenth century. The Malay women were expert cooks and when they arrived at the Cape they carried with them precious spices from the East, including cardamom, anise, fennel, turmeric, ginger, cumin, garlic, coriander, curry mixtures, mustard seed, saffron, saltpetre and tamarind. These were integrated into local cooking and before long a glorious array of spiced and fragrant dishes emerged to find their place for all time in Cape cuisine.

Curry is made up of between 12 and 20 different spices and the ingredients can be varied according to the desired flavour and strength of the curry. In India and Sri Lanka curry powders are freshly ground each day and vary from dish to dish. Ground chilli gives curry its typical biting hot taste, which can vary in strength. Commercial curry powder is an easy and convenient way of using this exciting blend of spices and this too can be obtained in varying degrees of hotness. Specialist shops and Indian markets in South Africa will blend a curry for you and with their expertise will open up for you a wealth of subtly different flavours.

It is also possible to buy garam massala, a mixture of ground spices that are not as hot as curry powders, and this can be used alone for a curry-like flavour or mixed with curry powder to give an extra bite. I find massala on its own a wonderful flavouring that lifts plain and uninspiring dishes to exotic heights.

Curry powder recipes abound, and it is infinitely satisfying to mix your own. Here are three variations, in all of which the amounts can be varied according to your taste and preference.

In all three recipes, crush the spices with a pestle and mortar, blend well and store in an airtight jar. Use one of your favourite blends whenever a recipe calls for curry powder.

# Curry Powder Mixture No. 1

1 tablespoon each coriander, cardamom
  and ginger

3 tablespoons turmeric
1 teaspoon cayenne

# Curry Powder Mixture No. 2

2 tablespoons each black peppercorns,
  and coriander fenugreek and turmeric
1 tablespoon cinnamon powder
2 tablespoons dried chillis, broken up
  fairly small

2½ tablespoons cumin seed
1 tablespoon poppy seed
1 tablespoon cardamom seed
1 dessertspoon mustard seed
1 dessertspoon powdered ginger

# Curry Powder Mixture No. 3

1 tablespoon each of coriander, cumin
  and turmeric
1 teaspoon dry ginger
1 teaspoon peppercorns

½ teaspoon cayenne
1 teaspoon fennel seeds
¼ teaspoon each mustard, fenugreek,
  cloves, poppy seed and mace

# Curry Enhancer

This can be strained and added to recipes that call for curry, or added just as it is to vegetable, meat or fish dishes. It gives an amazing taste to good old mincemeat dishes, and I use it in vegetarian dishes and as a sauce over brown rice.

⅓ cup olive oil or butter
4 tablespoons chopped onion
3 tablespoons chopped celery or fennel
3 tablespoons chopped apple
⅓ or ½ cup flour
2½ cups milk

¼ teaspoon nutmeg
bay leaf
2 – 3 teaspoons curry blend
juice of 1 lemon
1 teaspoon soy or Worcestershire sauce

Heat the olive oil or butter in a saucepan. Add the chopped onion and brown. Add the chopped celery or fennel, and the chopped apple. Blend the flour into the milk, add the nutmeg and bay leaf and stir into the vegetables. This will thicken as you stir. Lastly add your curry blend, the lemon juice and the soy or Worcestershire sauce. Cook for about 5 minutes.

# Curry Sauce

This curry sauce recipe has been the closely guarded secret of a famous American restaurant. It has a sensational flavour and may be used over pasta, rice, vegetable and meat dishes. It is a real party dish and is sure to turn you into a curry fanatic!

4 tablespoons butter
½ teaspoon mustard seed
½ teaspoon cumin seed
½ teaspoon fenugreek seed
4 whole cloves
1 teaspoon salt
1 teaspoon turmeric

1 teaspoon ground coriander
¼ – 1 teaspoon cayenne (according to taste)
3 cups clear apple juice
2 tablespoons sugar or 1 tablespoon honey
1 cup plain yoghurt
3 tablespoons rice flour

Melt butter in a heavy pan. Add whole spices and sauté until they pop. Add ground spices and turn heat to low. Mix the apple juice and honey or sugar into the yoghurt and add the flour. Beat gently, pour this into the spice mixture and simmer, stirring with a wooden spoon until it thickens. Add this to chicken, fish and vegetable dishes – it turns an ordinary dish into one fit for a king!

# Vegetarian Curry

This is a nourishing, warming dish that is a meal in itself. Served with brown rice and a side dish of cottage cheese, it has all the nutrition one needs. This combination of vegetables is popular all over India and by experimenting you will find the combination most palatable to you. Any vegetables can be used, even hubbard squash or courgettes.

4 tablespoons maize oil
2 large onions, chopped
½ teaspoon turmeric
1 teaspoon curry powder
½ teaspoon freshly ground black pepper
1 tablespoon brown sugar
1 teaspoon salt
1 large tomato, chopped

4 leeks, thinly diced
2 potatoes, cubed in tiny pieces
1 cup fresh garden peas
1 eggplant, cubed
1 cauliflower, broken into flowerets
1½ cups water*
juice of 2 lemons

Heat oil in a large, heavy-bottomed saucepan, and sauté the onions. Add turmeric, curry powder, pepper, sugar, salt, and brown these slightly with the onions. Add vegetables, stir to coat each piece with the oil and spice, add water, cover and cook slowly over a medium heat. Add a little more water and the lemon juice, stirring every now and then to prevent burning. Cook until the vegetables are tender. Serve hot.

* I use a waterless cooking pot with a temperature gauge in the lid, and 1½ cups water works perfectly here. In an ordinary pot you may need to add more water and watch for too vigorous a heat.

# Dandelion

*Taraxacum officinale*

Although dandelion is considered a nuisance weed, it is one of the most important plants in our diet. It is an extremely effective diuretic, and probably the best herb with which to treat liver complaints. The leaves can be included in salads and are an excellent tonic and laxative. They are also good for soothing and healing jaundice, treating the early stages of cirrhosis of the liver, rheumatism, aching joints, improving the digestion and strengthening tooth enamel. They are fairly bitter, however, so use them sparingly in salad.

The milky juice from the stems and leaves is an effective application for warts and blisters and should be applied daily. The diluted juice is also an effective eyedrop for sore, red eyes.

Dandelion is native to Europe and Asia and has been introduced elsewhere. The roots, dried and powdered, have been used as coffee in many countries for centuries. It can be used to make fermented and unfermented beer and the whole plant can be cooked and enjoyed in soups, stews and vegetable dishes.

The name *dandelion* comes from the French *dents de lion*, the teeth of the lion, and if you look at the leaf shape you will see why.

# Green Soup

This is an excellent soup for those undergoing stress or writing exams, and for those who are depressed or grieving.

2 cups chopped onions, including
  green tops
1 cup of each of the following, chopped:
  comfrey
  celery stalks
  watercress
  borage
  salad burnet

celery leaves
carrot tops
chervil
lucerne
2 cups chopped dandelion greens
salt and cayenne pepper
2,5 – 3 litres chicken stock
1 tablespoon marmite

Fry onions in oil until they start to brown. Add all the other ingredients and simmer until tender – about 30 minutes. You can put the soup through a liquidiser, or ladle straight into bowls and decorate with a little parsley.

## Dandelion Salad

1 cup chopped watercress
1 cup mung bean sprouts
1 cup avocado scoops
½ cup chopped parsley
½ cup diced feta cheese

2 cups chopped dandelion greens
1 cup diced cucumber
½ cup chopped celery
½ cup calendula petals
salt, paprika

Mix all ingredients. Toss with a vinegar and oil dressing, and sprinkle with a little ground caraway or dill seed. Decorate with sprigs of parsley.

## Dandelion Wine

This can be drunk before dinner or as a night-cap. Warmed in winter it is a soothing remedy for coughs and chest complaints.

2,3 litres dandelion flowers
4,5 litres water
2 large oranges
3 large lemons

6 kg sugar
2 tablespoons dry yeast
50 g raisins

Bring the flowers and water to the boil in a large pot. Peel the orange and lemon rind thinly, add to the boiling flowers, and add the sugar. Simmer in a closed pot for 1 hour. Cool and strain. Add the yeast to the lukewarm brew. Stir, and cover with a cloth. Next day add the orange and lemon juice and the raisins. Bottle and leave uncorked. Three weeks later when fermentation has ceased, cork the bottles loosely.

# Dill

*Anethum graveolens*

Dill is another ancient herb mentioned in the Bible. It is often included in children's medicines as it is stomachic and is excellent for flatulence, and it is therefore a constituent of gripe water. Even chewing a seed will ease the condition. Dill is an important herb in Scandinavian and Central European cuisine and it is native to the Mediterranean region and Southern Russia, where it is a common ingredient in many local dishes.

Dill seeds and leaves are used in pickles, with cabbage, onion and root vegetable dishes, in chutneys, breads and cheeses. It is a delicious herb and pleasing to most palates.

Perhaps it is best known in pickled cucumbers as dill pickle.

# Dill Pickle

*1 kg pickling cucumbers*  
*brine*

*1,75 litres spiced vinegar*  
*dill seeds*

Choose small, crisp cucumbers. Larger ones need to be sliced lengthways into convenient-sized pieces to fit the pickling jars. Prick the skins all over. Place the cucumbers in a brine solution made by dissolving 450 g salt in 4 litres water. I use sea salt or rough rock salt, as refined table salt gives a cloudy effect to the water, does not strengthen the skin of the cucumbers so well and is not as easily absorbed. Leave in the brine solution for 3 days.

At the end of the third day, drain off the brine and pack the cucumbers into sterilised glass jars. (Sterilise the jars by washing them in a strong detergent, rinsing well and placing in a warm oven for 20 minutes.)

Pour the spiced vinegar to which the dill seeds have been added over the cucumbers, seal, and stand for 24 hours. Then strain the vinegar off and bring to the boil. Again pour it over the cucumbers, seal and stand for 24 hours, and then do the same again. In this way the cucumbers develop the rich green colour so typical of dill pickles and absorb the spicy vinegar flavour. After the third time add a few more dill seeds and make sure that the vinegar completely covers the cucumbers, seal well, label and store.

# Basic Spiced Vinegar

To 1 litre good quality vinegar add the following whole spices:

*thumb-length stick of cinnamon*  
*1 teaspoon cloves*  
*2 teaspoons allspice*

*1 teaspoon black peppercorns*  
*1 teaspoon mustard seed*  
*3 bay leaves*

Bring to the boil and immediately remove the pot from the stove and stand for 3 – 4 hours. Strain and use for pickles or wherever a spice-flavoured vinegar is needed.

# Dill Sauerkraut

Well-flavoured and well-made sauerkraut is a most useful and delicious dish. So often it is a complicated and difficult recipe but here is one that is quick, easy and very tasty. The dill seeds help to digest the cabbage, and a sprinkling of freshly chopped dill leaves can be added just before serving. Dill cannot really be combined with other herbs as its flavour is so delicate and unique; and in this sauerkraut recipe it is perfect. It can be served as a vegetable dish with all meat dishes and is particularly delicious with fish dishes. Cold, it makes an unusual salad that combines well with other salads like potato and carrot.

Sauerkraut should really only be made in the cooler months as it ferments very quickly in the heat of summer. It is best to wait for the winter cabbages and make it then.

You will need a stoneware crock, a plate that will fit into the crock and a heavy stone to weight the plate.

*1 medium-sized cabbage*
*½ litre water per cabbage*

*½ litre apple cider vinegar per cabbage*
*2 tablespoons dill seed per cabbage*

Shred the cabbage finely and pack into the crock in layers alternating with light sprinklings of coarse salt. Pour over this the cider vinegar/water/dill mixture, cover with a clean cloth, then the plate and the stone weight. Every 2 days spoon off the scum that rises and replace the cloth with a clean one. In about 5 days it will be ready to eat.

If you cannot eat up your crock contents on the first day, bottle what you do not use in sterilised jars as it does not keep.

Sauerkraut is best made in the winter months

This recipe is not at all complicated

# Elder

*Sambucus nigra*

Elder has been a highly esteemed and much-loved herb since early Egyptian times. The flower has excellent cosmetic properties and, combined with peppermint in tea, is still used throughout Europe to treat colds and coughs. Wine and an excellent cough mixture can be made from the berries, and the leaves and flowers make a good wash for skin conditions such as eczema. They are also laxative, diuretic and antispasmodic when drunk as a tea. Elder flowers can be used in pancakes, cakes, creams and custards. Added to a butter icing on cakes they make an unusual treat and the whole flower dipped into batter and fried as a fritter is a most delicious tea-time treat. I dust them with icing sugar and cinnamon, spoon on whipped cream and serve them with bergamot tea. It's a show stopper!

Although elder is native to Asia, Europe and the British Isles, it has been introduced everywhere and I have seen it shading a mud hut in the Transkei, a sea cottage on the Wild Coast and an isolated farmhouse in the Orange Free State. I am sure not one of those who live in its shadow knows that it keeps witches at bay, that the leaves made into a brew will keep mosquitoes away, or that the flowers can be made into champagne or the best face cream ever!

Young elder buds can be added to pickles and to fruit salads, and the flowers have a honey-like taste when added to cakes and puddings. The berries make excellent jam, syrup and ice-cream. In very hot areas the berries don't set very well, so one would have to grow an avenue of elders to get enough for jam or syrup, but do try to grow it as it is one of nature's most wonderful remedies for cystitis, bronchitis, coughs, colds, skin ailments, rheumatism and eye complaints.

## Elder Flower Champagne

6  *large flower heads*
4  *litres water*
750 g *sugar*
2  *lemons*

2  *oranges*
2  *tablespoons white wine vinegar*
1  *cup raisins*
1  *tablespoon dry yeast*

Boil up the flowers in the water with the sugar and thinly sliced lemon and orange. Stand and cool. Strain. Add vinegar, raisins and yeast. Cover and leave for a fort-night. Strain and bottle, and keep in the fridge. Serve chilled.

## Elderberry Curd

Like lemon or orange curd, this is a delicious filling for cakes and puddings, pan-cakes and pies.

500 g *ripe elderberries, cleaned*
100 g *butter*

300 g *sugar*
4  *eggs*

Wash the berries and cook in a little water until they are soft. Put through a sieve to separate pulp from pips – put the purée in a double boiler, add butter and sugar, and stir well. Add eggs and stir with a wooden spoon until it thickens. Pour into jars. Seal and store in a cool place.

# Fennel

*Foeniculum vulgare*

There are several varieties of fennel but the one most commonly used is sweet fennel or Florence fennel. Florence fennel has been used for culinary purposes for about 2 000 years, though its origins are shrouded in legend. Its medicinal properties are widely known, and it is the best-known herb for slimming.

The whole plant can be used and as it grows so prolifically and vigorously it can be used lavishly. Fennel has a strong flavour and does not blend well with other herbs, so it is better to use it alone or with chives and parsley.

One of the easiest ways of using fennel is in a sauce for grilled, baked or fried fish. The chopped leaves can be added to the sauce or used as a garnish. The stem thinly sliced is delicious in salads and the root and stalks thinly chopped can be boiled and eaten as a vegetable. The seeds are used in pickles and sauces and for flavouring breads, and they help digest starchy foods like pastries, bread and pasta. As it is a digestive herb, fennel can be added to cabbage, cauliflower, broccoli, onion and turnip dishes. A tea made from 1 teaspoon of bruised seeds to 1 cup of boiling water is wonderful for flatulence.

A few fennel seeds chewed will freshen the mouth wonderfully, and a few chewed and swallowed at the end of a heavy meal will aid digestion like a dream. In Italy tiny fennel seed sweets are served in little paper cases at the end of a meal. One can experiment by adding a few fennel seeds to a favourite sweet recipe at the hard ball stage.

The well-known Five Spice Powder from China is a mixture of star anise, black pepper, fennel seed, cloves and cinnamon and this is a most exciting seasoning. The ingredients vary in quantity with pepper being the smallest, and once again you can experiment with the blend.

Fennel and dill should not be grown next to each other in the herb garden, as fennel will devitalise dill and dill's daintier strength and flavour will be lost through cross-pollination.

## Quick Fennel Dressing

3/4 cup chopped fennel leaves
1/2 cup white vinegar (preferably tarragon vinegar)
1/2 cup water
1 tablespoon sugar

Put all the ingredients into a screw-top jar and shake vigorously. Serve separately in a small jug or sauce boat with fish dishes, or over cheese dishes and salads.

## Fennel Sauce                                    **Makes 3 cups**

This is a delicious sauce that combines beautifully with so many dishes, including baked potatoes, cauliflower, broccoli and turnips. It is rich and nourishing and can be put through a blender and used as a 'white sauce' over pasta or with grilled fish or steak.

1 onion, chopped
3 tablespoons oil
2 cups vegetable or chicken stock
1 clove fresh garlic
1 tablespoon chopped fennel root
1 teaspoon fennel seed
2 tablespoons chopped parsley
1/8 teaspoon pepper
1 1/2 teaspoons salt
4 potatoes, peeled and cubed

Sauté the onion in oil, add all the ingredients except the parsley, cook until soft, then put through a blender until smooth. Add parsley.

# Fennel and Spinach Pie

2 – 3 cups thinly chopped fennel (the
   swollen root end)
6 – 8 well-packed cups chopped Swiss
   chard spinach
1 onion, chopped
2 well-beaten eggs

2 cups cottage cheese
juice of 1 large lemon
$1/2$ teaspoon salt
paprika
1 cup fresh wholewheat breadcrumbs

Cook fennel and chard in a little water until tender. Stir every now and then while cooking so it does not burn. Drain well. Sauté the onion in a little oil, add the fennel and spinach and stir well. Beat together eggs, cottage cheese, lemon juice, salt and paprika. Stir a cup of this mixture into the fennel, onion and spinach. Grease an oven dish and pack this well down into it. Pour over the remaining cheese and egg mixture and sprinkle with breadcrumbs. Dot with butter. Bake for about 30 minutes at 180 °C/350 °F or until set. Allow to stand for 10 – 15 minutes before cutting into squares and serving.

Fennel is a wonderful
aid to digestion

# Fenugreek

*Trigonella foenumgraecum*

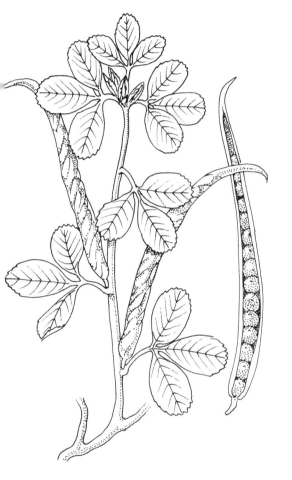

Fenugreek is really a fodder crop and the Latin, *foenumgraecum,* means 'Greek hay', which emphasises its agricultural use.

Fenugreek was introduced into Europe by Benedictine monks and in the ninth century Charlemagne urged the use of the herb not only as a fodder but also as a medicine. A favourite herb of the Arabs, it was studied at the Salerno School of Medicine by Arab physicians. The Egyptians favour fenugreek and not only use it as medicine but roast and grind it into coffee, and eat the sprouted fresh seed and leaves as a tasty vegetable. Fenugreek is favoured in Indian cookery as well and is often an ingredient in curries.

The seed is used as a source of yellow dye, and is valuable in the treatment of dyspepsia and diarrhoea. Boiled seeds can be applied as a poultice to skin inflammations. The celery-flavoured leaves are tonic and carminative and can be used in salads, soups and stews. The ground seeds and leaves are often ingredients in chutneys and in many Middle Eastern confectioneries, particularly halva.

Fenugreek has a subtle yet pungent flavour and should really be used on its own as its flavour is so distinctive. However, it does combine with other spices.

During our midsummer months mangoes are available in quantity and a delicious mango chutney flavoured with fenugreek can be made quickly and reasonably. This piquant condiment will enhance every dish it is served with – particularly mince meat, roast beef, grills and vegetarian dishes.

# Mango and Fenugreek Chutney

1,35 kg mangoes that are just ripening
3 tablespoons salt
2 litres water
450 g brown sugar
600 ml vinegar
3 tablespoons root ginger, peeled and
    finely chopped
1 tablespoon fenugreek seeds
3 tablespoons fenugreek leaves (if
    you have them)

4 cloves garlic, crushed
1–2 teaspoons curry powder (start with
    1 teaspoon and taste as you may not
    want it too hot)
1 cinnamon stick
125 g dates, chopped
125 g seedless raisins or sultanas

Peel the mangoes and cut away from the stone into bite-sized pieces. Sprinkle with salt, cover with the water and leave for 24 hours. Drain and set aside. Dissolve the sugar in the vinegar and bring to the boil. Add the rest of the ingredients and the mango pieces and simmer in a covered pot for 30 minutes, stirring occasionally as it thickens. Discard the cinnamon stick, bottle, seal and label.

I melt a cheap candle and pour this on top of the chutney in the neck of the jar to seal it completely. In this way the chutney will keep for years, if you can restrain yourself from relishing it!

# Tonic Tea                                        Serves 1

1 cup boiling water
1 teaspoon fenugreek seeds

Pour the boiling water over the fenugreek seeds and sweeten with a little honey if desired. This is blood-cleansing and a wonderful tonic if taken for several days at a time. In nursing mothers it aids lactation.

# Fenugreek Seed Cordial

This aids digestion and is a wonderful winter warmer. It can be quickly and easily made.

600 ml good brandy
3 tablespoons brown sugar
1 teaspoon crushed fenugreek seed

1 teaspoon aniseed
1 teaspoon caraway seed

Add the ingredients to the brandy, bottle, and shake well. Store for a month, shaking occasionally. Strain through muslin and rebottle. Slowly sip 1 tablespoon before meals.

# Garlic

*Allium sativum*

Garlic is perhaps the most favoured and widely used of kitchen herbs. There are several varieties, including small and giant forms with flavours that range from mild to very strong.

Garlic is native to Asia and has been cultivated for many centuries. It was employed medicinally by the Egyptians and Romans and widely revered for its amazing medicinal powers. It is one of the few herbs that can treat almost all the disorders of the body; and it is particularly beneficial in treating diseases of the respiratory system, nervous ailments, high blood pressure and infection, and in warding off parasites. Garlic is a natural antibiotic and is also a beneficial tonic, antiseptic and preventative medicine. It should be included daily in our diets!

The pungent smell that one exudes after eating garlic can be helped by eating fresh parsley. Mint, basil and thyme also help clear the breath.

So many dishes include garlic and it can be used so widely that I hesitate to give any recipes except for garlic butter, garlic vinegar and a wonderful garlic mayonnaise that can be served with salads, chicken and fish dishes. It is also delicious served in avocado pear halves as an entrée, or used as a sandwich filling with cucumber or tomato slices, or as a dip.

# Garlic Mayonnaise

3 egg yolks
pinch salt
300 ml olive oil

juice of 1 lemon
8 cloves garlic, peeled and crushed

Beat the egg yolks and salt for 3 minutes in a blender. Add the oil a few drops at a time, beating constantly. When a quarter of the oil has been blended, pour in the rest in a thin stream. Beat until thick and then add the lemon juice, and finally the crushed garlic. Bottle and store in the refrigerator.

  Note: If the mayonnaise should separate, beat a fresh yolk in another bowl and slowly add the curdled sauce to it. This can be done with any mayonnaise.

# Garlic Butter

1 cup soft butter
4 – 8 cloves garlic, peeled and finely
    chopped (or 1 teaspoon garlic flakes)

about ¼ teaspoon salt

Choose a fresh French loaf or bake a loaf of wholewheat bread. Slice fairly thickly, but do not slice right through. Butter each slice on both sides with the well-blended garlic butter. Wrap in aluminium foil and place in a hot oven for 10 – 15 minutes or until the bread is crisp and golden. Serve hot.

# Garlic Vinegar

This can be used on its own as a salad dressing, or combined with oils and mustard into a delicious dressing, or used whenever a dish calls for a flavoured vinegar. It is strong and wonderfully versatile, and can be stored for many months. Whenever I have a crop of matured garlic I immediately make enough vinegar to last me for a season. Remember you will have to make enough to give away, as this is a cook's favourite!

1 bottle white vinegar
2 garlic bulbs, broken into cloves

Push the garlic cloves into the bottle of white vinegar, bruising and peeling each clove before popping it into the bottle. Stand the bottle in the sun for 100 hours of strong sunlight – I leave it for about 2 weeks in a good sunny position. Taste and, if it is not strong enough, repeat the procedure. Strain through muslin into a clean, attractive bottle, push in a few thinly peeled fresh cloves and, if you can, a garlic flower and a few leaves. This makes the bottle attractive and easy to identify on the kitchen shelf.

# Geranium

Scented Geranium
*Pelargonium* species

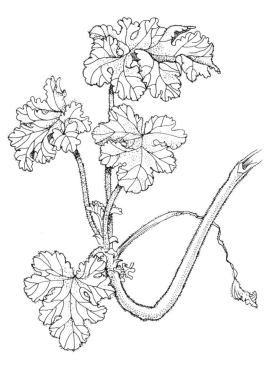

This glorious plant is indigenous to South Africa. It has many varieties and each is distinguished by its particular scent, such as rose, lemon, apple, peppermint, nutmeg and eucalyptus. As they grow with such ease and beauty in our country, I urge you to make use of their exquisite flavours in cooking. They add a bouquet to rice puddings, custards, cakes, fruit dishes, and summer cooldrinks and jellies. Although the subtle fragrance and flavour of the geranium really needs to be savoured on its own, it does combine well with ginger and vanilla.

Four varieties lend themselves to cooking and perhaps the favourite is rose-scented geranium, *Pelargonium graveolens*. The flavour and fragrance of this variety is a mixture of rose and spices. There is also a peppermint variety, *P. tomentosum*, and this is delicious in drinks. *P. limonseum* has a lemony scent and is widely used in jellies and baked puddings. Apple geranium, *P. odoratissimum*, smells and tastes like Granny Smith apples and is delicious in apple dishes.

In cakes and jellies I make a rosette of leaves at the bottom of the tin or bowl and pour the dough, liquid jelly or fruit pureé over them. This can be baked or cooked as usual. You will find a wealth of recipes where geranium leaves can be used and each one will have a floral bouquet of its own.

Oil of geranium is important in the perfume industry and the dried leaves are an important ingredient in pot-pourri. A small pillow stuffed with dry geranium leaves is an aid to sleep.

A delicious tea can be made by pouring 1 cup of boiling water over 4 medium-sized leaves. Allow it to steep and drink frequently through the day as a treatment for diarrhoea.

# Geranium Health Drink

10 rose geranium leaves
 3 cups boiling water
 2 cups barley water
 3 cups grenadilla, apple or pear juice,
   unsweetened and unpreserved

2 – 4 tablespoons honey
juice of 2 lemons

Pour boiling water over geranium leaves and allow to steep overnight. Make barley water by boiling up 1 cup of pearl barley in 6 cups of water. Simmer for an hour, cool, strain and keep in the refrigerator for adding to summer drinks.

   The next day strain the geranium tea and barley, combine all the ingredients, mix and serve in tall glasses with a slice of lemon and a sprig of mint. This is a particularly refreshing drink in summer and is nourishing and healthy, so make it daily for the summer holidays.

# Baked Rose Geranium Custard

This is a quick and easy dessert that is healthy and delicious and can bake alongside the roast for Sunday lunch.

3 large eggs
3 cups fresh milk
3 tablespoons honey
little butter

6 geranium leaves
½ cup raisins
½ cup sunflower seeds

Whisk together the eggs and milk, and then beat in the honey. Grease a baking dish with butter, press the geranium leaves onto the butter so that they do not float up into the custard. Sprinkle the raisins and sunflower seeds over them. Pour in the milk, egg and honey mixture, sprinkle with cinnamon, and bake at 180 °C/350 °F for about an hour or until the custard is set. Serve with whipped cream and discard the geranium leaves when serving.

# Baked Apple and Geranium

Quinces, pears or yellow peaches are as delicious as apples in this pudding. Serve it hot in winter and cold in summer.

## Filling

10 apples, pears or quinces, or 12 yellow
    peaches, or a combination

1 cup brown sugar
little water

## Crust

2 cups large flake oats (not the quick cook
    variety)
1 teaspoon cinnamon

¾ cup soft butter
½ cup brown sugar

Peel, core and thickly slice the fruit. Boil with the sugar and drain. Press the crust into a greased pie dish, saving ½ cup to crumble over the fruit. Spoon a layer of fruit into the crust cover followed by a layer of rose geranium leaves and another layer of fruit. Sprinkle with the rest of the crust crumbs, dot with butter and bake at 150 °C/300 °F for half an hour or until browned on top. Serve with heavy cream.

    The geranium leaves can be discarded when serving but are pleasantly edible.

Geranium health drink is particularly
refreshing in summer

# Ginger

*Zingiber officinale*

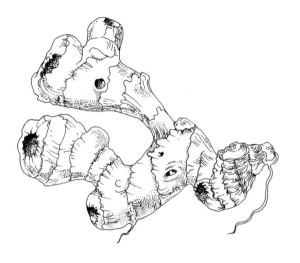

Ginger is perennial in the south-eastern part of Asia, and is now cultivated in many countries – from Australia to Jamaica – with a tropical and subtropical climate. In China ginger has always been an important herb in medicine and to show how long ginger has been used both as a medicine and flavouring, the Greeks had imported the rhizome from the East for many centuries before Dioscorides described its medicinal uses in the first century.

The rhizome is used fresh or dried, sliced or powdered, and it has been included in many dishes for its wonderful relief in flatulent colic. It is an excellent tonic, it stimulates and aids digestion, and it is used in purgatives to prevent griping and as a treatment for dyspepsia.

Ginger's wide spectrum of flavouring makes it a favoured herb. Delicious in biscuits, cakes, puddings and drinks, it is also a wonderful ingredient in chutneys and meat dishes.

It complements many fruits and in jam-making combines beautifully with rhubarb, quince, watermelon, vegetable marrow, plum and pineapple.

# Cape Chutney

**Yields approx. 8 bottles**

This well-loved Cape chutney recipe with its Malay influence is the perfect condiment and adds piquancy to any savoury dish.

250 g seedless raisins
250 g sultanas
250 g dried apricots
250 g dried peaches
2 tablespoons salt
750 g brown sugar
5 tablespoons ground ginger
2 red chillis ground or 1 teaspoon
    cayenne

2 teaspoons paprika
2 teaspoons mustard powder
6 allspice berries, crushed
6 cups onions, finely chopped
1 cup green pepper, finely chopped
3 cups vinegar

Soak the fruit overnight in water. In the morning strain and boil up the fruit, spices, onions and peppers in the vinegar. Simmer slowly in a covered pot until it thickens. Stir often to prevent it sticking to the bottom of the pot. When thick, spoon into clean, hot jars. Seal with melted wax, label and store. Serve with meat, fish, cheese tarts, egg dishes and cold meats.

# Rhubarb Jam

**Yields about 2,5 kg**

Rhubarb jam is an unusual and delicious treat that uses up those extra rhubarb stalks in the garden when the family is tired of rhubarb puddings and pies. This jam can be used in pebble tarts and on hot buttered toast with cream cheese is food for the gods!

1,75 kg trimmed rhubarb cut into
    2,5 cm pieces
250 ml water
2 5-cm pieces fresh root ginger, peeled
    and bruised

juice of 3 lemons
1,35 kg sugar
6 tablespoons thinly sliced crystallised
    ginger pieces

Boil the rhubarb in the water with the fresh ginger root and the lemon juice until the rhubarb is soft. Remove the ginger roots. Add sugar and stir until dissolved. Add crystallised ginger and boil rapidly for 10 – 15 minutes – or until a teaspoon of the juice sets on a cold saucer. Bottle while hot, seal and label.

# Ginger Bread

Ginger bread and biscuits are long-time favourites and both keep well in an airtight tin. If you can manage to keep your ginger bread a week, it greatly improves in flavour if wrapped in foil and kept in an airtight tin. Serve thinly sliced either plain or buttered.

175 g butter
225 g soft brown sugar
6 tablespoons treacle
6 tablespoons golden syrup or honey
450 g flour
4 level teaspoons baking powder

1 teaspoon salt
1 tablespoon ground ginger
2 eggs, lightly beaten
300 ml milk
4 – 6 tablespoons crystallised ginger,
    thinly chopped

Preheat the oven to 170 °C/325 °F. Heat the butter, sugar, treacle and syrup in a saucepan on a low heat and stir frequently until blended and dissolved. Allow to cool. Sift flour, baking powder, salt and ginger into a mixing bowl. Make a well in the centre and pour in the eggs, milk and the syrup and butter mixture. Stir gently to combine the ingredients, then beat well until smooth and blended. Lastly stir in the crystallised ginger. Pour into a lined, greased 900 g baking tin. Bake for approximately 1 hour or until a skewer inserted into the middle of the loaf comes out clean and dry. Cool a short while in the tin, then turn out onto a wire rack.

If you serve it immediately, drizzle a little of the syrup in which the crystallised ginger is preserved over the loaf while it is still warm – I find about 3 tablespoons is sufficient. Otherwise cool the loaf and wrap it in foil. This is also delicious served as a dessert with plain ice-cream and ginger syrup.

## Ginger Shortbread Biscuits     Yields about 30 biscuits

32 g ground ginger
350 g plain flour

175 g castor sugar
250 g butter

Sift ginger and flour. Stir in the sugar and rub in the butter. Turn onto a floured board and knead until smooth. Roll out to 5 mm thick, cut with a pastry cutter into rounds, place on a greased baking tray and bake at 190 °C/375 °F for about 20 minutes or until light brown. They will keep well in an airtight tin with a little castor sugar sifted between them.

# Horseradish

*Armoracia lapathifolia,*
*A. rusticana, Cochlearia armoracia*

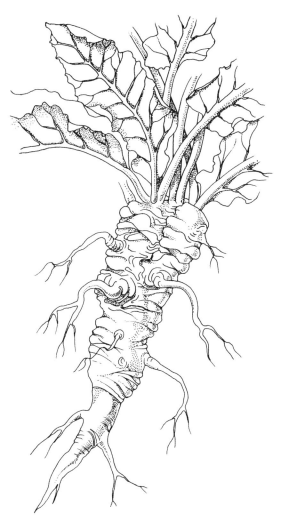

Horseradish is easily grown by root cuttings in any soil, and is a worthwhile addition to the herb garden. Like all herbs, it has been known and valued through the ages.

It is an antibiotic herb and works particularly well on the respiratory tract and urinary system. The grated root dissolves internal tumours and is an effective poultice if applied to swellings, wounds and external tumours. It is also an appetite stimulant and its warming properties destroy bacteria in the digestive tract and expel worms. To stimulate the appetite and aid digestion take a teaspoonful of grated horseradish on a little bread before meals. A little grated horseradish in salads, soups and stews will build up your resistance to coughs and colds.

Horseradish belongs to the mustard family and is rich in sulphur. It is a valuable herb that should be used more frequently. Its pungent taste tends to overpower other herbs, but it is strengthened by mustard, so it combines well in sauces and vinegars.

# Horseradish Sauce

Horseradish sauces are a wonderful accompaniment to roast beef, pork, eggs, poultry and fish, and give an unusual taste to salads.

This traditional horseradish sauce is simple to make. Wash and scrape a good quantity of freshly dug up roots. Put these through a mincer or grate finely. Pack into clean, hot bottles. For every 6 bottles of roots boil up 3 cups vinegar with:

*1  tablespoon salt*
*a few peppercorns*
*4  teaspoons mustard powder*

Strain and pour over the horseradish to the top of the bottles. Seal with a layer of grease-proof paper and tighten the screw top. Store for a month before using.

## Red Horseradish Sauce  Yields approx. 4 x 400 g bottles

A ruby red horseradish sauce is available commercially, but this home-made version is infinitely nicer. Store it for a month before serving.

*4  cups minced fresh horseradish*
*2  cups finely grated or minced fresh*
 *raw beetroot*
*5  cups vinegar*
*1  stick cinnamon*

*1  tablespoon salt*
*4  teaspoons mustard powder*
*2  teaspoons whole cloves*
*5  tablespoons brown sugar*

Mix the horseradish and beetroot and pack into hot jars. Boil the cinnamon, salt, mustard powder, cloves and sugar in the vinegar and pour over the horseradish and beetroot mixture to overflowing. Seal with a round of wax paper and screw the lids on tightly.

# White Horseradish Sauce

This is a delicious sauce that will spoil you for all time and put paid to plain white sauce in your cooking! The base is a béchamel sauce.

*600 ml milk*
*1 small onion, chopped*
*2 small carrots, scraped and chopped*
*1 stick celery, chopped*
*4 cloves*
*1 bay leaf*
*4 peppercorns, roughly crushed*

*½ teaspoon ground mace*
*1 teaspoon salt*
*2 tablespoons butter*
*2 tablespoons flour*
*½ cup cream*
*1 cup grated horseradish*

Boil the onion, carrots, celery, cloves, bay leaf, peppercorns, mace and salt in the milk. Remove from the heat, cover and allow to infuse for half an hour. Strain.

Melt the butter in a saucepan, blend in the flour and add the strained milk, stirring as it thickens. Bring to the boil and allow to boil for a minute or two, stirring all the time. Add the cream. Keep stirring briskly, then add the grated horseradish. Adjust seasoning – a little more salt and pepper may be necessary. Heat through and serve with fish, pork, poultry or potatoes.

Horseradish, a great antibiotic, is easily grown

Minced root can be preserved in vinegar

# Hyssop

*Hyssopus officinalis*

Hyssop is not a well-known herb but has the wonderful property of dissolving fats and oils in rich meats and fish. In counteracting these oily substances it aids the digestion and for this reason it is an important herb to include in a book about cooking with herbs.

Hyssop is a perennial plant, and is available at some nurseries. It establishes quickly and grows fairly easily from seed, so do try and search it out. Its flavour is strong and unique and its uses in cooking have not been fully explored.

A few chopped hyssop leaves are delicious in stuffings, sausages and pork pies and, at the other end of the scale, impart an unforgettable flavour to stewed fruit dishes, fruit pies and *compote*. A thumb-length sprig added to a pot of stewing fruit makes all the difference.

Hyssop derives its name from the Hebrew word *Ezobh*. It is referred to in the Old Testament ('Purge me with hyssop and I shall be clean'), when it was esteemed in purification rites and used to cleanse the temples. Paulus Aegnita wrote of it in the seventh century and it was used in the fourteenth century as a strewing and cosmetic herb.

Hyssop is native to central and southern Europe, and thrives on rocky, calcareous soils in the mountains of Siberia. It has been introduced into the Americas, Russia and India, where it is cultivated commercially.

Hyssop is a respected medicinal herb used to treat coughs, colds, sore throats, asthma and catarrh. It is a valuable antiseptic and is used as a poultice over wounds and grazes. As a tea or in the bath it is an effective treatment for rheumatism. It may be used to flavour liqueurs, it is a valued fixative in perfumery and a treatment for excessive perspiration. It is one of the most valuable herbs for aiding digestion, and should be included sparingly in all rich, fatty dishes. A teaspoon of fresh herb per dish or half a teaspoon of dried herb is usually sufficient but here your own taste will guide you.

Hyssop is a strong herb and combines fairly well with other herbs like thyme, the mints, sage, bay, most spices and oregano, but reacts unfavourably with bergamot, celery, fennel, fenugreek, chillis, caraway and basil.

# Hyssop Ratafia

Ratafias are made by steeping herbs and fruit in brandy for several weeks in the sun. The result is a richly flavoured drink that has wonderful pick-me-up qualities. They are of tremendous benefit in winter for treating chills, colds, coughs and poor circulation, as well as aiding digestion and stomach cramps. Hyssop ratafia is particularly beneficial for old people who suffer from rheumatism and lack of appetite. A liqueur glass taken before the evening meal will work wonders.

4 cups washed and hulled
   strawberries or 4 cups stoned
   apricots or 4 cups diced
   pineapple (choose fruit that is
   firm but not overripe)
1 cup brown sugar

4 thumb-length sprigs of hyssop
3 or 4 hyssop flowers
10 cloves
1 stick cinnamon
1 litre good quality brandy

Place a layer of fruit in a wide-mouthed jar, sprinkle with half the sugar, cover with another layer of fruit, and sprinkle with the rest of the sugar. Add hyssop, cloves and cinnamon. Pour over the brandy and seal tightly. Place daily in the sun for at least 4 weeks, being careful not to shake it up too much. The secret of the blending of the fruit juices and herb oils is the warmth by day and the cooling by night. At the end of the 4 weeks strain through muslin, discard the fruit and herbs, bottle and store in a dark cupboard. Use as required.

This combination of everyday vegetables is delicious enough to serve at a dinner party, particularly with roast pork. Hyssop dissolves and helps digest the fats and oils in pork and oily fish, and this quick and easy side dish can be served with all rich dishes.

*1 large onion, finely chopped*
*4 tablespoons maize oil*
*1 bay leaf*
*1 teaspoon mustard powder*
*1 teaspoon celery seed or*
  *4 tablespoons chopped celery*
*2 medium potatoes, diced*
*2 carrots, thinly sliced*
*1 small cauliflower head broken into*
  *florets*

*2 green apples, peeled and chopped*
*2 cups sliced courgettes*
*2 ripe, fairly large tomatoes, peeled and*
  *sliced*
*1 tablespoon finely chopped hyssop*
  *leaves or 2 teaspoons dried hyssop*
*salt*
*paprika to taste*
*cornflakes or breadcrumbs*

Fry onion in the oil with the bay leaf, mustard and celery. Stir in the vegetables in this order, leaving about 2 minutes between each addition: potato, carrots, cauliflower and apple. Stir until they are all turned and softening. (The trick of getting the vegetables to cook evenly is to dice the potato, carrots and cauliflower small, as these take longer to cook.) Add courgettes, tomatoes and hyssop. Heat through on low heat for a few minutes. Season. Transfer to a baking dish, sprinkle with paprika, crumbled cornflakes or breadcrumbs, dot with butter and bake at 190 °C/375 °F for about 20 minutes.

Hyssop vegetable dish is an ideal accompaniment to rich dishes as hyssop helps digest fats and oils

# Lavender

*Lavendula officinalis,*
*L. vera, L. spica*

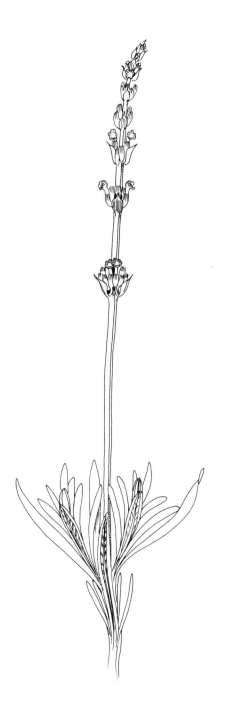

Although lavender might seem a strange herb to include in a cookery book, its delicate and beautiful flavour is a delight and once you have tried it as a flavouring, you will want to grow and use it abundantly. It is probably the most popular of the traditional herbs and it has been used as a medicinal plant and an aromatic for hundreds of years. It is sedative, antiseptic, beneficial in gastric ailments characterised by flatulence, and an effective insect repellent and cough suppressant. It is also a wonderful cure for headaches.

Try a few lavender flowers in a fruit salad. Choose fresh young flowers, break them up finely and sprinkle them over the fruit salad.

Lavender is an exciting ingredient in marinades in which game is turned. It combines well with the oil and flavouring and helps tenderise tough meat. The leaves can be added to stews and braised meat dishes. Use about 1 tablespoon of fresh leaves per dish.

Lavender is a wonderful ingredient in pot-pourri and is important in perfumery. Scented lavender sachets are effective moth repellants and dried lavender in bowls about the house gives a delightful fragrance.

# Lavender Sugar

Lavender sugar can be used in baking and confectionery and gives a delicate flavour to plain cakes and puddings.

Fill a large glass jar with lavender flowers and sugar (see that you have enough for your everyday needs for it will soon become a favourite flavouring).

*750 g white sugar*
*4 cups lavender flowers (on the stalks)*

Mix the sugar and lavender flowers in a blender or crush in a mortar. Fill an airtight jar with the mixture and, when a recipe calls for sugar, sieve the correct quantity, returning the flowers to the jar.

# Lavender Honey

This is an excellent cough remedy and soothing agent for sore throats, and gives a delicious flavouring to herb teas and fruit drinks.

*1 cupful lavender flowers*
*500 g honey*

Place the lavender flowers in a pot. Pour the honey over them. Heat gently over a pot of boiling water (a double boiler is perfect), cover and simmer for half an hour. Pour into hot jars and seal. Store for at least one month before using. Strain through a sieve, discard the flowers and store in screw-top honey jars.

# Lavender Tea

This refreshing tea is quick and easy to make and will alleviate fatigue and stress.

*2 fresh lavender sprays, or*
*2 – 4 teaspoons flowers stripped of*
*their stems, or a thumb-length leafy*
*twig*

*1 cup boiling water*

Pour the boiling water over the lavender. Stand a few minutes, sweeten with lavender honey if desired, and sip while inhaling the aroma. Herb tea should never be drunk with milk and the only sweetening should be honey.

Rose petal, orange blossom, honeysuckle and jasmine honey can also be made in this way. Orange blossom is bitter so do not leave it too long.

# Lemon Balm

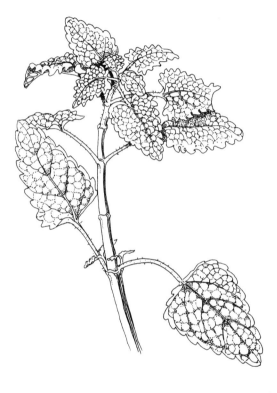

Its strong lemony flavour and fragrance gives this mint its name and it is a favourite herb world-wide. It originated in the mountainous regions of southern Europe.

*Melissa* is the Latin for 'bee' and in some countries it is known as 'bee balm'. 'Balm' is the shortened form of 'balsam', the fragrant oil, which signifies the herb's aromatic sweetness. It has wide medicinal uses including treatment for nervousness, headaches, neuralgia and high fevers, and a tea made from lemon balm lifts the spirits, relieves tension and brings down temperatures.

The fresh leaves are delicious in fruit salads and fruit drinks. A brew can be made of fresh or dried leaves and drunk as a tea, or used as a base for punch. The dried leaves give a delightful lemony fragrance to potpourris and a bush of melissa in the garden is a treasure. Cut the strong growth as it flowers, and dry; in this way the bush constantly produces new lush shoots.

Lemon balm is essentially a 'sweet' herb and combines beautifully with other herbs and spices, for its lemony flavour enhances rather than dominates. In asparagus soup, for instance, a few chopped leaves are delicious; and I use minced balm in mayonnaise for a piquant flavour.

Because of the lemony flavour, balm is often delicious with fish and cheese dishes and I find that a quantity of dried balm kept handy in a screw-top bottle is most useful. For salads, balm combines well with cucumber, sorrel, celery, asparagus, beetroot and fresh spinach leaves. Try it with rosemary and oregano in savoury dishes, but avoid contact with basil as it tastes too pungent in this combination.

For summer drinks it is so easy to freeze into an ice cube a sprig of lemon balm or other herbs like rosemary, mint, peppermint, spearmint and bergamot. It is both decorative and an easy way of adding flavour and interest to an otherwise uninteresting drink. Lemon balm added to freshly squeezed lemon juice (4 thumb-length sprigs to 1 lemon and 1 cup of boiling water) is a delicious cure for colds and also helps sleeplessness.

Lemon balm can be propagated from seeds, cuttings and division. It grows lushly in partial shade but can take full sun. It likes a moist, rich soil and will grow up to 75 cm in height.

## Lemon Balm Tea                                                                 Serves 3

Lemon balm tea will uplift the spirits, bring down fevers and relieve nausea. It is a tonic and is good for slimming. It can also be used as a base for fruit drinks.

10 *thumb-length sprigs lemon balm*
 1 *litre boiling water*

Pour the boiling water over the lemon balm sprigs and allow to steep. Drink hot as a tea, or cool and strain, and drink a small wineglassful several times during the day.

## Fruit Punch                                                                  Serves 6 plus

*lemon balm tea*
*1 litre fresh pineapple juice,*
  *unsweetened and unpreserved*
*honey*
*½ litre grenadilla juice*

*pulp of 6 grenadillas*
*1 pineapple, chopped*
*fresh lemon balm sprigs*
*½ litre iced water or 10 cubes ice*

Add the fresh pineapple juice to the lemon balm tea recipe above. Sweeten with a little honey if desired. Add the grenadilla juice, grenadilla pulp, and the finely chopped pineapple. Add fresh sprigs of balm and the iced water or ice cubes.

## Gooseberry and Lemon Balm Sherbet                                            Serves 6

*6 cups fresh, husked gooseberries*
*300 ml thick cream*
*3 tablespoons boiling water*
*2 tablespoons powdered gelatine*

*2 eggs, separated*
*2 tablespoons fresh chopped lemon balm*
*sprig fresh lemon balm, for decoration*
*extra cream for decoration*

Cook the gooseberries for 5 minutes in a syrup of 2 cups boiling water and 1 cup brown sugar. Drain the gooseberries and place in a blender with the cream and 4 tablespoons of the syrup and whirl. Pour the boiling water on to the gelatine and stir until dissolved. Add to the cream and gooseberries in the blender. Add the egg yolks and fold in the stiffly beaten egg whites. Add the chopped lemon balm. Pour into individual pudding glasses or bowls and set in the fridge. Just before serving decorate with a little whipped cream and a sprig of fresh lemon balm.

# Lemon Grass

*Cymbopogon citratus*

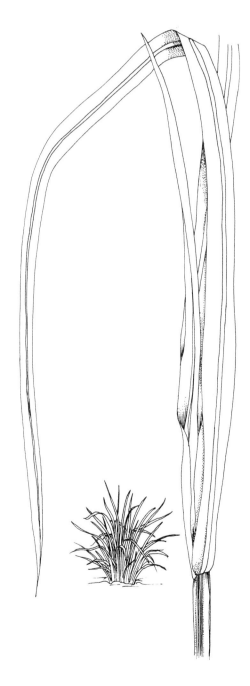

Herb lovers are searching out lesser-known plants with enthusiasm and the once rare and little known lemon grass is one such herb that is becoming a firm favourite.

Its growing conditions are so undemanding that it can be cultivated in any soil. It does not need much water and the clump can be divided up over and over again and new plants started from side roots and shoots. Like most grasses, lemon grass is frost tender and is dormant in winter, but in frost-free areas it remains evergreen and attractive. It can be used lavishly as it benefits from shearing.

Lemon grass is perhaps best known as a fragrant flavouring in teas and drinks. It is a wonderfully calming herb that soothes the digestion, aids assimilation and alleviates stress and anxieties that affect the stomach. Lemon grass tea as a substitute for ordinary tea will soon become a favourite and cooled tea is a delicious summer drink. A few blades of lemon grass added to any dish, particularly curries and fish soups, give a delicious lemony flavour.

A small bundle of lemon grass can be added to vegetable soups and stews while they are cooking. Combinations with sage, rosemary, bergamot, chervil, mint, parsley, salad burnet, nasturtium, winter and summer savory and tarragon are best, as lemon grass has a delicate flavour which can easily be neutralised by the stronger herbs.

## Lemon Grass Tea

8 blades of lemon grass approximately
   15 cm long, chopped into short,
   manageable pieces
juice of 1 lemon

1 sachet honeybush or rooibos tea
5 cups boiling water
honey to sweeten
few lemon slices

Place the lemon grass, lemon juice and sachet of tea in a teapot. Pour over it the boiling water, allow to steep for a few minutes, sweeten with honey and float a lemon slice in each cup.

## Lemon Grass Fruit Punch

Serves 6 plus

Use the recipe for lemon grass tea as a base for fruit punch. Make two or three times the quantity and allow to cool. Then add:

1 litre pineapple juice (the fresh, boxed,
   unsweetened, unpreserved variety)
several sprigs mint

honey to sweeten
1 cup grenadilla pulp
½ pineapple, chopped

This is a basic punch and several herbs can be substituted for the lemon grass, such as bergamot, mint, lemon verbena, pineapple sage, spearmint, balm and geranium.

Lemon grass makes a wonderfully soothing tea

# Lemon Verbena

*Aloysia triphylla*
*Lippia citriodora*

Lemon verbena is native to Central and South America, and has been esteemed throughout the ages for its nostalgic fragrance, its value as a flavouring in cooking, its medicinal properties and as an insect repellant. It is excellent for nausea, flatulence, colic spasms, palpitations and vertigo. For these conditions it can be made into a tea by adding 4 – 8 leaves to 1 cup of boiling water, sweetened with honey if desired, to be drunk after meals.

Lemon verbena was introduced to Europe by the Spaniards, who added a sprig of it to finger bowls and washing waters.

A sprinkling of finely chopped lemon verbena leaves and freshly squeezed lemon juice will transform ordinary dishes like grilled fish, and rice is delicious cooked with a spray of lemon verbena (remove before serving). Oatmeal porridge with just a sprig added while it is cooking and removed before serving, topped with cream and honey, is food fit for a king. A helpful thought when coaxing children to eat their porridge is that the lemon verbena will alleviate a gripy tummy.

Lemon verbena is the only herb that can be picked fresh and green and placed directly in the linen cupboard. It does not mildew or rot but dries with its full and glorious fragrance.

My favourite way of using lemon verbena is with onions (see the Onion Soup recipe below). It is also delicious in jellies, jams and with stewed fruit. Just add a sprig or two to the pot while cooking, and remove once the delicious lemon flavour has penetrated. It also goes particularly well with citrus drinks and puddings. A sprig of lemon verbena in orange juice is unbeatable!

# Onion Soup

6 *large onions, finely chopped*
2 *tablespoons oil (sunflower or maize)*
2 *tablespoons flour*
8 *cups chicken stock*
4 *tablespoons celery leaves, chopped*

4 *tablespoons fresh lemon verbena
   leaves, chopped*
*salt and pepper*
3 *tablespoons fresh parsley, chopped*

In a large pot lightly brown 4 tablespoons of the chopped onions in the oil. Add flour and stir well. Then add all the ingredients except the parsley. Cover the pot and simmer for 20 minutes. Ladle into bowls, sprinkle with a little chopped parsley and serve with croutons.

# Onion Casserole

1 *350 g pickling onions*
4 *tablespoons butter*
4 *tablespoons wholewheat flour*
3 *cups milk*
1/2 *cup cream*
2 *tablespoons finely chopped fresh lemon
   verbena leaves*

1 *teaspoon celery salt*
*pepper*
2 *cups grated cheddar cheese*
*wholewheat breadcrumbs*

Boil the pickling onions in salted water with a spray of lemon verbena. To skin the onions, pour over them a kettleful of boiling water, stand for 10 minutes, then pour off the water and rub off the skins.

Melt butter, stir in flour and cook for 3 – 4 minutes over medium heat. Blend milk and cream and slowly add, stirring with a wooden spoon all the time. Bring to the boil to thicken. Add lemon verbena, salt and pepper and grated cheese.

Arrange the onions in a casserole dish, pour the sauce over them, sprinkle with the wholewheat breadcrumbs and more lemon verbena. Dot with butter and bake at 180 °C/350 °F for 20 minutes or until browned. Serve as a vegetable dish with roast chicken or meat or as a luncheon dish with green salad.

# Lovage

The Maggi Herb
*Levisticum officinale*

Lovage was one of the many Mediterranean plants introduced to Britain and Northern Europe by the Romans, who served fresh lovage stalks after overindulging at a banquet! A leaf or two and a bit of stalk chewed after too much rich food will give immediate relief and aid the digestion. Lovage was grown in the earliest monastic herb gardens and was used to treat rheumatism, digestive disorders and coughs, as well as to impart a rich, celery-like flavour to savoury dishes.

Lovage is one of my favourite herbs. Because of the richness of its flavour I find it is at its best not combined with other herbs, except perhaps for the blander tasting ones like borage, salad burnet, watercress, chervil and comfrey.

The whole lovage plant can be used fresh or dried. The seeds can be ground and used as a pepper substitute – excellent for those on a careful diet for ulcers or digestive problems. Chopped leaves and stalks are delicious raw in salads and can be added to soups, stews, casseroles and savoury tarts to give the delicious Maggi sauce-like flavour that gives lovage its other name, the Maggi herb. The stalks can also be cooked as a vegetable and served with butter, lemon juice and a little black pepper. The root can be chewed as a tobacco substitute and, peeled and bruised, tossed into the bath to soothe rheumatism.

Lovage dies down in winter, so cut it back and dry the leaves two or three times in the year to keep a supply of dried herb for winter soups and stews.

# Lovage Savoury Tart                                      Serves 6

3 large eggs
3 cups milk
2 teaspoons mustard powder
3 tablespoons flour
salt and pepper to taste

2 chopped onions
1 cup chopped lovage leaves and
  stalks
2 cups grated cheddar cheese

Whisk eggs, milk, mustard, flour, salt and pepper. Chop onions and lovage and stir into the milk and egg mixture. Add the cheese. As a variation add 1 cup crisp fried bacon chips or 1 cup finely diced ham. Pour into a baking dish. Bake at 180 °C/350 °F for ½ – ¾ hour or until set and lightly browned. Serve immediately either as a savoury tea-time treat or as a luncheon dish with a green salad and freshly baked brown bread.

# Italian Bean and Lovage Bake                           Serves 8 – 10

This dish is delicious hot or cold. It is the perfect answer for a nutritious, fully balanced meal and is excellent for vegetarians. It can be made in advance and kept refrigerated. There are many variations to the basic recipe, so one never tires of it.

4 cups white kidney beans
8 cups water
1 cup chopped lovage
2 cups chopped onions

1 cup olive oil or maize oil
1 cup fresh lemon juice
1 cup honey

Soak the beans overnight in the water. Next morning strain off the water and boil up the beans in fresh water, to which 2 teaspoons salt have been added, for 1 hour or until tender. Drain.

Whisk together the oil, lemon juice and honey. Add the chopped lovage and onions, and mix into the kidney beans. Spoon into a casserole, cover and bake for 1 hour at 200 °C/400 °F.

## Variations

Any one of the following can be stirred in before baking.

2 cups grated cheddar cheese
3 cups chopped tomatoes

2 cups flaked tuna
2 cups cooked savoury mince

# Mace

*Myristica fragrans*

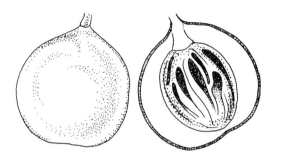

Mace is the outer covering or membrane of the shell that surrounds nutmeg. It has a stronger, sweeter flavour than nutmeg and can be used in a host of ways – possibly in as many dishes and beverages as nutmeg – and it has the advantage of being easily removed after cooking, much like bay.

The tall evergreen tree *Myristica fragrans* is native to the Moluccas Islands in Indonesia and is cultivated in the West Indies and other tropical countries as a commercial crop. There are male and female trees, they grow to about 8 metres high and bear fruit for at least 70 years. The fruit is annual and is succulent, large and yellow skinned, with a heavy seed. Inside the seed is the nutmeg, which is protected and surrounded by a bright red fleshy network, the mace or 'aril'. In tropical areas growth is rapid and the trees are harvested three or four times a year.

Nutmeg and mace are dried separately and once dried are packaged and sent all over the world. As a protection from insects, nutmeg is dusted with lime and mace is flattened into 'blades' and sealed in cellophane.

Mace can be powdered and used in cakes, patés and fish, meat and cheese dishes. It blends well with other spices so it can be included in many dishes. A pinch of powdered mace in coffee, or sprinkled over whipped cream served in coffee, or on puddings, adds a glorious taste.

Mace is yet another spice that aids the digestion, and a blade added to a stew or casserole will not only taste delicious but will quell nausea, indigestion and flatulent colic. Even chewing a small piece will quickly alleviate the problem.

# Mace Chews

3 eggs, separated
1 cup honey
9 tablespoons wholewheat flour
½ teaspoon salt

1 cup chopped pecan nuts
1 cup sunflower seeds
1 cup chopped almonds
1 teaspoon ground mace

Beat egg yolks until thick. Add honey and beat again. Combine the dry ingredients. Stir into the egg and honey mixture, blending well. Lastly fold in the stiffly beaten egg whites. Turn into an oiled pyrex dish, or two pie dishes, spread evenly and bake at 180 °C/350 °F for 20 – 30 minutes or until lightly browned. Cut into squares when cool. This is a perfect school tuckbox treat as it is nutritious and very quick and easy to make.

# Meat Loaf

4 medium-sized carrots, grated
1 kg minced topside
3 onions, chopped
2 celery stalks and leaves, chopped
4 tomatoes, skinned and chopped
2 blades mace

2 teaspoons salt
pepper to taste
juice of 1 lemon
1 tablespoon fresh oregano, chopped, or
   1 teaspoon dried
2 eggs, well beaten

Blend all the ingredients. I find it easiest to use my hands, well washed of course! Either make into flat patties and fry in oil in a pan on top of the stove (in this case use 1 teaspoon powdered mace instead of 2 blades), or shape into a loaf in a large oven-proof dish. Surround with peeled, halved or quartered potatoes, pour about ¾ cup of sunflower oil over the loaf and the potatoes, and bake at 180 °C/350 °F for about 45 minutes or until browned. Remove the mace blades when serving.

# Marjoram

*Origanum marjorana*

There are many cultivated *Origanum* species but here I write of the sweet or knotted marjoram, a well-loved flavouring native to the Mediterranean that is used to treat digestive problems, depression, bedwetting, colds and sore throats.

All varieties of marjoram possess a strong aromatic oil which, because of its strength of flavour, has been used from ancient times to flavour food and treat disease. Marjoram flowers macerated in oil make a soothing rub for rheumatism and aching joints, and warmed, softened leaves make a wonderful poultice for bruises. Marjoram was used to ease toothache in Roman times and was strewn in homes and public places as a disinfectant.

Being a strong herb, marjoram does not combine well with other herbs, except for chives and onions, so it should be used either alone or combined with blander herbs.

It dries well and keeps its flavour longer than most other dried herbs. Try ½ – 1 teaspoon dried marjoram beaten into scrambled eggs or into tomato sauce.

Try marjoram over grilled chicken, steak and fish; add it to soups and stews; cook a sprig with new potatoes, peas and squash. It is a wonderfully versatile herb that will give you much pleasure.

107

# Marjoram Oil

*good quality sunflower oil*
*marjoram flowers*

Pack a glass bottle with sprigs of flowering heads, top with sunflower oil, stand in the sun for 10 – 14 days, then strain and rebottle. Should the flavour not be strong enough, this can be repeated by packing fresh flowering tops into the bottle, topping with the strained oil and again standing in the sun. This makes a wonderful salad oil and I use it for frying onions, chops and fritters. It gives a rich, full flavour and is a good base for soups, stews and casseroles.

# Marjoram Dripping

*500 g white cooking fat*
*2 large onions, finely chopped*
*2 large carrots, finely grated*

*3 sprigs marjoram, about 20 cm long*
*2 teaspoons salt*
*1/2 teaspoon pepper*

Melt the fat, then add the chopped onions, grated carrots, salt, pepper and the marjoram leaves stripped from their stalks. Cook in a covered pot over medium heat until the vegetables are brown and crisp. Pour through a sieve into a dripping jar, discard the browned vegetables, cool and store in the fridge. Use this full-flavoured dripping for roasts, stews and casseroles. It adds a mouth-watering taste to ordinary dishes.

# Marjoram Rarebit                                                      Serves 4

Marjoram enhances egg and cheese dishes particularly well. This is a quick and easy dish that will satisfy even the hungriest of people!

*2 tablespoons butter*
*1 cup cottage cheese*
*1½ cups grated cheddar cheese*
*½ teaspoon salt*
*½ teaspoon paprika*
*1 teaspoon mustard powder*

*½ – 1 tablespoon chopped or minced*
  *marjoram leaves*
*2 eggs*
*1½ cups milk*
*4 slices buttered wholewheat toast*

In a double boiler melt butter and stir in cheeses and flavourings. Beat eggs and milk and add slowly, stirring with a wooden spoon until it thickens. Pour over the buttered toast, sprinkle with a little fresh marjoram and serve immediately.

# Mint

*Mentha*

There are many *Mentha* species but for culinary purposes I really only use garden mint *(Mentha rotundifolium* or *M. crispa)*, peppermint *(M. piperita)* and spearmint *(M. spicata)*.

Peppermint and spearmint are glorious in fruit drinks, teas, fruit salads and ice-creams. The garden mints are savoury mints and combine well in salads, casseroles and sauces, like the well-known and loved mint sauce and mint jelly.

Try using chopped fresh mint in potato salads or with cream cheese in split baked potatoes, with cucumbers and plain yoghurt, with peas, beans and in lentil dishes.

One of my favourite ways of using mint is on watermelon, green melon and sponspek. Mince or chop finely one cup of mint and stir into this about ½ – ¾ cup sugar, so that it is almost dry. Sprinkle over melon just before serving. You will get rave notices!

Mint is excellent for flatulence, colic, disturbances of the gastro-intestinal tract and is an antispasmodic. It is also used medicinally to treat agitation and nervous headaches, and mint in the bath soothes rashes and grazes and tones and freshens the skin. Fresh leaves chewed will sweeten the breath and freshen the mouth, and a leaf or two well chewed and swallowed after a rich and heavy meal will soothe heartburn and aid digestion.

Mint is used in confectionery and even in cosmetics. To help you sleep or just as a bonus, try stuffing a pillow with lemon or eau de cologne mint or spearmint. You will wake clear-headed and refreshed.

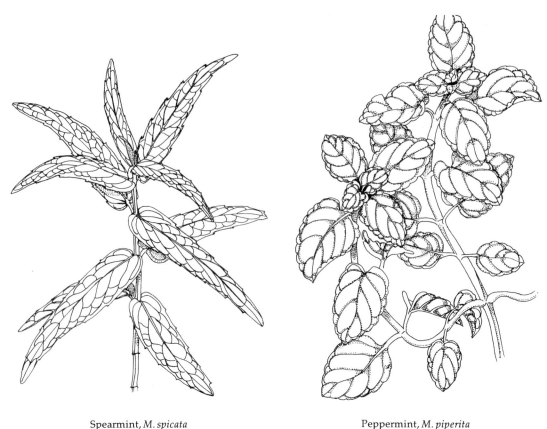

Spearmint, *M. spicata*          Peppermint, *M. piperita*

## Mint Tea                                   **Serves 1**

*thumb-length sprig of mint*
*1 cup boiling water*
*honey*

Pour the boiling water over the sprig of mint and allow to stand to enable the flavour to strengthen. Remove the sprig and sweeten with honey if desired. This is an excellent drink after a heavy meal and, served after a dinner party in coffee cups, will soon become a favourite. To make it partyish I have a small bowl of freshly picked and washed mint leaves and I float a leaf in each cup as I pour it out.

## Mint Sauce                                **Serves 8 – 10**

*1 cup vinegar*              *¾ cup brown sugar*
*1 cup water*               *¾ cup chopped mint*

Place all the ingredients in a screw-top jar and shake vigorously. Pour into an attractive jug and serve separately with lamb roasts or chops, or as a dressing for potato chips or salads.

# Mint Biscuits

Any mint species can be used in these biscuits, but I find spearmint, orange mint or eau de cologne mint the most appealing. The dough is basic and you can enjoy experimenting with various mints – or other herbs like lemon thyme, rosemary, bergamot, scented geranium, pineapple sage or lemon balm.

6 *heaped tablespoons brown sugar*
8 *level tablespoons butter*
2 *eggs, beaten*
2 *tablespoons vanilla essence*
12 *heaped tablespoons flour*

4 *teaspoons baking powder*
*pinch salt*
4 *heaped tablespoons chopped mint*
*crushed cornflakes or coconut*

Leave butter to soften and then beat together the sugar, butter and eggs. Add the vanilla essence. Mix together the flour, baking powder, salt and the chopped mint. Add this to the egg and butter mixture and work into a thick dough. Take teaspoons of dough, roll in crushed cornflakes or coconut, place 5 cm apart on a greased baking sheet and bake at 200 °C/400 °F for 10 – 15 minutes.

These are favourite tuck box biscuits and their popularity never wanes! They keep well in a sealed tin.

# Iced Mint Drink

10 *thumb-length sprigs fresh mint*
6 *cups sugar*

10 *cups water*
*juice of 10 lemons*

Mince the mint and blend into 1 cup of the sugar. Boil up the rest of the sugar in the water for 5 minutes. Cool. Add the lemon juice, sugar and mint, stir well, and adjust the sugar to taste. Chill before serving. Serve in long glasses with a slice of lemon and a sprig of fresh mint. This is a very refreshing and invigorating drink.

# Mustard

*Brassica nigra, B. alba*

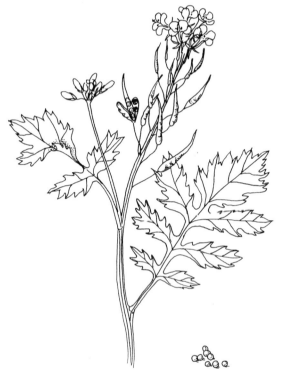

The word 'mustard' comes from the Latin *mustum ardens*, which means 'burning must'. The ground seed was originally combined with 'grape must', an unfermented wine, and used medicinally.

Mustard is indigenous to Europe, Asia Minor, China, North and South America, North Africa and Western India. It has had a multitude of uses over the centuries. Seeds and leaves were used as a rubefacient poultice for rheumatism, sprains and chilblains; it is emetic (encourages vomiting), it stimulates the digestive system and can be added to foot baths to aid circulation and fatigue. A few leaves chewed will avert a cold and are tonic and antiseptic. Probably the nicest way of enjoying these benefits is to add chopped fresh mustard leaves to a green salad.

Ground mustard powder is a condiment found on kitchen shelves throughout the world. A mere pinch added to sauces, stews, stuffings and casseroles gives a wonderful flavour; and whole mustard seeds flavour vinegars, chutneys, pickles, savoury spreads and marinades.

Commercially prepared dry mustard powder is by far the quickest and easiest way of using mustard. To give it extra flavour, add a teaspoon of honey to every 3 teaspoons of mustard powder instead of just mixing it with water, then add a little water and mix to a fine paste.

Mustard is one of the easiest herbs to grow and it seems a pity that we do not make more use of it. Grow sprouts by sprinkling the seeds over a tray lined with damp cottonwool or thick lint. Keep moist and within 3 days the seeds will have sprouted. Continue to keep moist and when they reach about 5 cm in height and are green and juicy, cut them off at the roots with kitchen scissors and serve in salads, sprinkle over roasts or float them in soup.

Mustard is particularly good with cheese and egg dishes, in pizza dough and with mayonnaises and potato salads, and of course as the traditional accompaniment to roast beef and ham.

# Green Mustard Salad Serves 8 plus

This is an unusual and wonderfully satisfying salad that is good enough for a party as well as being wonderfully nourishing and healthy.

*1 lettuce*
*1 – 2 cups chopped celery leaves and stalks*
*1 cup mustard leaves or sprouts*
*1 cup chopped nasturtium leaves and a few seeds*
*1 cup chopped peeled cucumber*
*½ cup chopped green pepper*
*1 cup chopped green onions (spring onions or chives)*

*1 – 2 cups watercress*
*1 cup chopped parsley*
*½ cup finely chopped very young comfrey leaves*
*½ cup finely chopped very young borage leaves*
*1 cup salad burnet leaves*
*2 cups crumbled or diced feta cheese*

## Dressing

*1 cup lemon juice*
*2 teaspoons mustard powder*

*½ cup brown sugar*
*¾ cup sunflower or maize oil*

Shake together in a screw-top jar and pour over the salad, which has been well mixed, just before serving. Finally sprinkle with the feta cheese crumbs. Served with freshly baked bread and a herb butter, this salad is a meal in itself.

I sometimes add my favourite weeds to this salad, which makes it even more appetising:

*1 cup chopped sow's thistle*
*1 cup fat-hen leaves*

*1 cup purslane leaves, stripped from stems*

# Nasturtium

*Tropaeolum majus*

You may be surprised to find the common or garden nasturtium in a book of cooking with herbs. Well, the nasturtium is a wonder-plant: it is a natural antibiotic and an aid to digestion, nervous anxiety and depression; it treats poor eyesight, lack of appetite, sore throats and tiredness; and its biting rich flavour enhances salads and vegetable dishes. It is decorative and can be used in many ways, from wrapping hors-d'oeuvres like cheese, asparagus and ham in the leaves, to blending and pickling the seeds for exciting sauces. Float flowers in punch bowls when serving fruit punch and lavishly decorate summer salads with their brightness.

Nasturtium combines well with tarragon, basil, oregano, dill, fennel, parsley, mint and garlic, so it can be included in many dishes where these herbs are used. Both the leaves and flowers can be chopped and added to salads, soups, stews and savoury dishes. Fresh leaves chopped into cream cheese make a delicious sandwich spread. Add a nasturtium flower to herb teas like sage or thyme for colds and sore throats.

Its common name makes nasturtium easily confused with watercress, *Nasturtium officinale*, and indeed their taste, which is hot and peppery, is remarkably similar.

114

# Nasturtium Salad Serves 6

1 cup cooked garden peas
1 cup cooked diced green beans
1 cup chopped nasturtium leaves
1 cup nasturtium flowers for decoration
1 cup diced cucumber
½ cup parsley, finely chopped

1 cup grated sweetmilk cheese
½ cup chopped chives
juice of 1 lemon (about ½ cup)
½ cup oil
½ cup honey

Combine the last three ingredients in a screw-top bottle and shake until blended. Add a little salt, black pepper and a pinch of mustard, and mix well. Combine all the salad ingredients, mix lightly with a fork, pour over the salad dressing, decorate with the nasturtium flowers and serve immediately.

# Nasturtium Seed Capers 1

Pack fresh nasturtium seeds into a bottle. Vary the flavouring by adding any one of the following:

1 sprig thyme
1 sprig rosemary

1 sprig oregano
1 sprig sage

Then add:

1 or 2 bay leaves
6 – 10 cloves or 1 stick cinnamon
  or root of ginger or a piece of
  horseradish root

1 – 2 teaspoons salt
1 dessertspoon mustard seed

Cover with hot white wine vinegar or hot apple cider vinegar. Seal well and store for a month before using, as you would capers. Use when a spicy condiment is needed; or add to white sauces to serve with fish; or to tomato sauce to serve with pasta. The seeds have a rich, biting flavour that gives a unique taste to whatever they are added to.

## Nasturtium Seed Capers 2

nasturtium seeds, green and freshly picked
sprig of thyme
2  bay leaves

few cloves
white wine or apple cider vinegar

Pack a glass jar full of nasturtium seeds and add the thyme, bay leaves and cloves. (For variation use a sprig of oregano and a roughly crushed nutmeg; or a sprig of sage and a few peppercorns; or a sprig of rosemary and a few coriander seeds; or a sprig of winter savory and a tablespoon of brown sugar.) Pour over this hot white wine vinegar, or hot apple cider vinegar, and a sprinkling of salt. Seal and store for a month before using as a substitute for capers.

## Nasturtium Egg Salad                                Serves 4 – 6

6  hard-boiled eggs
1  cup watercress
2  tablespoons chopped parsley
salt
lemon pepper

20  nasturtium leaves
3  tablespoons oil
2  tablespoons lemon juice
1  cup mayonnaise
12  nasturtium flowers

Mash the eggs and add the watercress, parsley, salt and pepper. Line a salad bowl with nasturtium leaves, blend the oil and lemon juice and sprinkle over the leaves. Spoon in the egg and mayonnaise and tuck the flowers all around the edges. Serve with crusty bread and butter as a light luncheon dish.

Nasturtium flowers, seeds and leaves can be used in countless ways

# Nettle

*Urtica dioica*

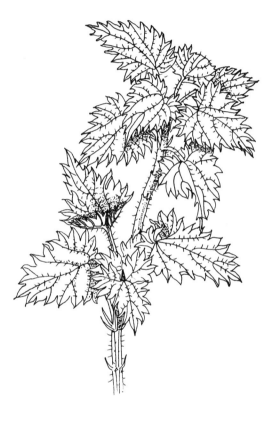

This much maligned perennial is indigenous to many countries in the world and is in fact a delicious herb and vegetable. With its amazing medicinal qualities, it deserves to be reconsidered as a nourishing part of our diets.

Nettle is good for arthritis, gout and rheumatism, it repels kidney stones, clears the lungs, purifies the blood, tones the system, builds the blood in anaemia, stops nosebleeds, improves the hair, removes dandruff and aids infertility. And that's not all! The leaves are used in the manufacture of cloth and paper and a strong brew can be made to rid the body of worms and to treat diarrhoea.

Because of its bland and unobtrusive taste, nettle combines well with thyme, oregano, sage, marjoram, basil, shallots, onions, garlic, celery and savory. It thickens soups and stews, adding its beneficial medicinal value to every dish.

It can be cooked as a spinach and served with a squeeze of lemon juice, salt and butter or simply added to cabbage and spinach dishes. Use nettles as often as you can for they are richly endowed with vitamins and minerals and will relieve tiredness.

To make an excellent hair rinse just pour a kettle of boiling water over stalks and tough leaves and allow to stand until cool, then strain. Massage into the scalp frequently to encourage hair growth and to tone and revitalise the hair. Keep the excess in the fridge.

Wear gloves when picking nettles and wash the plants well before using. The sting immediately disappears once the nettles are immersed in boiling water, but should you have a skin irritation, rub the area well with dock leaves, plantain leaves or aloe vera, or quickly dab on some vinegar.

## Nettle Tea                                                          Serves 3

6  tablespoons nettle tops
3  cups water

juice of 1/2 a lemon
honey

Simmer the nettle tops in the water for 5 minutes. Strain, and add the lemon juice. Sweeten with honey and drink a cupful once or twice a day. This is a wonderful blood purifier.

## Nettle Soup                                                    Serves 10 – 12

8  cups diced leeks
2  tablespoons butter
6  large potatoes, peeled and diced
8  cups nettle tops and leaves, well packed
    down
1,8 litres chicken stock

salt and freshly ground black pepper
2  teaspoons fresh thyme
3  cups watercress, well packed down
12  large sorrel leaves
2  cups thick cream

Lightly brown the leeks in the butter; add potatoes and nettles and stir well. Cook for about 10 minutes, add the stock and seasoning, bring to the boil, cover and simmer gently for 20 minutes. Chop the watercress and sorrel and add to the pot for the final 2 minutes of cooking time. Pour into a blender, and blend. Return to the pot and stir in the cream. Reheat gently but do not boil. Serve with a sprig of fresh watercress floating on top of each bowl. Stand by for second helpings!

## Irish Nettle Champ                                             Serves 4 – 6

This was once a favourite dish in Ireland, served for the children's supper with a glass of buttermilk, and is in itself a delicious light meal if a sprinkling of cheese is added and served with a salad and crusty bread.

675 g potatoes
3  onions, sliced
3  tablespoons butter
200 ml milk

3  cups nettle tops, well packed down
salt and freshly ground black pepper
grated cheese
chopped parsley

Boil the potatoes in their skins with the onions. When they are soft, drain and skin them. Return to the pan with the onions and mash, adding butter and a little of the milk. Chop the nettles and boil them in the milk for 8 minutes – the milk will curdle but it does not matter. Add the milk, nettles and seasoning to the potatoes and onions and stir well on low heat, adding a little more milk if it dries out too much. Spoon into a serving dish or onto individual plates, make a well in the centre of each portion and place a knot of butter in this. Sprinkle with grated cheese and chopped parsley and serve piping hot.

# Nettle Beer

This is a refreshing, unusual, rather potent drink and a very enjoyable party treat, which is nourishing at the same time!

*4,6 litres water*
*juice of 4 lemons*
*lemon rind, thinly pared*
*3 thumb-length pieces of root ginger,*
*    well bruised*

*675 g young nettles*
*25 g cream of tartar*
*450 g brown sugar*
*1 tablespoon dried yeast*
*extra 4 – 6 teaspoons sugar*

Pour the water into a large pot. Add the lemon juice, thinly pared lemon rind, ginger and the chopped, washed nettles and boil for 30 minutes, keeping the pot covered.

Mix the cream of tartar and sugar in a large bowl and pour the nettle water through a sieve over this, pressing the nettles down well to extract as much of their juice as possible.

Stir until the sugar dissolves and cool to about body temperature. Sprinkle the yeast on top, cover and leave to ferment in a protected place for 3 days.

Strain through muslin and pour into bottles. Add a teaspoon of sugar to each bottle, cork well and leave undisturbed for about a week until the beer is clear.

Place in the fridge before serving and serve with a slice of lemon and a sprinkling of ground ginger stirred in.

Always wear rubber gloves when you handle nettles

# Nutmeg

*Myristica fragrans*

The beautiful nutmeg tree, native to the Moluccas Islands in Indonesia, is cultivated in tropical countries and nutmeg and mace (the outer covering of nutmeg) are exported all over the world.

Nutmeg has been used since the earliest times. There are records of Arabs and Indians trading it in the sixth century and it was introduced into Europe in about 1190. It has long been recognised that even moderate doses of nutmeg can cause hallucinations and a feeling of unreality – so use nutmeg sparingly! These effects have been found to be caused by a protoalkaloidal constituent called myristicin.

Used in small doses, nutmeg stimulates the digestion, is carminative and relieves flatulence, nausea and diarrhoea. Oil of nutmeg is poisonous, so do not use it without the guidance of a doctor or qualified herbalist.

Nutmeg particularly complements milk and cheese dishes and, being strongly aromatic, can be combined with other spices as a fixative in pot-pourris and pomanders. As a condiment, however, its strong, distinctive flavour makes it more suited to use on its own. Nutmeg has stimulant properties and aids digestion, so use a little on slightly indigestible dishes such as cabbage or sauerkraut, cheese tarts and toasted cheese sandwiches, pickles and condiments. A sprinkling over a meat loaf or fish cakes gives a rich and delicious flavour and will aid digestion. Best of all, sprinkle a little ground nutmeg over yoghurt, icecream, vanilla custards and fruit dishes. I find that to grate a little whole nutmeg on a fine grater as you need it is the best way of preserving its unique flavour.

For old people who have no appetite, or for invalids, try a pinch of nutmeg in soups, stews and even fruit desserts.

# Nutmeg Flip

This is a wonderful pick-me-up and a meal in a glass for those who are too rushed to eat a meal, for invalids or for old people.

1  glass fresh full-cream milk
1  fresh egg
1  dessertspoon honey
1  teaspoon debittered powdered yeast

sprinkling of nutmeg (about ½ a
    teaspoon)
1  dessertspoon brandy (optional)

Whisk all ingredients well, pour into a glass, sprinkle with nutmeg and drink immediately. I find this particularly good at the end of a day if you have to go out to dinner, if dinner is to be delayed or if you are too tired to eat. It revitalises and invigorates you and protects you against shocks!

# Rice Cream Pudding                                     Serves 6

1  cup brown rice
2  cups water
1  teaspoon sunflower oil
½  teaspoon salt
3  cups milk
2  eggs

¾  cup raisins
4  tablespoons honey
2  tablespoons cornflour
½  cup cream
1  teaspoon nutmeg
½  cup chopped almonds

Cook rice in the water with the oil and a pinch of salt for 20 – 30 minutes, keeping tightly covered on low heat. Drain. Beat the milk and eggs together and add to the rice. Add the raisins, bring to the boil again, then cover and simmer for 15 minutes. Stir in honey. Add a little cold milk to the cornflour and blend well. Add to the simmering rice, beat well with a fork and cook gently until it thickens. Cool slightly, stir in cream and sprinkle with nutmeg and nuts. Serve hot.

This is a delicious pudding for cold winter evenings. If I have a roast in the oven, I first cook the rice, then blend all the ingredients, pour into a baking dish, sprinkle with nuts and nutmeg, dot with a little butter and bake it alongside the roast until it is set and browned.

# Potato Cheese and Nutmeg Fritters

4 cups mashed potatoes or left-over
  potatoes
2 eggs, well beaten
1½ cups grated cheddar cheese

1 cup finely chopped onions
salt and pepper to taste
1 teaspoon grated nutmeg
sunflower oil

Mix everything well – I find a fork is the easiest way of blending the onions and cheese into the potato. If the mixture is too soft, add a little wholewheat flour. Form into spoon-sized fritters and fry in sunflower oil in a large frying pan. Turn when browned. Serve hot with a salad as a lunch dish.

Whole nutmeg has much more flavour than ground nutmeg

# Onion

*Allium cepa*

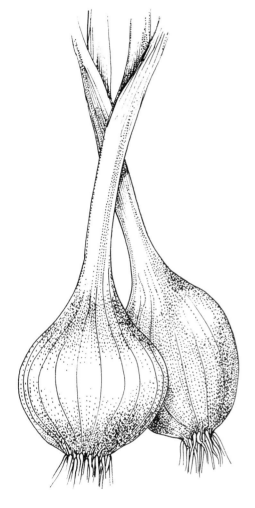

The onion is included here as it is a most important healing herb, and one which has been in cultivation for so long that its origins have been lost. The plant was recorded by the Egyptians, the Chaldeans and the ancient Greeks, and has been used medicinally since then. There are numerous cultivars of *Allium cepa*, which include shallots, spring onions, tree onions, Welsh onions, scallions, ever-ready onions and chives.

I find tremendous enjoyment in growing all the varieties I can find, as their subtle flavours enhance any dish, and I have discovered a wonderful range of tastes. I find spring onions, shallots and Welsh onion tops become bitter if they are fried, so I add these just as the cooking time is over to get the full benefit of their subtle tastes.

The onion is antibiotic, diuretic and expectorant and is a most useful treatment for coughs and colds, bronchitis, gastro-enteritis and jaundice. It helps reduce high blood pressure and the blood sugar level. A slice of onion heals cuts and acne, and promotes hair growth.

Include chopped or sliced fresh onion in the diet, and to freshen and sweeten the breath after eating onions, chew a piece of parsley. Use onions in savoury dishes, soups, stews, salads, pickles and marinades. It is one of the tastiest of all vegetables and no cook can be without it. Always remember that the healthiest way of eating onion is raw.

# Onion Flan

This is a delicious lunch or supper dish and a very quick and easy recipe. It can be baked without the pastry case, but with it it makes a substantial meal.

### Pastry case

½ cup butter  
1 cup flour (wholemeal)

little salt  
cold water

Rub the butter into the flour and salt until it resembles breadcrumbs and add sufficient cold water to make a stiff dough. Roll out on a floured board. Line an oven-proof dish, trim and fork the edges.

### Filling

2 cups chopped onion  
2 cups chopped green onion leaves or  
    spring onions  
little maize oil or butter  
¼ cup cream  
¾ cup milk

3 beaten eggs  
little nutmeg  
½ – 1 teaspoon savory  
salt and pepper to taste  
cheddar cheese

Sauté the onion in the oil or butter, until it turns a golden colour. Add cream and milk to eggs, whisk well, and add this to the onion. Add nutmeg, savory and salt and pepper. Pour into the pastry case. Sprinkle with a little cheddar cheese and more nutmeg. Bake at 375 °F/180 °C for about 30 minutes or until set. Serve either hot or cold.

# Onion Batter Rings

2 – 3 large onions

### Batter

4 tablespoons wholewheat flour  
little salt

1 egg, separated  
6 tablespoons cold water

Mix flour and salt, add water and beaten egg yolk, and mix to a smooth paste. Leave to stand for an hour. Beat the egg white stiffly and fold into the batter just before using it.

    Peel and slice the onions about 5 – 7 mm thick. Carefully separate into rings. Dip the rings into the batter and fry in deep, hot maize oil until golden brown. Drain on crumpled paper towels and serve as an accompaniment to a roast or grill.

# Oregano

*Origanum vulgare*

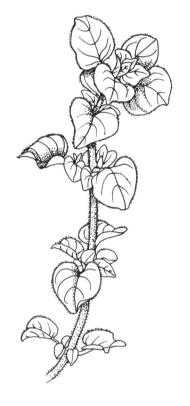

There are several species of *Origanum*, all of which have a similar pungent fragrance and flavouring. All are good for the digestion and just chewing a piece will ease heartburn.

Oregano has the amazing property of dissolving fats in the body so it is particularly good with fatty meat dishes like pork – sprinkle half a cup of chopped herb over the meat while it is roasting. Try a little sprinkled over fried foods such as potato chips and fritters. Add oregano to gravies and sauces – an approximate guide is 2 teaspoons fresh herb finely chopped or 1 teaspoon dried herb to 1 cup of gravy or sauce.

The generic name *Origanum* is derived from the Greek words *oros* and *gamus*, meaning 'mountain glamour' or 'joy of the mountain', and this is a herb that indeed adds glamour and joy by enhancing ordinary dishes with its rich flavour and fragrance. I find that dried bundles of oregano from the mid-summer garden have a stronger flavour than the fresh plant, so I always keep a screw-top jar with dried oregano at hand next to the stove.

Oregano is well loved in Italy where it is used lavishly in pasta dishes. It combines well with garlic, chives, onions, shallots and watercress but not very well with other strong-flavoured herbs. It is good with all meat and poultry dishes and, because of its aid to digestion and its wonderful medicinal uses in gastro-intestinal and respiratory disorders and colic, it can be used lavishly in any number of dishes.

Fresh oregano can be added sparingly to salads, vegetable dishes, pasta, rice dishes and dips. I use a good 2 tablespoons of fresh or 1 dessertspoon of dried oregano in chicken stuffings, meat loaf and lamb stew.

# Chicken Stuffing

1 cup fresh brown breadcrumbs
¾ cup yoghurt
1 cup mung bean sprouts
2 tablespoons debittered powdered yeast
1 teaspoon salt

½ teaspoon pepper
½ cup chopped onion
2 tablespoons fresh oregano leaves
juice of 1 large lemon

Combine all the ingredients and stuff the chicken with it. Baste the chicken with more lemon juice and salt and pepper. Bake in an unglazed clay casserole in a medium oven for 2½ hours.

# Oregano Avocado                                                    Serves 6

This is a delicious entrée dish for a summer dinner or, served with freshly baked crusty bread and cream cheese, makes a substantial luncheon dish.

3 large ripe tomatoes
1 tablespoon chopped fresh oregano
1 – 2 teaspoons salt
freshly ground pepper to taste

3 ripe avocados
juice of 1 large lemon
1 cup chopped fresh chives
1 tablespoon sugar

Peel and chop the tomatoes and simmer to a purée with the oregano, salt and pepper. Cool then chill. Just before the meal cut the avocados in half and sprinkle over the lemon juice (this will keep them from turning black). Add the chopped chives to the chilled tomato purée and fill the pip cavity of the avocado with this. Place on a lettuce leaf, decorate with a tiny sprig of fresh oregano and serve immediately.

# Tomato Cocktail                                                    Serves 6

When tomatoes are plentiful and cheap I make this refreshing, appetising tomato cocktail. The left-overs can be added to soups and stews.

10 – 12 large, fully ripe tomatoes, roughly
    chopped
1 tablespoon salt
6 tablespoons sugar

2 teaspoons freshly ground pepper
1 – 3 tablespoons fresh, chopped
    oregano
2 medium onions, finely chopped

Combine all the ingredients and bring to the boil. Boil for 10 – 15 minutes. Pour through a sieve and force pulp through. Chill and serve in cocktail glasses with a few drops of Worcester sauce.

# Paprika

*Capsicum annuum*

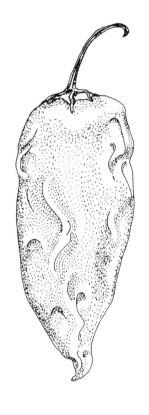

Paprika is a brilliant red, dried ground seasoning derived from sweet red pepper and combined with other capsicum species. It first became known in about 1494 when a physician who sailed with Columbus on his second voyage to the West Indies noted its use by native tribes. Capsicum chillis are American in origin but are now grown throughout the world in tropical zones.

Paprika can be made from a combination of several capsicum species according to the flavour and colour desired. It is most satisfying to grow a selection of species oneself, and to make one's own blend.

Paprika is not as strong as cayenne pepper, although many countries blend in quantities of hot chillis to give it a stronger bite and flavour. In South Africa, commercially bought paprika is mild and pleasant, and is delicious sprinkled over roasts, grills and baked savoury dishes.

Paprika seems to combine particularly well with cheeses, and my favourite way of using it is sprinkled over cauliflower cheese.

Sweet pepper is rich in vitamins and many believe in its soothing qualities for rheumatism and backache, as well as an aid to digestion, liver complaints and blood conditions.

Paprika is sometimes wrongly known as 'grains of paradise'. The 'grains of paradise' are in fact a completely different variety of pepper, *Aframomum melegueta*, which derived its name from the ancient African empire of Melle in the upper Nile region, where it was cultivated and exported by ship to Europe. It became an expensive and much-prized spice, hence the name 'grains of paradise' or *grana paradisi*. It was much used in European cuisine from 1245. This pepper is still cultivated in Ghana today, where it is much prized as a condiment, and its pungent resin as a stimulant. Paprika is a far cheaper substitute of this spice and is available throughout the world. It has a similar beneficial effect on the digestive system.

I have had much success in harvesting my own red peppers and the green pepper so commonly grown in summer, allowing it to ripen on the bush until it begins to crinkle. I then cut the flesh into thin strips, discard the seeds and dry the pieces on a gauze tray in an airy place. You can also mince them fresh and spread them out on trays to dry. I then grind the pieces in a coffee grinder, store the powder in bottles and blend it with other chillis or spices to make my own grains of paradise.

## Grains of Paradise

10  red peppers, fully ripened
1 – 3 hot peppers (small variety)
3  teaspoons coriander seeds
3  teaspoons dried thyme

2  teaspoons crushed cumin
1  teaspoon crushed aniseed
1  teaspoon crushed cloves
3  teaspoons powdered ginger

Dry and pulverise the peppers, discarding the seeds. Combine all the ingredients and crush well with a pestle and mortar. Fill a salt cellar or pepper shaker with the powder and keep it handy on the kitchen shelf for use on grills, fish, meat, poultry or cheese dishes.

## Paprika Toast                                                                 Serves 4

This is a revamped old favourite that makes a quick and easy supper dish.

4  fairly thick slices wholewheat bread,
   preferably home-made
little mayonnaise
slices of cheese (sweetmilk, gouda or
   mozzarella)

2  large tomatoes, sliced
1  onion, thinly sliced
paprika

Toast the bread evenly on both sides. Butter well and spread with mayonnaise. Lay slices of cheese and on top of this, lay the slices of tomato and onion, and sprinkle with paprika. Place under the grill for 4 – 7 minutes, or until bubbly and starting to brown. Serve piping hot with a green salad.

# Paprika Sauce

This delicious sauce can be used over cauliflower, cabbage, broccoli, Brussels sprouts, kidney beans, macaroni, spaghetti, hard-boiled eggs, toast, turnips, brown rice, or butter beans. These must be cooked first and kept hot.

*4 tablespoons butter*
*4 tablespoons wholewheat flour*
*2 cups milk*
*1 egg, beaten*

*pinch of salt*
*1 cup grated cheese*
*1 teaspoon paprika*

Melt butter in a pot, stir in flour, and cook for 3 minutes over medium heat. Blend in milk, into which the egg has been beaten, and add the salt and paprika. Keep stirring with a wooden spoon until it thickens. Lastly, fold in the cheese and pour the sauce over the prepared dish. Sprinkle with a little more paprika and grated cheese. Brown under the grill if desired and serve piping hot.

The flavour of this sauce can be varied by experimenting with different herbs.

Grain of paradise is made with a variety of spices crushed together in a pestle and mortar

# Parsley

*Petroselinum crispum*

Parsley is the most commonly used of all the herbs. It is loved and respected in both the culinary and medicinal worlds, and it is the favourite garnishing for every savoury dish. It is also the oldest of all known herbs, and has been in cultivation for at least 2 000 years.

There are several kinds of parsley and lately I have come to enjoy the flat-leafed Italian parsley, *Petroselinum crispum neopolitanum*, sometimes known as Greek parsley or Cypriot parsley as the continentals consider it to be of superior flavour. It is easy to grow and seeds itself readily in the garden. I treat parsley as a biennial, but in colder areas it is best as an annual, and it seems to do well as a potplant, so no cook need ever be without it.

It is a most wonderful herb for clearing kidney, bladder and urinary tract problems, and for stimulating a sluggish liver. It is also useful for all female complaints, and the easiest and most effective way of using it in the diet is in its fresh, green state.

For the arthritic diet parsley is of paramount importance and parsley tea can be used for slimming and to treat anaemia, soft bones, jaundice and for aiding milk flow in breast-feeding mothers. Always add parsley to a dish at the last possible minute to retain all its goodness and freshness.

# Parsley Tea                                                    Serves 1

¼  *cup freshly picked parsley*
1  *cup boiling water*

Pour the boiling water over the parsley and allow to stand and steep. Strain, and drink a cup once or twice daily.

# Parsley Eggs                                                   Serves 4

This is a tasty change from ordinary fried eggs and is a quick and easy supper or breakfast dish.

3  *tablespoons butter*
4  *fresh eggs*
*salt, pepper*

1  *large onion, sliced into rings*
2  *tablespoons chopped parsley*
1  *clove garlic, finely chopped*

Melt half the butter in a heavy-bottomed saucepan. Break the eggs into the pan and fry gently. Lift out onto a hot serving dish, sprinkle with salt and pepper and keep hot.

Fry the onion rings, adding more butter if necessary. (Alternatively, dip the onion rings into a light batter and fry them in oil.) Lift out and drain. Keep hot.

Mix the rest of the butter with the chopped parsley and garlic and a little salt. Drop this in small lumps over the hot eggs. Serve immediately with hot toast and a salad.

The garlic parsley butter is so popular, that I make a double quantity to spread on toast.

# Parsley Potted Cheese

This is a most delicious spread. It is nourishing and tasty and can be used as a sandwich filling or as a pastry case filling or for savoury tarts.

1  *cup butter*
1  *cup coarsely grated mozzarella cheese*
2  *cups coarsely grated cheddar cheese*
1  *egg, beaten*
½ – ¾ *cup medium sweet sherry*
*little pepper*

1  *heaped tablespoon fresh thyme or*
   *marjoram*
1  *heaped tablespoon fresh chives*
3  *heaped tablespoons parsley, finely*
   *chopped*
½  *teaspoon dried mace*

Melt butter and cheese over a double boiler and add the egg. Beat well and remove from heat. Beat in sherry, pepper and herbs. Press into small pots, cover with melted butter and tin foil. Refrigerate and decorate with a sprig of parsley before serving.

# Parsley Soup

This is an excellent soup for slimming or for cleaning out the system after an over-indulgence of eating or drinking! Parsley soup will rid the body of toxins and aid kidney and bladder function. I find it particularly good on days when one feels 'liverish' or off-colour and it is very pleasant cold with a little plain yoghurt stirred into it. I usually double the quantity and keep it in the fridge for a quick pick-me-up. After a long day when one wants only a light supper, it is perfect.

2  cups chopped onions, green tops as well
2  litres water
2  cups grated carrots
1/2 – 3/4 cup chopped carrot tops
2  cups chopped celery

1/2 – 1 tablespoon marmite
3  cups chopped parsley
juice of 1 lemon
a little vegetable salt
pepper

Lightly brown the onions in a little oil, add water, carrots and celery, and bring to the boil. Boil for 5 – 7 minutes, remove from the stove and stir in marmite, chopped parsley, lemon juice and a little salt and pepper to taste.

Parsley eggs make a tasty change from fried eggs

# Pepper

*Piper nigrum*

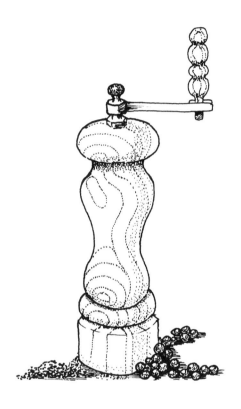

Pepper is the world's most valuable spice, although not the most expensive, and was once used as a substitute for money. Whole peppercorns are the berries of pepper vines, and can either be ground down to powdered form or freshly ground in a pepper mill. The perennial pepper vine only grows within 10° of the equator and is mainly grown in India, Sri Lanka, Indonesia, Brazil and Malaysia.

The berries grow in racemes like grapes and as they ripen they turn from green to yellow to red. Those destined to be sold as black pepper are picked before they are ripe. As they dry, so the hull changes from yellowy-red to black.

For white pepper the berries are left on the vine to ripen before they are picked, and then are immediately soaked in water, which softens their hull. This can then be easily rubbed off, revealing the parchment-coloured corn with its milder flavour.

The flavour of ground pepper deteriorates rapidly but peppercorns keep well, so one can buy them in quantity. It is a good idea to buy the green, unripe peppercorns which are marketed in brine or vinegar, if they are available, as they are utterly delicious, tender, and with a delicate fresh taste – completely unlike pepper. Sprinkled on grilled mushrooms or baked potatoes, they are a treat never to be forgotten!

Surprisingly, pepper has medicinal uses, which made it a highly sought after spice in Roman times. It helps increase the flow of gastric juices and aids digestion and constipation.

# Diatron Piperon

This is an old-fashioned recipe which was once singularly popular for treating memory loss and helping digestion. There are variations, but this is the basic recipe.

2 cups sugar
1 cup chopped hyssop
1 tablespoon chopped thyme
1 tablespoon aniseed, roughly crushed

2 teaspoons black peppercorns
2 teaspoons sliced ginger root or 1 – 2 teaspoons ground ginger
4 cups water

Boil the ingredients together in a covered pot for 2 minutes, turn down heat and simmer for 10 minutes. Stand, steep and strain. Bottle and dilute 1 tablespoon of this brew in a cup of herb tea, such as mint, sage or lemon grass and drink daily.

# Pepper Steak                                                 Serves 2 –3

2 – 3 portions tenderised steak
black peppercorns
butter

salt to taste
freshly squeezed lemon juice

Trim the meat of fat, wipe clean, and place on the grilling pan or rack. Roughly crush 2 – 3 teaspoons of peppercorns in a mortar, and sprinkle over the meat. Dot with butter. Sprinkle the lemon juice over the meat, and grill quickly on both sides. Serve with salads, baked potatoes, more lemon juice and more black pepper.

# Baked Pepper Potatoes

Baked potatoes are the healthiest way of eating potatoes, and this recipe is extremely quick and easy and can be varied to suit your taste. Select undamaged, medium-sized potatoes – one per person.

butter
salt and pepper
little lemon juice

### Filling alternatives

cream cheese with chopped chives
cottage cheese with chopped tarragon

grated cheese with mustard
butter with chopped oregano

Wash and dry the potatoes, place on a baking tray in a medium oven (180 – 220 °C) and bake until soft. Squeeze the potato at both ends to split it open. Fill the inside with either butter, a little salt and lots of freshly ground black pepper and a squeeze of lemon juice, or a prepared filling. Serve immediately.

# Peppermint

*Mentha piperita*

I have found peppermint one of the most superb digestive herbs. It can be used to treat indigestion, flatulence, nausea, overeating, dyspepsia, heartburn, anxiety, timidity, colic and travel sickness.

It is a delicious addition to drinks, cakes, ice-creams, fruit salads, fruit cocktails and jellies.

Peppermint is one of the easiest plants to grow, and it enjoys both shade and sun, its long runners forever seeking new ground. The black peppermint gives the oil that flavours many pharmaceutical products, and is also the source of the peppermint sweets we all enjoy.

Rub fresh peppermint leaves onto your skin to protect against mosquitoes and insects, and chew a leaf or two to clear the breath and freshen the mouth.

# Peppermint Ice-cream Serves 8 plus

1 – 2 cups peppermint leaves
2 litres milk
4 eggs, beaten

1 cup honey
1 cup cream (optional)

Boil up the peppermint in the milk. Remove from the stove, stand, steep and cool. Strain. Whisk the beaten eggs and honey together, and whisk into the milk. Whisk the cream and add to the milk mixture, whisking all the time. You may like to add chopped peppermint leaves or a little grated lemon rind at this point. Pour into trays and freeze.

# Peppermint Apple Cake Serves 8

This is always a favourite and can be served for tea with whipped cream or as a pudding with custard.

½ cup soft butter
½ cup soft brown sugar
2 eggs, beaten
1 cup wholewheat flour
pinch salt
½ cup finely chopped fresh peppermint
    leaves

2 teaspoons baking powder
3 apples, peeled, cored and sliced
3 – 5 tablespoons extra sugar
grated rind of 1 lemon
cinnamon
juice of ½ lemon

Cream the butter and the half cup of sugar. Add eggs and blend well. Stir in flour, salt, peppermint and baking powder. Mix apples with the extra sugar (leaving a little over) and lemon rind. Place in a pyrex dish. Cover with the cake mixture, and bake at 350 °F/180 °C for 30 minutes.

    While the cake is still warm, sprinkle with the rest of the sugar, a teaspoon or two of cinnamon and the lemon juice. Serve warm.

# Peppermint Tea

1 – 2 thumb-length sprigs of peppermint
1 cup boiling water

honey to sweeten
squeeze of lemon juice (optional)

Pour the boiling water over the peppermint. Stand and steep. Sip when cool enough. Honey and lemon can be added if desired. This tea can be sipped for all digestive ailments.

    For nausea, leave out the honey and sip frequently.

    A stronger brew can be made for colic. Take a teaspoonful to a tablespoonful at a time until the condition eases. This tea can also form a base for cool drinks: just add apple or grenadilla juice.

# Pineapple Sage

*Salvia rutilans*

This beautiful, bushy perennial is a species of *Salvia* and is a tremendous asset in the garden, as its long sprays of brilliant red flowers make it attractive to bees and in the border, and it can be used in pot-pourris and fresh in fruit salads.

Originally indigenous to the Mediterranean regions, the tender pineapple sage has been cultivated all over the world, and is only now becoming a sought-after addition to the South African herb garden. Because it is frost tender, it dies down completely in winter, except in very warm, moderate regions, and the new growth appears again in the spring. It makes an attractive but large container plant, which can be successfully wintered in a sunny, sheltered position.

I take several cuttings in April and keep these well bedded in sand under cover, so that I can start the spring garden with a good selection of sturdy new plants. It roots easily and quickly, and by midsummer the new bush is a good size.

Like the rest of the sage family, it is good for digestion, and makes a delicious tea, hot or cold. I keep a quantity of dried pineapple sage leaves in a glass jar for winter teas as a treatment for coughs, colds and flu, as it clears mucous and phlegm from the throat and nose and, with honey, it is very soothing.

Experiment with pineapple sage in all sorts of puddings. A sprig in rice puddings, sago, and bread and butter puddings imparts a subtle pineapple flavour and aids digestion. A sprig or two added to jam while it is cooking gives a wonderful flavour and a leaf or two tucked into the bottle further enhances the taste.

Add finely chopped pineapple sage leaves to punches, fruit salads, tarts, jellies and ice-creams. Add 2 or 3 sprigs to stewed fruit dishes, and remove just before serving.

At the end of the day a tea made with ¼ cup pineapple sage, fresh, or 2 teaspoons

137

dried, and one cup boiling water, allowed to stand and steep, then strained and sweetened with honey if desired, will revitalise and relax you and ensure a good night's sleep.

## Pineapple Sage Punch

I make this punch in quantity all summer long as a cool drink.

4  cups pineapple sage leaves
8  cups boiling water
1  stick cinnamon
honey

1  cup freshly picked mint leaves
few ice cubes or crushed ice
1  litre pineapple juice
liquidised fresh pineapple (optional)

Cover the pineapple sage leaves with the boiling water. Add the cinnamon, stand, steep, and cool. Strain, and discard the leaves and cinnamon stick. Add honey to sweeten, freshly picked mint leaves, a few ice cubes or crushed ice, and pineapple juice. A delicious addition to this is liquidised fresh pineapple. Float a few pineapple slices on top of the punch, and serve chilled in long glasses.

## Pineapple Sage Jelly                                    Serves 6

This is a refreshing summer pudding, and is quickly and easily made.

4  cups pineapple sage leaves
1  litre boiling water
honey to taste (about 2 tablespoons)
2  tablespoons gelatine dissolved in hot
    water

few fresh fruit slices, e.g. peach, straw-
    berries, nectarine or mango
few pineapple sage flowers

Pour the boiling water over the pineapple sage leaves, stand, steep and strain. Sweeten with honey and stir in the dissolved gelatine. Lay slices of fruit in a glass dish and pour the warm tea over this. Decorate with a few pineapple sage flowers and a leaf or two. Place in the refrigerator for 3 to 4 hours until set. Serve with whipped cream or custard.

   Note: Do not use fresh pineapple or the jelly will not set.

# Quick Cooling Pick-me-up Drink

1 *fresh pineapple, thinly sliced and liquidised*
4 *cups pineapple sage tea\**
2 *cups plain yoghurt*
1 – 3 *eggs*

¼ *cup brandy*
*a little nutmeg*
4 *tablespoons honey or honey to taste*

\* To make pineapple sage tea, pour 4 cups boiling water over 2 cups pineapple sage leaves. Stand, steep, cool and strain.

Blend everything in a liquidiser, pour into long glasses, dust with nutmeg and drink immediately.

I find this a most wonderful end-of-the-day energiser if I have to go out in the evening and feel tired. It is a meal in itself and will sustain you for the entire evening. It is also an ideal convalescent drink.

Pineapple sage punch is a refreshing drink which aids digestion

# Poppy Seed

*Papaver somniferum*

Commercial poppy seeds are from the opium poppy, an annual originally from the Mediterranean region and native to the Middle East, but now cultivated widely all over the world. Opium was known to the Greeks, Romans and Egyptians before AD 800, as it was already being cultivated in Persia, India and China by that time.

Opium consists of the gummy latex which oozes out of the unripe seed pod when it is slit and this latex contains some 24 different alkaloids which are used medicinally and, of course, narcotically. There is no need to worry about the narcotic content in cooking as the seeds cannot form until the plant has matured to the point where it has lost all its opium content.

The deep blue-black seeds are delicious sprinkled over breads, cakes and pasta and can be crushed and mixed with syrup as a filling for pastry and cakes. Most European kitchens have a poppy seed grinder, a gadget which is seldom found in South Africa, where poppy seeds are not used nearly as much. Without a grinder they can be equally well ground by soaking the seed in water, draining it next morning and crushing it with a rolling pin.

To toast poppy seeds, spread them on a baking sheet and bake at 190 °C/ 375 °F for 5 – 8 minutes. This brings out the flavour.

Try using poppy seed in gravies, stews and curries. You will find it thickens and improves the texture and imparts a rich nutty flavour to the dish.

Incidentally, on first pressing the seeds exude a rich, clear, flavour-filled oil known as 'olivette'. The second pressing under heat produces an inedible red oil which is used for paints and in industry, and is available at art supply shops.

## Poppy Seed Sauce

This is a nourishing, rich, tasty sauce that will transform a plain cauliflower, cabbage, carrot or pea dish.

3  tablespoons butter
1 – 2 tablespoons poppy seeds
2  tablespoons lemon juice
1 – 2 teaspoons finely chopped marjoram
       or oregano

1/2  teaspoon salt
dash of paprika
little finely chopped garlic

Melt the butter and add the other ingredients. Pour over hot, cooked vegetables.
   I often combine diced carrots and peas in a silver dish, pour over the sauce and decorate it with chopped parsley or chervil – it's a party dish every time!

## Poppy Seed Snack                                     Makes 3 – 4 doz.

So often one wants a salty, tasty nibble with drinks before dinner and I find this an ideal biscuit for such occasions. I make a big batch and find they keep for weeks in an airtight tin.

1/2  cup poppy seeds
6  tablespoons butter
1  cup wholewheat flour
1/2 – 1 teaspoon salt
1  teaspoon baking powder

1/2  teaspoon cayenne
1  cup grated cheese
cold milk or water
paprika

Place the seeds on a baking tray and bake at 200 °C/400 °F for 15 minutes. Allow to cool. Rub butter into the flour, add salt, baking powder, cayenne, cheese, and poppy seeds. Stir in enough cold water or milk to form a fairly stiff dough. Turn onto a floured board and roll out very thin. Cut into strips, sticks or small diamond shapes, or use a small pastry cutter.
   Dust baking trays with extra flour, place biscuits on trays, and bake at 200 °C/ 400 °F for 10 – 13 minutes or until they start to change colour. Remove from the oven, sprinkle with a little salt and dust with paprika. When cold, store in a sealed container.

# Poppy Seed Ginger Bread

110 g butter
170 g treacle
50 g honey
140 ml milk
2 eggs, beaten
225 g wholewheat flour

50 g brown sugar
1 teaspoon baking powder
1 tablespoon ground ginger
2 tablespoons poppy seeds
2 teaspoons mixed spice

Line an 18 cm or 20 cm round cake tin or two 18 cm loaf tins. In a pot, melt together the butter, treacle and honey. Add milk and cool. Beat eggs and blend with the mixture. Sieve all the dry ingredients together and into this blend the egg, butter, honey and treacle mixture.

Turn into the prepared tins and sprinkle with poppy seeds. Bake at 300 °F/150 °C for 1 – 1½ hours, depending on the size of the tin, or until just firm when pressed. Serve sliced and spread with butter.

Poppy seed sauce is a nutritious addition to a variety of vegetables

# Rose

Rosaceae family

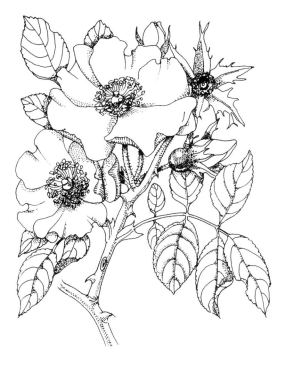

Surprisingly, the petals of cultivated and wild roses give a wonderful flavour to jams, drinks, cakes and puddings. The heavily scented Crimson Glory is my favourite, as it tastes exactly like it smells – rich, headily fragrant and simply beautiful.

The rose has perhaps always been the most loved of all flowers and its scent the most highly esteemed. Rose hips have long been made into syrups and jellies and used in medicine, but the full importance of rose hips as a source of vitamin C was only realised during the Second World War.

Roses are indigenous to Europe and Western Asia and have been naturalised and introduced elsewhere in the world. The rose contains vitamins C, B, E and K, nicotinamide, organic acids, pectins and tannins, which make it a valuable addition to the diet. It is a most attractive asset in the herb garden.

There has been a revival of interest in the old-fashioned roses, and most nurseries offer these for sale. *Rosa canina*, or dogrose, is a single rose that produces an abundance of hips. The petals are delicious in salads.

*R. eglanteria* or sweet briar is a vigorous grower with a glorious scent, and its leaves smell of apples. It is well worth growing as it too produces a wealth of hips which can be turned into a tasty, tart jelly, or syrup for cool drinks.

*R. rugosa*, the Japanese rose or Turestan rose, is a hardy and very prickly rose and a heavily scented continuous bloomer. This rose, too, produces hips, and its petals can be used in cooking.

# Rose-water

Recipes often call for rose-water, and you can so easily make your own with the roses in your garden. Choose only red ones as the other colours turn the water an unattractive colour. Pick a basketful of fully opened roses at their prime. Rinse, and place in a glass, heat-proof bowl. Pour enough boiling water over the petals to cover them. Place a towel over the bowl and leave to cool for at least 5 hours. Strain through a sieve and press out all the juice from the petals. Bottle and refrigerate.

## Rose and Strawberry Ice-cream

3  cups strawberries, hulled and washed
2  cups plain yoghurt
2  cups red rose petals, well pressed down
    and heeled

200 g soft brown sugar
2  eggs, beaten
1  cup thick cream

Liquidise the strawberries. Add the yoghurt and the heeled rose petals (heeling the petal means cutting off the small bitter, whitish tip at the base of the petal). Add the sugar and the beaten eggs. Lastly, blend in the cream with a spoon.

Pour into trays and freeze. Serve with crystallised rose petals and fresh strawberries.

## Crystallised Rose Petals

few fully opened roses
2  egg whites
castor sugar

Separate the petals and make sure they are clean and dry. Beat the egg whites until they are opaque, but not foamy. With tweezers dip each petal into the egg, making sure the entire surface is well covered. Place on grease-proof paper on a baking tray. Sprinkle with castor sugar and turn the petals so that both sides are evenly coated. Place each coated petal carefully on a clean, lightly oiled baking tray.

Preheat your oven to 200 °F/100 °C and place the tray in it, leaving the oven door slightly ajar. After 3 hours check to see that the petals are not too brittle. Once they are stiff and crisp, store in an airtight jar. Use to decorate cakes, ice-creams, puddings and fruit salads.

# Rose Custard Pancakes

### Filling

2 eggs
4 tablespoons sugar
2 – 4 teaspoons rose-water
1 – 2 tablespoons wholewheat flour

1 tablespoon cornflour
300 ml milk
6 tablespoons chopped, heeled rose petals

Beat eggs, sugar and rose-water until creamy. Whisk in flour and cornflour. Bring the milk to a boil slowly and then stir into the egg and flour mixture, beating all the time, until it thickens. Lastly add the rose petals and stir well. Remove from heat and allow to cool.

### Batter

225 ml cold rose-water
225 ml milk
4 eggs, well beaten

1/2 teaspoon salt
250 g sifted wholewheat flour
6 tablespoons melted butter

Mix the milk and rose-water, and beat this together with the eggs and salt. Add flour and melted butter. Whisk well for one minute. Cover and let it prove for 2 hours. Then pour a little batter into a hot, greased pan, and make the pancakes in the usual way. Keep warm.

Fill each pancake with the rose custard and dust with cinnamon. Sprinkle with a squeeze of lemon juice and decorate with chopped pecan nuts and cream. Serve hot.

# Rose Petal Syrup

This is a syrup that can be served with ice-cream, rice puddings or cakes, or diluted with soda water or iced water as a cool drink.

1 cup rose-water
2 cups sugar or honey
1 1/2 cups orange or lemon juice, or a
    combination

2 cups chopped, heeled red rose petals
1 sprig lemon verbena

Dissolve the sugar in the rose-water and fruit juice over low heat. Add the chopped rose petals and lemon verbena, stirring with a wooden spoon. Ensuring that it does not boil, keep over heat for 1/2 – 3/4 hour, stirring frequently so that it does not burn. Cool and strain. Pour into a sealable bottle.

# Rose Hip Jelly

rose hips
water

lemon juice
sugar

Collect a basketful of ripe rose hips at the end of autumn. Clean and trim them, and put into a pot with just enough water to cover them. Allow to simmer for about 30 minutes. Pour into a liquidiser and strain through a jelly bag overnight. Next morning, for each 600 ml of liquid add the *juice of one large lemon* and *4 g sugar*. Boil together and allow to simmer until a drop settles in a saucer of cold water, which indicates that the syrup is setting. Pour into clean, warm glass jars. Stand covered until cool. Seal with a circle of grease-proof paper dipped in brandy, and screw on the lid tightly. Serve with mutton or beef, or as a spread on toast.

My favourite edible roses are the Crimson Glory and the new Margaret Roberts' Rose

# Rosemary

*Rosmarinus officinalis*

Rosemary was one of the best loved and most highly respected and esteemed herbs in ancient times and was commonly associated with protection and healing. It was sometimes used in the place of costly incense at religious ceremonies and is still said to protect against witches and evil spirits – so no garden dare be without it!

It has a strong, distinctive flavour that is apt to overpower other herbs, so it is best used alone, and fairly sparingly. It lends itself equally well to savoury dishes as it does to jams, jellies, biscuits and fruit dishes and it makes a delicious tea, claret cup, cool drink and fruit punch.

A piece of rosemary steeped in wine or claret adds a delicious taste, and if you warm it just a little, add a little sugar and a piece of cinnamon, it makes a delicious winter drink that soothes a sore throat and helps a stuffy nose.

Rosemary is a tonic herb which is strengthening, revitalising and soothing to the digestion.

# Rosemary Tea Energiser

1 cup boiling water
1 thumb-length sprig rosemary
few raisins
1 stick cinnamon

honey to sweeten
1 teaspoon apple cider vinegar
(optional) or squeeze of lemon juice

Pour the boiling water over the rosemary, raisins and cinnamon. Allow to stand for about 6 minutes, or until drinkable. Strain, eat the raisins and sweeten the tea with honey. Add apple cider vinegar or lemon. This is an excellent tea for coughs, colds and for times when you feel chilled, over anxious, overtired and headachy.

# Rosemary Fish Grill
Serves 6

My love for cooking in unglazed clay pots has made this dish into a favourite. I find the flavours of the fish, rosemary and vegetables combine to make a mouth-watering, nutritious dish and one that is tremendously quick and easy to prepare. You can substitute mutton, pork chops or steak for the fish if you prefer – they will all be superb.

6 sprigs fresh rosemary
2 large onions, sliced into thick rings
1 green or red pepper, sliced
6 pieces of fish, skinned and trimmed
salt
pepper

paprika
butter
6 large brown mushrooms
6 small or medium-sized potatoes
juice of 2 lemons

Soak a large, clay cooking pot in water for half an hour. Drain the pot and pour in one cup of cold water. Lay the rosemary sprigs in the bottom. On top of these lay the thickly sliced onion rings and the sliced green or red pepper (pips removed). Over this place the fish pieces, sprinkle with salt, pepper and paprika, and dot with butter. Around the sides of the pot arrange the brown mushrooms and the scrubbed potatoes. Pour the lemon juice over everything. Dot the mushrooms with butter and sprinkle with a little salt and paprika. Sprinkle a little finely chopped rosemary over the fish. Cover with the wet lid, and bake at 375 °F/180 °C for ½ to ¾ hour or until the potatoes are soft and the fish is tender.

Serve from the clay pot with a green salad and fresh lemon juice, discarding only the rosemary twigs.

The baking steaming method is foolproof and a very healthy way of eating. Once you begin cooking this way you'll find experimenting with clay cookery a continual pleasure and every dish will be a winner.

# Rosemary Buttermilk Rusks

I bake these frequently, particularly in winter. The subtle rosemary flavour makes them a favourite with everyone and they keep very well in a tin.

*500 g butter*
*6 cups wholewheat or brown bread flour*
*6 cups cake flour*
*8 teaspoons baking powder*
*1 – 1½ cups sugar*
*2 cups coconut*

*pinch salt*
*6 tablespoons finely chopped fresh*
  *rosemary*
*little powdered nutmeg*
*3 eggs beaten with 1 litre buttermilk*

Rub butter into flour. Add all the ingredients, the beaten eggs and buttermilk last, to form a stiff dough. Roll into balls about the size of golf balls and pack into well-greased tins. Sprinkle with a little nutmeg, and bake for 1 hour at 375 °F/180 °C or until done.

When cool, remove from the tins, breaking apart gently. Place on the oven rack or on a cake cooler in a 200 °F/100 °C oven overnight to dry out. Keep the oven door slightly ajar. When dry and cool, pack into tins.

When you're low on energy, rosemary is what you need

149

# Saffron

*Crocus sativus*

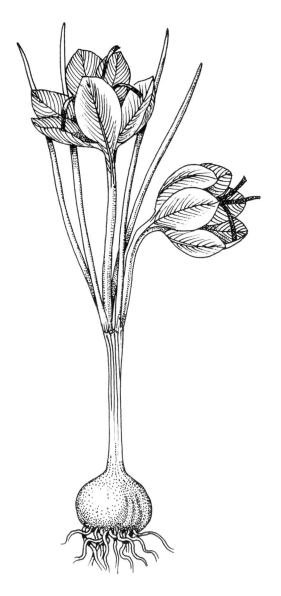

Saffron is the world's most expensive spice. It is made from the stigmata of the autumn crocus, a beautiful, bulbous plant native to Asia and the Mediterranean which produces mauve lily-like flowers in autumn. Each flower contains three long stigmata, which are picked by hand, and if one thinks of the huge number of stigmata – about 225 000 – that are needed to make up 450 g of spice, one can understand the price!

Spain and Portugal are the chief exporters of saffron and both countries use it extensively in their cooking.

Good saffron must smell fresh and have a bright orange colour. Its smell is sweet, pungent and unmistakable. One way to use it is to add the dried threads to a little warm milk or water and leave it for a few minutes to scent and colour the liquid. You can crush it into the liquid with a pestle or alternatively you can put the saffron threads into a low oven for a few minutes to crisp, and this can then be crumbled directly into the food. A little saffron goes a long way – just a pinch will colour and flavour 450 g of rice. The flavour is subtle and a bit too much will make the dish bitter.

Spanish paella, Milanese risotto and French bouillabaise are traditional saffron-flavoured dishes, and although calendula and marigold petals and ground turmeric have been substituted for saffron, their flavour is not nearly as distinctive as that of saffron.

Saffron was recorded on papyrus paper in 1552 BC in Greece. The Romans used it extensively in that period too, and it was they who brought it to Britain and Europe. In the eighth century the Muslims introduced saffron to Spain and the Crusaders carried it with them to Britain again in the thirteenth century. It was cultivated in the fifteenth century and used medicinally to treat gout, and it is still used in folk medicine in some countries today.

Saffron can be fairly easily grown in a fairly cold climate with winter snow.

Incidentally, the typical saffron yellow dye is produced by the stigmata, but don't try to use it as it is water soluble!

Saffron can be used to spice meat and fish dishes, buns, puddings and cakes and it imparts a subtle and beautiful flavouring to wine.

# Saffron Rice

1  cup brown or white rice
little salt
freshly ground black pepper

pinch saffron
2  cups water

Simmer the rice, salt, pepper and saffron in the water until cooked. Drain, and steam to separate the grains and make it light and fluffy.

As a variation you can add 1 cup raisins, or 1 cup chopped walnuts or almonds, or 1 cup chopped sweet pepper, or 1 cup sunflower seeds, or combinations of these.

# Saffron Lamb Stew                                           Serves 4 – 6

2  onions, sliced
little sunflower or maize oil
1 kg cubed lamb (e.g. shoulder)
1  cup wholewheat flour
2  large tomatoes, skinned and chopped
3  large potatoes, cubed
3  carrots, diced
1  teaspoon crushed coriander

freshly ground black pepper
salt to taste
pinch saffron
3  sprigs rosemary
little grated lemon peel
juice of 1 lemon
water or vegetable stock

Slice the onions and fry in a little oil. Roll the pieces of lamb in the flour and add to the browning onions. Fry until golden. Add all the other ingredients and cover with water or vegetable stock. Cover and simmer for about 30 – 40 minutes or until the vegetables are tender, stirring every now and then to prevent burning. Add a little more water if necessary. Serve with a sprinkling of chopped parsley and saffron rice.

# Saffron Sauce

This is elegant and unusual sauce, and is most delicious on steamed vegetables such as courgettes, cauliflower, carrots, peas, beans and kohlrabi.

2 *tablespoons butter*
2 *tablespoons wholewheat flour*
1 *cup milk*
1 *cup sharp cheese, finely grated (e.g.*
   *mature cheddar)*

½ *cup well-cooked split peas*
½ *teaspoon salt*
*freshly ground black pepper*
*pinch saffron, finely ground*

Melt butter in a thick-bottomed saucepan. Stir in flour and cook for 2 – 3 minutes over medium heat. Add milk, stirring all the time. Add cheese, split peas, seasonings and saffron. Pour over the vegetables, sprinkle with chopped chervil or parsley and serve hot.

Saffron rice can be made with a range of variations

# Sage

*Salvia officinalis*

Sage has a powerful flavour, especially if it is grown in hot, dry conditions. It contains strong, camphor-like oils which, if not used cautiously, will easily overpower your cooking. Indeed, opinions vary enormously as to the value of sage in cooking. Some cooks say it is too strong, crude and overpowering, while others love it! For me the joy in cooking with sage is its magical medicinal quality. Sage is one of the most esteemed herbs for health. It aids digestion, it is an antiseptic, tonic and antifungal, it reduces excessive perspiration, cleanses the liver, cures respiratory tract diseases, soothes anxiety and depression, restores the memory, and treats skin problems, hypoglycaemia and sore throats.

Sage has been used for milennia. Its 750 species are distributed widely throughout the world. Most varieties have medicinal uses and many are used in cooking. The most important and best known species is *Salvia officinalis*, and it is this that you should use in the recipes below.

Sage grows well in sandy soil as it does not like wet feet. I treat it as a biennial and make cuttings every summer to ensure that I have new plants coming on. Sage flowers are lovely in a fruit salad or pushed into honey. Discard the tough calyx and use only the soft petals.

It combines well with parsley, chives and chervil, but do not mix it with any other herbs as it is too strong.

Sage, like borage, comfrey and salad burnet, can be dipped into batter and fried in deep oil for a tasty snack to serve with drinks.

Wrap fish or pork in whole sage leaves to marinade for 1 – 2 hours before frying or baking. Shake off the leaves before cooking.

153

## Sage Honey

½ – 1 cup sage flowers
1 – 4 tablespoons lemon juice, depending
    on taste

1 jar of new honey (not solidified)
1 stick cinnamon

Stir the flowers and lemon juice into the honey and see that each flower is well coated. Press in the cinnamon stick. Store for a fortnight, and then use as a spread or to sweeten herb teas.

## Sage Cough Mixture

This is the most effective cough mixture I know.

½ cup chopped sage leaves
2 tablespoons freshly squeezed lemon
    juice
3 – 4 tablespoons honey

Mix well. Take a teaspoonful frequently.

## Sage Tea

¼ cup chopped fresh sage leaves
1 cup boiling water
2 – 3 teaspoons honey

1 teaspoon apple cider vinegar
pinch of nutmeg

Pour the boiling water over the chopped leaves. Stand, steep and strain when cool enough to drink. Sweeten with honey, add apple cider vinegar and a pinch of nutmeg.
    Drink a cup daily, particularly during winter, to combat coughs and colds and to aid the memory.

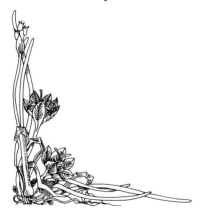

# Tuscan Sage and Bean Bake

Sage combines beautifully with butter or white haricot beans, and this is a delicious, very rich and filling dish which tastes even better served cold the next day with onion rings and a green salad. One of my favourite ways of cooking it is in a wet, unglazed clay pot.

| | |
|---|---|
| 2 cups dried butter beans or white haricot beans | 1 tin tuna (small) |
| 2 teaspoons salt | juice of 2 lemons |
| 4½ cups cold water | freshly ground black pepper |
| 10 fresh sage leaves | little garlic, finely chopped |
| | 2 tablespoons olive or maize oil |

Soak the beans overnight in enough water to cover them. The next morning bring to the boil, boil for about 10 minutes, and drain. Place the hot beans in an unglazed clay pot that has been soaked in water. Sprinkle with salt and pour in the 4½ cups of water. Add the sage and bake at 375 °F/180 °C for 1½ hours or until the beans are tender. Check halfway through the cooking time, stir the beans and add a little extra water if necessary.

In the meantime, break the tuna up with a fork and add the lemon juice, black pepper and garlic. Remove the baked beans from the oven and stir in the tuna and olive oil. Bake covered for an additional 15 minutes. Remove from the oven, stir and add additional seasoning. Stand covered with a towel to retain the heat for at least half an hour before serving.

# Sage and Onion Stuffing

I find this a particularly pleasing stuffing for duck and turkey, and it turns an ordinary roast chicken into a gala dish. It is very quick and easy to make, and can be sprinkled over the top of a chicken casserole or braai for extra taste, as one would sprinkle breadcrumbs.

Substitute cream for the yoghurt, sprinkle over fish and bake uncovered for 10 minutes to brown and crisp or over grilled chicken or sausage.

| | |
|---|---|
| 1 cup plain yoghurt | salt and pepper |
| 1–2 cups brown breadcrumbs, depending on the preferred consistency | cardamom or allspice to taste |
| ½ cup chopped sage | ½–1 tablespoon debittered brewers yeast |
| 1 cup chopped onion | juice of 1 lemon |

### Optional

| | |
|---|---|
| ½ cup sunflower seeds | or ½ cup alfalfa (lucerne) sprouts |
| or ½ cup mung bean sprouts | or ½ cup buckwheat greens |

Mix all the ingredients together and stuff the bird, or add a little wheat germ and use it as a topping for casseroles and grills.

# Sage Sauce

This is delicious served with fish, pork or sausage dishes. I use it as a 'gravy' for grills and braais, and I find it is excellent for indigestion. It also spices up a plain dish.

3  medium onions, finely chopped
½  cup grated carrots
½  cup chopped chives
2  cups stock or water
¼  cup chopped sage leaves

1  tablespoon parsley
2  teaspoons marmite
2  tablespoons butter
2  tablespoons brown flour
1  cup milk

Cook the onions, carrots and chives in the stock or water until tender (about 20 minutes). Pour into a liquidiser with sage, parsley and marmite. Blend for 2 minutes. Heat butter, stir in flour and after a minute or two add the milk. Stirring all the time, add the liquidised mixture. Allow to thicken slowly. Adjust seasonings and serve as a gravy.

Sage sauce can spice up
all sorts of plain dishes

# Salad Burnet

*Sanguisorba officinale*

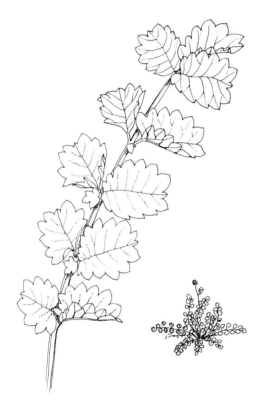

A handy perennial, salad burnet is native to the British Isles and Europe and is one of the few salad plants able to withstand the snow. It makes a most attractive garden plant with its cushion of green, fresh, fern-like leaves and these ensure a continual supply of salad greens in all seasons. It has a pleasant, bland cucumber-like flavour and combines well with many other herbs and spices.

It is a most valuable tonic herb, and helps to cool and cleanse the blood, bring down fevers, soothe the liver and aid digestion. Even just chewing a few leaves will help digest a heavy meal or relieve an 'uptight' feeling. It aids menopause and blood conditions, and burnet tea will soothe sunburn and cool the skin.

Salad burnet is most pleasing as a salad herb but can also be added to soups and stews. Use young leaves and strip them from their middle rib.

# Salad Burnet and Cucumber Salad

A daily salad is extremely important and this is a cooling, refreshing, energy-giving salad for a hot day. With cottage cheese and home-baked bread it is a sustaining midsummer meal.

1 cucumber, peeled and chopped
1 cup celery leaves and stalks, chopped
2 cups salad burnet leaves
1 cup mung bean sprouts or alfalfa
   (lucerne) sprouts

1 cup grated fresh pineapple
1 cup finely chopped borage leaves
squeeze lemon juice
freshly ground black pepper
little oil

Toss all the ingredients and serve immediately.

# Winter Rice and Egg Dish with Salad Burnet

225 g brown rice, soaked for an hour in
   cold water
2 tablespoons sultanas
salt and pepper to taste
2 tablespoons sunflower seeds
1 cup finely chopped onion

2 tablespoons maize oil
3 thinly diced carrots
1/2 cup chopped lovage
1 cup salad burnet leaves
4 chopped hard-boiled eggs

Soak the rice and raisins in water for an hour. Then add salt, pepper and sunflower seeds and cook until the rice is tender. Meanwhile brown the onion in the oil with the carrots and lovage. Stir in the cooked rice. Add the salad burnet leaves and hard-boiled eggs. Serve with a curried meat dish, or on its own with a salad or steamed mixed vegetables.

# Salad Burnet Health Drink

This is a wonderful drink, especially for those who are under tremendous pressure, students at exam time, or those on whom summer's heat and rush are merely taking their toll! It is a pick me up, a meal in a glass and is excellent for athletes too.

1  *cup sunflower seeds*
2  *cups apple or grape juice*
    *(unsweetened and unpreserved)*

1  *cup salad burnet leaves*
2  *tablespoons honey*
1  *banana*

Blend the sunflower seeds and fruit juice in a liquidiser. Add the salad burnet leaves, honey and banana and whirl for 2 minutes. Drink immediately.
    For extra strength and energy, the following can be added:

½  *cup wheat germ oil*
1  *tablespoon debittered brewers yeast*
½  *cup yoghurt*

Salad burnet health drink is ideal for students at exam time

# Summer and Winter Savory

*Satureja hortensis/S. montana*

Winter savory is a perennial herb with a stronger, more pungent taste than its relative, summer savory. Both are known for their effects on the bowel, dispelling wind, aiding constipation and regulating the bowels. Both are antiseptic and the leaves have an immediately soothing effect when rubbed onto wasp stings. Summer savory is quick and easy to grow and needs little attention once it is well established. The flower is a combination of thyme and mint with a hot peppery taste and this makes it delicious with bean dishes, sausages, stuffings and meat pies. Try chopping a few leaves into cheese dishes; it seems to draw out the flavour of the cheese.

Savory has been employed in food flavouring for over 2 000 years. Suprisingly, it was considered to be an aphrodisiac, probably owing to its stimulant effect.

Savory is native to the eastern Mediterranean region, south-west Asia and south-east Europe, and has been introduced elsewhere.

Oil which is of commercial value can be extracted from the leaf and the leaves themselves are used to flavour salami.

My favourite way of eating green beans is steamed with savory. Gather a basketful, top and tail them, and steam them until tender on a bed of either winter or summer savory (I would suggest that you start with two sprigs until you are familiar with the taste). Lift the beans off the savory twigs, dot with butter, sprinkle with a little salt and pepper and a squeeze of lemon juice and serve immediately. You will never again eat green beans any other way! The secret seems to lie in picking and steaming them directly, as they absorb the taste of the savory best this way.

# Savory Broad Bean Sauté

Serves 6

1 large onion, chopped
1 clove garlic, finely chopped
2 tablespoons maize oil
2 thumb-length sprigs winter savory or
    4 sprigs summer savory

2 tablespoons parsley
3 tablespoons sour cream
6 cups shelled broad beans
3 cups stock
salt and pepper to taste

Sauté the chopped onion and garlic in the oil until they start to brown. Add all the herbs and sauté. Add the sour cream and the beans and continue to sauté. Add stock and seasoning and simmer in a covered pot until the beans are tender. Check and stir every now and then to ensure that the beans do not burn. Serve with sausages, mashed potatoes and grilled tomatoes.

# Savory Cheese

Serves 4

1 cup grated cheddar cheese
1 cup cream cheese
2 beaten eggs
½ cup milk or yoghurt

½ cup chives
2 teaspoons chopped savory
4 – 6 slices buttered wholemeal toast

Blend all the ingredients in a double boiler and allow to thicken, stirring all the time. Have the buttered wholemeal toast ready. Pour the cheese mixture over this and serve piping hot with a green salad.

# Sesame

*Sesamum indicum*

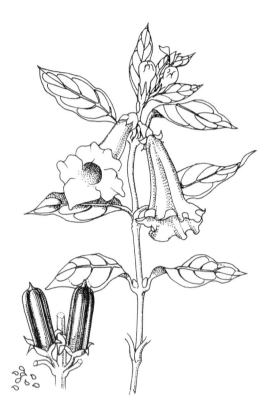

Man has known and used sesame since 1800 BC and it is still much favoured today. It is an annual crop, cultivated in Africa, Asia and America and the oil is a valuable export that is suitable for both medicinal and culinary purposes. Sesame is a most valuable herb and one which should be included more often in our diets for it is nutritive, it aids genito-urinary infections, constipation, liver ailments and sluggishness, soothes bleeding haemorrhoids and its vitamin E content strengthens the nerves and heart.

A popular way of using sesame seeds is to sprinkle them over rolls, cakes, breads and biscuits just before baking. After baking their taste resembles toasted almonds, so sesame is a useful substitute for nuts and can be used to offset the more expensive ones. If you can find sesame oil keep it at hand for soothing sunburn, cradlecap in babies, smoothing wrinkles and for hair dressing. It also acts as a barrier cream if you have to go out into the sun all day. I have also used it effectively for minor burns and scalds.

Tahini is a popular paste made from sesame which gives a glorious taste to casseroles and sauces, pâtés and spreads. It is worth investing in a jar (available through health food shops) for just a little will make ordinary dishes out of the ordinary, and it is nourishing as well.

The Greeks, Egyptians and Persians have recipes for sesame which are so ancient they have become part of their culture. A particular favourite is halva, a middle Eastern sweetmeat. Although there are many varieties, the basic ingredient is finely ground sesame. Halva is particulary nourishing for athletes and those who are stressed or rushed, and most people will agree that it is far superior to modern confectionery.

The recipe below is an easy method of making your own halva. Experiment by

162

adding raisins, walnuts, almonds, cashew nuts or dates for variation, and use this as a base for making your own nutritious sweets.

# Halva

---

1 cup sesame seeds
1 cup sunflower seeds
2 tablespoons soft brown sugar
2 tablespoons chopped nuts, e.g.
   almonds, pine nuts

raisins (optional)
3 – 4 tablespoons honey

Grind the sesame and sunflower seeds in a coffee grinder as finely as possible – it needs to be a powder. Stir in sugar, nuts and raisins. Knead the honey into the mixture until it has a hard dough consistency. Form into a small loaf and wrap lightly in grease proof paper. Chill. Serve in slices as a sweet, or roll small balls in coconut. Serve after dinner with coffee.

# Hummus and Mint

---

Hummus is a staple Arab dish and so easily made. It is packed full of nourishing vitamins and makes a wonderful dip for crudités.

225 g chick peas
225 ml plain yoghurt
2 tablespoons chopped mint
squeeze lemon juice
little finely chopped garlic
2 tablespoons olive or maize oil

1/2 teaspoon ground cumin
salt and pepper
1/2 – 1 tablespoon tahini
sprigs mint and roasted sesame seeds for
   decoration

Soak the chick peas overnight and cook in enough water to cover them for about 1 hour until tender.

Purée all the ingredients in a liquidiser. Serve chilled, garnished with mint and sesame seeds, with freshly baked wholewheat bread or biscuits; or use as a dip with carrot, celery sticks or raw mushrooms.

# Sorrel

*Rumex acetosa*

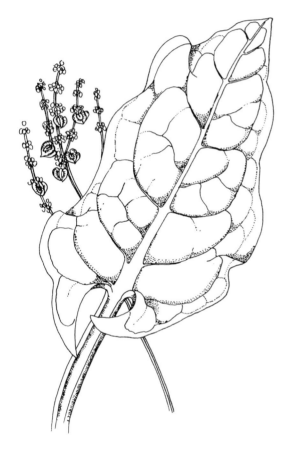

The sorrels are a large family and though some are sour and acid tasting, many can be eaten. The one described here is the large-leafed cultivated sorrel that is indigenous to Europe and much used in European cuisine. It is a diuretic, laxative, tonic and antiseptic, and combines well with other herbs like thyme, marjoram, chives, onions and lovage. The leaf can be eaten to treat skin complaints like acne, for cleansing the blood and toning the tissues. Because of its high acidity it should not be eaten too frequently and those who suffer from rheumatism, gout and kidney stones should avoid it.

Sorrel is known to have been eaten in ancient Greece, Rome and Egypt and was often the antidote for too much alcohol or rich food. It should only be cooked for a minimum time to preserve its fresh flavour. Always cut it with a stainless steel knife and use stainless steel or unchipped enamel pots for cooking in as the acidity of the herb reacts with iron and turns everything black and metallic-tasting.

# Spring Salad

1 cup sprouted buckwheat*
½ – 1 cup salad burnet leaves
5 large sorrel leaves, chopped
1 cup chopped dandelion greens

2 tablespoons chopped parsley
½ cup chopped celery or 2 tablespoons
  finely chopped lovage

\* see section on sprouting, p. 212.

Mix together and pour over your favourite salad dressing.

# Sorrel Omelette

Sorrel is a natural companion to eggs as its sharp taste offsets the blandness of the eggs. It makes a particularly delicious omelette.

2 tablespoons butter
6 eggs
salt and pepper

2 tablespoons cold water
4 tablespoons finely chopped sorrel

Melt the butter in a heavy-bottomed pan. Whisk the eggs, salt, pepper and water. Pour in the eggs before the butter browns and sprinkle the herbs over it. Lift the mixture around the edge of the pan so that the uncooked egg mixture runs to the edge. As soon as it sets, quickly flip over the one side and fold it in half. Lift onto a warm plate and serve immediately with hot buttered wholewheat toast.

The sharp taste of finely chopped sorrel is a natural companion to eggs in a sorrel omelette

# Waterblommetjie Bredie

This is probably the most sought-after dish in the Cape and a more truly South African dish would be hard to find. Ideally Karoo lamb should be the basis, and for those of us who do not live in the Cape with its vleis of waterblommetjies, we'll just have to wait impatiently for the holidays before we can make this delicious stew!

*1 – 2 kg rib of mutton*
*2 tablespoons honey*
*salt*
*freshly ground black pepper*
*maize or sunflower oil*
*2 onions, chopped*
*6 – 10 small potatoes*

*½ – 1 kg well-washed waterblommetjies*
 *that have soaked in salt water*
 *for 3 hours*
*5 – 10 large sorrel leaves*
*2 cups good white wine*
*little water*
*1 or 2 bay leaves*

Paint the honey over the mutton and sprinkle with salt and pepper. Place in a heavy-bottomed pot and brown in the oil. Add the onions and brown lightly. Put the potatoes and waterblommetjies on top of the mutton and add the sorrel leaves, wine and a cup or two of water. Tuck in the bay leaves and simmer gently until the meat is tender. Stir very carefully from time to time to prevent burning. Remove the bay leaves and serve steaming hot with rice.

# Tansy

*Tanacetum vulgare*

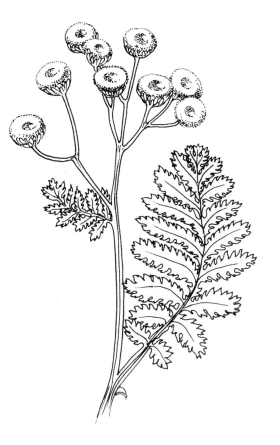

Although it is not very well known as a culinary herb, tansy will appeal to the gourmet cook. Like so many other herbs, its origins go back into the mists of time. In the Middle Ages it was well loved as a strewing herb, it was used as an insecticide, and was rubbed over meat to keep the flies off. It is native to Europe and Asia and grows freely in many countries, particularly in North America where it is a declared weed.

Small quantities or doses of tansy are all that is needed as its rather ginger-like taste becomes strong and bitter if used in too great a strength. A teaspoonful of chopped herb is usually enough.

It is wonderfully soothing to the digestion and eases flatulence and colic. A gargle can be made to cure mouth infections and small doses are effective for clearing worms in children. In some herbals tansy is said to induce abortion and it was once effective in the treatment of dropsy, but other herbs have now replaced it. It is often included in scented sachets.

The ginger-like flavouring of tansy leaves was immensely popular in the eighteenth century and Easter cakes and biscuits are still served today. Tansy combines well with ginger, nutmeg, cinnamon and allspice, and with sugar, cinnamon and pineapple juice it makes a sweet cordial which is refreshing on a hot day diluted with soda water.

As tansy is excellent for stomach complaints, try adding ½ – 1 teaspoon of herb to custard, rice puddings and milk sauces. Best of all, for keeping flies out of the kitchen have some in a vase or hanging in the kitchen and bruise the leaves from time to time. I rub tansy over the kitchen window sills to keep the kitchen fresh smelling and ant and fly free.

167

# Tansy Easter Biscuits

100 g soft butter
225 g sifted wholemeal flour
1 – 2 beaten eggs
50 g soft brown sugar
1 teaspoon cinnamon

100 g cake fruit
1 teaspoon mixed spice
2 teaspoons chopped tansy leaves
100 g chopped almonds
1 tablespoon milk

Rub the butter into the flour. Add the eggs and all the other ingredients. Add enough milk to make a stiff dough. Roll out 5 mm thick and cut into squares or rounds. Dust with castor sugar and cinnamon. Bake at 180 °C/350 °F for 20 minutes or until pale gold and crisp.

# Tansy Pudding

Serves 6 – 8

This unusual pudding forms a fudge-like sauce beneath a cake-like top.

1 cup flour (½ cup wholewheat:
  ½ cup cake flour)
pinch salt
¾ cup soft brown sugar
3 tablespoons cocoa
2 teaspoons baking powder

½ cup milk
2 tablespoons butter
1 teaspoon chopped tansy leaves
1 teaspoon vanilla
2 eggs, well beaten

Sift flour, salt, sugar, cocoa and baking powder. Heat the milk and melt the butter in it, add the tansy and stir into the flour. Add vanilla and the beaten eggs. Mix well. Butter a baking dish of approximately 22 cm x 22 cm and pour the mixture into this.

## Topping

Over this scatter without mixing:

½ cup soft brown sugar
½ cup castor sugar
4 tablespoons cocoa

Pour over this 1 cup of cold water. Bake for about 30 minutes at 375 °F/190 °C. Once it is out of the oven let the pudding stand at room temperature for 1 hour. Serve with whipped cream or plain yoghurt.

# Tarragon

*Artemisia dracunculoides*
*A. dracunculus*

There are two species of tarragon that are commonly used in cooking: Russian tarragon, *Artemisia dracunculoides*, and French tarragon, *A. dracunculus*, which has a coarser leaf and a richer, stronger flavour. Because of the easy and vigorous growth of Russian tarragon and its easy availability, many cooks use it in double the quantities they would use the more richly flavoured French species. French tarragon is difficult to grow as it is not vigorous, it does not propagate easily and unless the soil is exactly to its liking it more often than not does not come up again after its winter dormancy, or it reverts to the coarser flavour of Russian tarragon.

After years of battling with growing and using tarragon I now use only the new, fresh growth and replace my older plants with the very invasive new root stock. The flavour is better this way and my vinegars, oils and marinades are all very pleasing. I have also found that if I add the tarragon at the very end of the cooking time it retains its unique flavour far better.

Ideally tarragon for use in vinegars should be picked in midsummer when its flavour is at its peak. I find that my best tarragon vinegars are made around this time. Remember to make enough to last the year!

Tarragon is said to promote the appetite, but don't let that deter you as in French cuisine and for the serious cook it has no equal!

Add chopped fresh green tarragon to herb butters, chicken and fish grills, shellfish and salads. I find the nicest way of using tarragon is in a dressing which I prepare the day before using. It can also be used as a marinade (see recipe below).

Tarragon is native to Siberia and Asia, so it is included in many Asian dishes and many of our dishes are adapted from those cold countries. Tarragon is best with egg and fish dishes. Also try using it chopped as the Russians do over raw or cooked beetroot, with courgettes, mushrooms and cabbage.

Because tarragon has a subtle flavour, it is preferable not to mix it with other herbs and spices. In order to taste its unique flavour, double up on the quantities of tarragon given in recipes.

Tarragon is an excellent herb for aiding digestion, it helps in assimilating food, particularly when one is upset or anxious, and it is energy-giving.

## Tarragon Dressing/Marinade

½ – 1 cup chopped tarragon
3 – 6 tablespoons soft brown sugar
little cayenne pepper
1 cup sunflower oil
½ cup chopped chives or green onions

few pieces red chilli
1 tablespoon dry mustard
1 cup vinegar
1 cup warm water
little chopped garlic

Put all the ingredients in a large jar and shake. Refrigerate overnight. Shake well and use as a salad dressing or as a marinade for pork, fish or chicken. It is also delicious spooned over a braai while the meat is cooking.

## Tarragon Pea Lunch Dish                                        Serves 4 – 6

4 cups fresh garden peas
1 lettuce, shredded
salt
freshly ground black pepper

2 eggs
1½ cups milk
1 cup grated cheddar cheese
fresh tarragon, chopped

Lightly cook the peas in just enough water to cover them, with 2 – 3 sprigs of mint. Butter a casserole dish and lay some of the shredded lettuce leaves in it. Spread the peas evenly on top of the lettuce, and sprinkle with salt and freshly ground black pepper. Whisk the eggs into the milk and pour this over the peas. Sprinkle over this the rest of the shredded lettuce and grated cheddar cheese. Bake at 180 °C/350 °F for about 20 minutes – or until the custard has set. Sprinkle with chopped fresh tarragon and serve piping hot.

**Variations:** Add ½ cup feta cheese to the milk and egg mixture, or ½ cup wheat germ, or grate mozzarella cheese over the dish before baking. Substitute cauliflower or broccoli for the lettuce (cook first with the peas).

# Tarragon Health Salad

2  raw beetroots, finely grated
1  carrot, grated
½  cup chopped tarragon
1  green pepper, cut into thin strips

4 – 6 radishes, thinly sliced
1  apple, grated
½  cup chopped celery

Place layers of each ingredient in a glass bowl.

## Dressing

2  tomatoes
2  tablespoons tarragon
juice of 1 lemon

½  cup sunflower oil
2  tablespoons honey

Place all ingredients in a liquidiser and blend for 2 minutes. Pour over the salad and sprinkle over this alfalfa sprouts and a little parsley. Served with hard-boiled eggs this is a substantial and healthy meal.

# Tarragon Digestive Aperitif

This is an amazing pre-dinner drink for those who have heartburn, indigestion, or poor digestion in general. It keeps indefinitely and only a tablespoonful needs to be taken before a meal.

6  15 cm-long sprigs of tarragon
600 ml good brandy
piece of vanilla pod about 4 cm long

3 or 4 pieces thinly pared lemon skin
 (with no pith)
6 cloves

Combine all the ingredients and steep for 14 days. Strain and bottle. Slowly sip ½ – 1 tablespoonful before meals.

# Thyme

*Thymus vulgaris*

Thyme is one of the cook's best loved herbs, and has its place in the cuisine of many cultures. It is not known when thyme was first used in Europe. Some say the Romans took it to Britain, while others say it was in use in 850 AD in the Mediterranean regions. By the sixteenth century it was being cultivated in a number of countries far away from its native Italy and the Mediterranean.

Thyme is very versatile and can be combined with milder herbs such as tarragon, watercress, chives, parsley, chervil, bay, dill, fennel, mint and sage. Because of its pungent taste, it does not combine well with the spices, so use it with care.

*Thymus vulgaris* can only be used in savoury dishes such as meat (particularly pork and poultry), cheese, eggs, in stuffings for meat and fish, casseroles, soups and stews. Creeping thyme, *T. serphyllum*, and lemon thyme, *T. citriodorus*, are lighter in flavour and give a delicious taste to sweet dishes. Lemon thyme is particularly refreshing with fruit drinks and in fruit salads and jams. I use thyme freshly picked from the garden, but you can dry it. Its flavour is strong, so use it carefully.

Use sprigs of lemon thyme or creeping thyme when stewing fruit (soak a sprig or two in the water with the fruit) and add them to custards, baked puddings, punch and cool drinks. Use them to make a delicious after-dinner tea to help digest a heavy meal. This tea is also excellent for coughs and colds.

The various species of thyme, like many other culinary herbs, are excellent for digestive ailments, they are antiseptic and soothe mouth infections, flatulence, colic and sore throats if a sprig is chewed. Include thyme in the diet as a cleanser and tonic herb especially for infections; use strong thyme tea both as a drink and as a wash on the infected area. Thyme makes excellent vinegar as a base for salad

Creeping thyme, *T. serphyllum*

Lemon thyme, *T. citriodorus*

dressings. Sprinkle savoury thyme stripped from its stalks onto chicken and meat dishes, or fry it with more unusual dishes like mushrooms, sweet potatoes, the cabbage family, cheeses and pasta dishes.

## Mushroom Bake with Thyme                    Serves 6

450 g large brown mushrooms
2 tablespoons fresh green thyme
juice of 2 lemons
salt and pepper

1 cup stock – made with meat extracts or
   yeast extract and 1 bay leaf
1 large onion, sliced

Wipe and trim the mushrooms and place them stalk side up in a well-soaked un-glazed clay casserole dish. Sprinkle with thyme, lemon juice, salt and freshly ground black pepper and add the stock. Place the onion rings around the sides. Cover and bake at 350 °F/180 °C for 15 – 20 minutes. Serve as a lunch dish with salads.

# Herb Dredge

This is a very useful flavouring for all savoury dishes. I keep it in a flour dredger with a screw-on lid so that it is easy to sprinkle.

½ cup thyme, dried and stripped from
    its stalks
½ cup crushed sea salt
2 teaspoons milled coriander seeds

½ cup dried parsley
1 teaspoon milled peppercorns
2 teaspoons milled dill seeds
⅓ cup dried lovage leaves

Rub all the dried herbs and the salt through a sieve. Work all ingredients together in a mortar with a pestle. Work in some olive or sunflower oil and use this to brush over the meat or fish before grilling. Alternatively, fill your flour dredger with the ground herbs and keep them on hand for seasoning.

# Lemon Thyme and Rhubarb Tart

I find lemon thyme lends itself wonderfully to fruit tarts. This baked rhubarb tart is healthy and delicious and one of the nicest ways of serving rhubarb.

½ cup soft butter
1 cup soft brown sugar
2 eggs
1 cup wholewheat flour
½ teaspoon nutmeg
2 teaspoons baking powder

pinch salt
2 large ripe bananas
2 tablespoons fresh lemon thyme or
    creeping thyme leaves
4 cups fresh rhubarb stems, diced
½ cup wheat germ

Blend butter, half a cup of sugar and eggs in a mixer. Add flour, nutmeg, baking powder and a pinch of salt. Add and blend in the bananas. Pour half the mixture into a greased baking dish and sprinkle with the fresh lemon thyme or creeping thyme leaves stripped from their stalks. Place the diced rhubarb over the mixture, sprinkle with another half cup of brown sugar and a little more nutmeg. Pour the rest of the mixture over the rhubarb, sprinkle with a little wheat germ and bake in a moderate oven at 375 °F/190 °C for about 30 – 40 minutes or until the rhubarb is tender. Serve hot with custard or whipped cream.

# Lemon Thyme Tea

1  *cup boiling water*
¼  *cup fresh lemon thyme sprigs*
1  *piece cinnamon*

*juice of half a lemon*
*honey for sweetening*

Pour boiling water over the lemon thyme and cinnamon, stand, steep and strain. Sweeten with honey and add lemon juice. Drink hot.

If you make a large quantity, calculate 2 – 3 thumb-length sprigs per person, and add more boiling water if it is too strong. Save any that is over for a delicious cool drink base. Just add lemon or orange juice and a little honey and decorate with mint sprigs. Serve in long glasses with ice.

Lemon thyme tea can be taken hot or cold

# Turmeric

*Cucuma domestica*

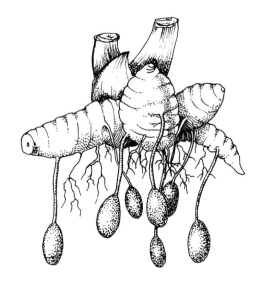

Turmeric is a tropical plant with a rhizome rather like ginger. The powdered turmeric available commercially is the mature rhizome that has been boiled, peeled, dried and pounded into a powder. Its taste is pungent and exotic and it gives its deep golden colour to various blends of curry and to mustard and pickles. The flavour is elusive and the older the turmeric the milder its taste, so buy it only in small quantities.

It is cultivated in China, Java, Peru and in India, where pieces of rhizome are chewed for indigestion and are also used for their glorious yellow dye. I have seen a turmeric plant with its long leaves and lily-like, honey-scented yellow flower grown near Durban, so it is possible to grow it in parts of South Africa.

Perhaps one of our best-loved traditional dishes in South Africa is yellow rice and raisins, and in this turmeric comes into its own. Try adding it to pasta dishes, fish and shellfish dishes, chutneys and piccalilli dishes. It combines well with cheese and eggs, but I am hesitant to combine it with too many herbs as it has a rather exciting taste that needs to be savoured on its own. It can be combined with the blander herbs like borage, chervil, comfrey and salad burnet, but rather start with a little and taste your way.

# Yellow Rice with Raisins

1 cup rice (traditionally white, but
  I use brown)
3 cups boiling water
1/2 – 1 cup seedless raisins

1 teaspoon turmeric
1/2 cup brown sugar
1 teaspoon salt
2 tablespoons butter

Soak raisins in warm water while you cook the rice. Boil the rice with the ripe turmeric, sugar, salt and butter until the rice is tender. Stir in the soaked raisins, turn into a sieve and steam until ready to be served.

# Rice and Turmeric Pancakes

This makes a wonderful side dish for curries, soups and stews and the pancakes can be stuffed with flaked fish, hard-boiled eggs and tomatoes or served as a dessert with apricot jam and whipped cream.

1 cup wholewheat flour
1 cup brown rice, cooked
1 1/2 teaspoons turmeric
pinch salt

1 beaten egg
1 – 2 teaspoons soy sauce
approximately 1 1/2 cups milk
oil for frying

Stir flour into the cooked, drained rice. Add turmeric, salt, beaten egg and soy sauce and enough milk to make a soft batter. Heat a little oil in a frying pan, pour in a little batter and flip over when it starts to bubble. Repeat, adding more oil when necessary. Keep the pancakes warm in a folded tea towel or napkin in the warming oven. Serve warm with a little mango chutney or apricot jam, or dip into curry.

# Vanilla

*Vanilla planifolia*

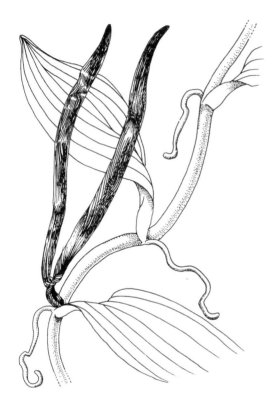

Vanilla is an orchid which originated in tropical South America. Its unique flavour made it highly sought after and it was cultivated elsewhere by artificial pollination. The pollination of the vine in its indigenous state is done by the vanilla moth, but those who are lucky enough to have grown a vine in a hot house will have found that pollination can be done by hand quite satisfactorily.

Vanilla is a perennial climbing plant with long, lime green pods that follow creamy white flowers. The pods are picked unripe and dried or cured until dark brown and covered with frosty crystals of vanillin. The concentrated flavour in a small piece of pod is enough to impart a strong taste to sweet dishes and the pod can be removed, washed and dried and used again and again. I feel a vanilla pod is an investment – and it gives so much for so little! I infuse the pod, either whole or a piece of it, in milk shakes, custards, milk, cream, buttermilk and ice-cream. Once the flavour is to my satisfaction I remove it, wash and dry it, and store it in a glass bottle for next time, or I push it into the sugar bowl and leave it there. Its flavour and fragrance give a delicious taste to the sugar, which in turn makes coffee or cocoa something special.

Commercial vanilla essence is usually made from a substance called eugenol which is present in clove oil and, like most synthetic substances, it lacks both the depth of fragrance and flavour of real vanilla. For the health conscious the vanilla pod is essential.

To cure your own vanilla pods (the green pod has no flavour) partially dry the mature green pods and allow them to 'sweat' a little in airtight boxes lined with greased paper. The flavour develops as a result of internal chemical activity by enzymes during the curing time. I have found curing tricky during the rainy season as the pods tend to mildew and experimentation is all one can do.

To make your own vanilla essence, steep crushed pods in alcohol. Shake daily and mature for 3 – 6 months. Use vanilla to flavour all sorts of sweet dishes, cakes, ice-creams and confectionery, biscuits and breads. It is at its best in creams and custards.

## Chocolate and Vanilla Roll

Chocolate lends itself particularly well to the subtle flavouring of vanilla and this is a party sweet or a tea party treat. I use it as a base for fruit in season and it is always a huge success. Try it for Christmas with cherries, nuts and raisins that have been soaked in brandy.

*4 tablespoons soft brown sugar in which*
  *half a vanilla pod has been lying*
  *covered for 3 – 4 days*
*4 eggs, separated*
*4 heaped tablespoons wholewheat flour*
*3 tablespoons cocoa*
*2 tablespoons boiling water*

*2 teaspoons baking powder*
*1 cup whipped cream*
*fresh fruit e.g. strawberries, cherries,*
  *sliced mango or sliced peaches*
*icing sugar*
*finely ground vanilla pod*

Beat sugar and egg yolks together. Add flour and cocoa, and beat well. Whisk egg whites until stiff. Mix the boiling water into the dough. Sprinkle over the baking powder, fold in the egg whites, and stir gently.

Line a 18 cm x 30 cm tin with foil or greased paper. Oil the tin and the paper. Pour the mixture into the tin. Bake for 10 – 15 minutes at 180 °C/350 °F. Turn out onto a clean cloth on a wire rack and roll up. As soon as it cools, open and spread with the cream and place the fruit over this in neat rows. Dust with icing sugar and a little finely ground vanilla pod. Roll up gently and loosely so as not to let the fruit ooze out or bake another vanilla cake to place over it. Serve in slices.

# Pavlova

The sweet taste of vanilla makes this old favourite into something special and by changing it according to the fruits in season you will always have a spectacular pudding that everyone will enjoy.

3 egg whites (extra large eggs)
175 g soft brown sugar in which a vanilla
   pod has been pushed for about
   3 days*
3 teaspoons baking powder
1 tablespoon vinegar
2 tablespoons honey or honey to taste

225 g cottage cheese
150 ml plain yoghurt
fruit in season, e.g. strawberries,
   peaches, mangoes, melons, pears,
   pineapple or a combination of your
   favourite fruits
icing sugar

\* Use 1 teaspoon vanilla essence if you have no vanilla pod.

Place 2 sheets of grease-proof paper on a baking sheet. Whisk egg whites until very stiff and gradually beat in the sugar. Fold in the baking powder, vinegar and, if you have no vanilla pod, the vanilla essence. Spoon this meringue mixture in a circle about 20 cm in diameter. Shape into a round with a dip in the centre. Bake at 150 °C/ 300 °F for about an hour or until firm. Cool, and place on a cake plate. Combine the honey, cottage cheese and yoghurt and fill the centre of the meringue with the mixture. Decorate with the fruit, dust with vanilla-scented icing sugar (keep a vanilla pod in your packet of icing sugar). Serve with sprigs of mint, lemon verbena or geranium leaves as decoration.

I feel a vanilla pod is an investment – it gives so much

180

# Vetiver

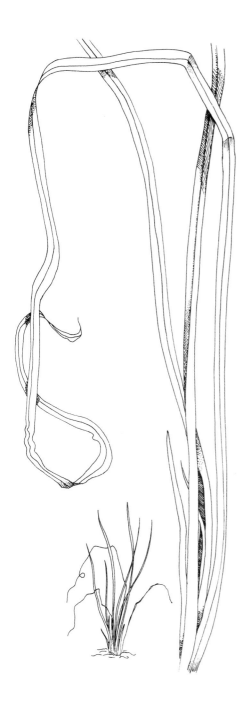

The deeply fragrant vetiver grass is indigenous to India, Java, Reunion and Brazil. It is much used as a fixative in perfumery and as an oil for flavouring sweets, drinks and sherbet. Khus-khus syrup can sometimes be bought from shops specialising in Indian food and it is much prized and appreciated both for its flavouring and its refreshing, energising qualities. In India blinds or shades were traditionally woven of the roots and leaves. Their cool, refreshing fragrance when splashed with water were thought to do much to restore energy and temper.

I grow vetiver very easily here in South Africa and every August I separate the vigorous clumps of attractive grass (it grows to about 1½ metres in height and width). I chop off the virous roots for pot-pourris and syrups and replant the abundant new clumps. It is a most wonderful pot-pourri ingredient and, if you are enterprising, bags and baskets, fans and shades, screens and blinds can be easily woven from the long, tough leaf blades.

Use washed root fibres in syrups and teas for energy and use the cold teas as a cool drink base. Sachets of roots give Indian clothes their typical fragrance and may be used as cupboard fresheners.

## Vetiver Syrup

This syrup is a delicious accompaniment to pancakes, fruit and baked puddings.

2  cups soft brown sugar
2  cups water
2  cups vetiver roots, well washed

4  allspice berries
1  stick cinnamon

Dissolve the sugar in the water. Add the other ingredients and bring to the boil. Simmer covered for 20 minutes on low heat in a stainless steel pot. Stand and steep. Strain the next morning and bottle.

## Vetiver Drink

 2  cups vetiver roots, well washed
10  cloves
 6  cups boiling water
juice of 4 lemons

fresh lemon slices
few thin lemon peel parings
few sprigs mint
1  cup sugar or honey

Boil the vetiver and cloves in the water for 10 minutes. Stand, steep until cold and strain. Add the lemon juice, lemon slices and peel parings, mint leaves, honey or sugar, and stir well. Drink chilled with ice.

Wash vetiver root well before using it

# Violet

*Viola adorata*

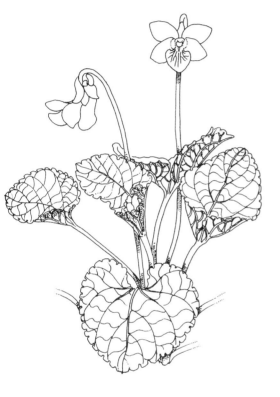

Few people ever think of the violet as a culinary herb. It originated in Britain and temperate Europe, though it has been introduced and naturalised elsewhere. It is shade loving and prolific and I have even grown it successfully in full sun as a border. I love violets for the colour they give to salads and fruit salads and as a decoration for vegetable dishes.

Medicinally, violets have a calming and relaxing effect on the nervous system. Five violet flowers (substitute leaves if the plant is not flowering) well chewed will relieve a headache (follow with three more an hour later). A tea made of leaves and flowers (1/4 cup violets to 1 cup boiling water) is excellent for expelling mucous from the nose, throat, chest and lungs. Whooping cough and postnasal drip are greatly alleviated if a cup of violet tea is taken 2 – 5 times a day with a little honey and lemon juice. Bruised leaves act as a soothing poultice for skin infections and inflammations and a strong tea is an excellent wash for eczema and rash. I use violets frequently in my cooking, as they aid insomnia, tension and nervousness, cure coughs and colds and act as a gentle laxative.

An infusion syrup of violets can be made by boiling up 1 cup violet leaves and flowers in 3 cups water. To this add 1 – 2 cups sugar, and use this to flavour puddings, creams, custards and ice-creams.

Because of their delicate taste I find violets best on their own, but they do combine well with lemon balm, bergamot, allspice, cinnamon, cloves, lemon grass, mace, nutmeg and the mints.

# Flower Salad

This is a spectacular salad and one which you can vary from season to season. It is a real party piece and you'll find your guests absolutely fascinated at the prospect of eating flowers!

2 cups nasturtium flowers
1 cup violets
2 cups rose petals with the bitter white
   heel cut off
1 cup borage flowers
½ cup rosemary flowers
½ cup calendula petals

½ cup sage flowers
few chive blossoms
few scented geranium flowers
½ cup bergamot flowers
few yarrow flowers
½ – 1 cup elder flowers

Mix all the flowers together and pour over a vinegar and oil dressing (see p. 205). Decorate with violets and violet leaves around the edge of the bowl.

# Violet Salad

2 cups violet flowers and leaves
2 cups young spinach leaves
4 large brown mushrooms, thinly sliced
juice of 1 lemon
salt
black pepper

½ cup chopped tarragon
2 tablespoons herb oil (e.g. tarragon or
   sunflower oil)
2 hard-boiled eggs
paprika
cayenne pepper

Shred the violet leaves and spinach leaves, add all the ingredients except the eggs, and stand at room temperature for at least an hour. Just before serving, chop the eggs and sprinkle over the top of the salad, season with paprika and a little cayenne. Decorate with violet flowers and serve with croutons, made from wholemeal bread fried in herb-flavoured oil.

# Violet Ice-cream

4 eggs, separated and beaten
150 g sugar
600 ml thick cream
1 cup violet infusion syrup (see p. 235)

1 cup violet flowers
1 cup flowers of your choice, e.g.
   carnation petals, rose petals,
   calendula petals, elder flowers

Beat egg yolks and sugar until thick and pale. Add cream and beat well. Add syrup and beat well. Stir in the flowers. Whisk egg whites and gently stir into the cream mixture. Pour into a freezer tray and freeze. Decorate with violets just before serving.

# Violet Jam

*250 g violet flowers*
*600 ml boiling water*

*750 g sugar*
*½ – 1 cup lemon juice*

Boil up the flowers in the water. Add sugar and stir well. Add lemon juice and simmer until thickening. Pour into small screw-top jars, seal with paper dipped into brandy and seal. Eat on hot toast or freshly baked scones.

Violet ice-cream is a floral treat

# Watercress

*Nasturtium officinale*

Although watercress is not usually considered a herb, both its medicinal and culinary uses are so varied and so valuable that I urge you to take a fresh look at this wonderful plant. It needs moving water at its roots, and yet I have grown it successfully under a dripping tap or in troughs or trays that stand in water which I swish out with the hose once a day. The seeds are easy to grow as dry root and stem cuttings. Treat it as an annual, sowing three or four batches every summer.

Watercress is indigenous to Europe and it has been introduced and naturalised elsewhere. It treats a wide diversity of ailments, and has been recommended for eye ailments, coughs, colds, sore throats, excess weight, bleeding gums, arthritis, rheumatism, kidney and bladder disorders, liver ailments, hardening of the arteries and high blood pressure – so it is worth including in the diet! The best way to eat it is fresh – in salads, sandwiches, with grills and as a side dish with feta cheese and olives. When using watercress in soups and stews, add it at the last moment to preserve its goodness. It contains vitamins A, B, C, D and E, nicotinamide, minerals, manganese, iron, phosphorus, calcium and iodine. It is a stimulant and diuretic, is easily digestible and combines well with most other herbs.

# Watercress Salad

This is a most filling and substantial salad and a wonderful accompaniment to grilled fish or meat. Surprisingly, raw eggplant (aubergine) is one of the main ingredients, which also contains essential vitamins and minerals.

1 eggplant
apple cider or tarragon vinegar
2 large bunches (4 – 6 cups) watercress
4 tablespoons chopped spring onions

1 tomato, thinly sliced
1 cup black olives
2 sliced hard-boiled eggs
2 teaspoons chopped fresh basil

Peel and slice the eggplant thinly, sprinkle with salt and cover for an hour. Rinse off the salt and dry with paper towels. Marinate in apple cider vinegar or tarragon vinegar for about 3 hours. Dry off again and chop into a salad bowl. Rinse the watercress, pick off the tough stems and yellow leaves, and add to the eggplant. Add the rest of the ingredients and toss. Sprinkle over this one or two tablespoons of chopped parsley and serve with a light vinegar and oil dressing.

# Watercress Soup                                                    Serves 6

This tasty and nutritious soup is so easy to make and is a favourite with everyone.

4 tablespoons chopped onion
2 tablespoons butter
2 tablespoons flour
690 ml milk
salt and black pepper
little nutmeg

little tabasco
6 cups watercress, washed and roughly
   chopped with tough stems removed
fresh cream
paprika

Fry the onion in butter. Add the other ingredients, except the watercress, paprika and cream. Bring to the boil and simmer for 10 minutes. Add the watercress, bring to the boil and remove from the heat. If you prefer a smooth soup, put everything through the liquidiser. Serve in soup bowls with a little cream stirred in (about 2 teaspoons per bowl) and a dusting of paprika. Serve with wholewheat croutons.

# Yarrow

*Achillea millefolium*

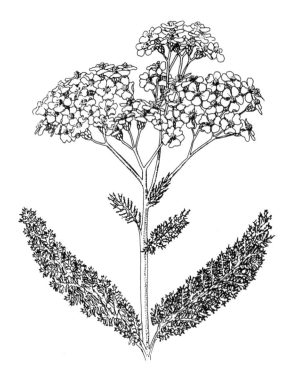

Yarrow is a tough, attractive and adaptable herb, yet not many people would consider planting it in their culinary herb gardens. Its spicy, spinach-like flavour is surprisingly pleasant and it is rich in vitamins and minerals. Because it has such a subtle and unique flavour I find it at its best used alone, but it is excellent in stuffings, particularly for poultry, in cream sauces and salads, and it combines particularly well with curries. It is perhaps best in beetroot salad and here I often add one or two spices or herbs like chervil, chives, comfrey, salad burnet and borage.

Yarrow is indigenous to Europe and has made itself at home in several countries. It is one of the 'old fashioned' herbs which once flourished in every cottage garden where it was easily available as a styptic, as its old names indicate: 'soldiers wound wort', 'knight milfoil', 'nose-bleed' and 'carpenter's herb'. Generations of country folk made use of its medicinal properties.

Its generic name *Achillea* is derived from Achilles, who is said to have been the first to use yarrow for healing the wounds of his soldiers in the battle of Troy. Yarrow formed part of the ancient materia medica which is the basis of medicine, and this esteemed herb has been grown through the centuries in physic, monastery and apothecary gardens and by housewives, all of whom pounded and mixed, blended and drew this precious herb to heal the sick. If yarrow was included in a wedding bouquet the bride was believed to be assured of seven years of happiness!

I have used fresh yarrow leaves on eczema, skin rashes and scratches with soothing and quick results, and have often found that wads of warmed yarrow leaves ease earache if placed and held behind the ear. A small wad of yarrow pushed up a nostril will staunch a nose bleed, and included in the diet as a tea will assist heavy menstrual flow, diarrhoea and palpitations, and will promote perspiration during colds and flu. It can be used in ointments, salves, lotions and washes and makes a pleasing tonic tea for ailments like chicken pox, measles, rheumatism and diabetes. It restores lost appetite and tones and strengthens flabby muscles. In the eighteenth century smokers were advised to substitute dried yarrow leaves for tobacco!

## Yarrow Kedgeree                                              Serves 4 – 6

675 g fish, e.g. cod, kabeljou, hake
2  bay leaves
freshly ground black pepper
salt to taste
2  onions, thinly sliced
2 – 3 teaspoons curry powder
2  teaspoons turmeric
2  tablespoons butter

1  cup strong stock
6  tablespoons chopped yarrow
2  cups brown rice, cooked
1/2  cup sultanas, soaked in hot water for
    2 hours
1/2  cup chopped almonds
parsley to decorate

Put the fish into a pot with the bay leaves, salt and pepper, cover with water and cook until tender (about 10 minutes). Drain, and flake the fish from the bones. Fry the onions, curry powder and turmeric in the butter, add the stock and mix well. Add the yarrow and simmer for 3 minutes. Combine the cooked rice, flaked fish and sultanas and pour the yarrow mixture over it all. Fork well to blend everything. Spoon into an attractive dish, sprinkle with almonds and parsley and serve hot with a salad.

## Curried Yarrow Soup                                              Serves 6

2  tablespoons butter
2  onions, finely chopped
1  clove garlic, finely chopped
1  teaspoon turmeric
2  teaspoons curry powder
2  tablespoons wholewheat flour
850 ml stock

2  cups chopped green beans
3  cups grated butternut squash
6  tablespoons finely chopped yarrow
    leaves
275 ml natural yoghurt
2  tablespoons honey

Melt the butter and add onions, garlic, turmeric and curry powder. Stir until the onions start to brown and soften. Add flour and stir in well. Add a little stock, blend well and then add the rest of the stock, beans and butternut and bring to the boil. Add the yarrow leaves as the beans start to soften and simmer for 10 minutes. Stir in the yoghurt and honey, spinkle with a little paprika and serve with croutons.

# Yarrow Tea

1/4 cup yarrow leaves
little honey to sweeten
1 cup boiling water

squeeze lemon juice (optional)
or 1 teaspoon apple cider vinegar

Pour the boiling water over the yarrow leaves and add the lemon juice or vinegar and the honey. Stand, steep and strain when cool enough to drink. Drink half a cup at a time 2 – 4 times during the day, or a full cup morning and night.

# Yarrow Salad                                                    Serves 6

2 – 4 beetroots, washed and scrubbed
1 apple, peeled
1 cup grated cucumber

3 tablespoons chopped yarrow
2 tablespoons chopped salad burnet
2 tablespoons chopped celery

Grate the raw beetroots on a fine grater. Grate the apple and blend with the beetroot. Add the grated cucumber, chopped yarrow, salad burnet and celery.

### Dressing

1 cup plain yoghurt
1/2 cup sour cream (optional)
1 tablespoon apple cider vinegar or
   lemon juice

2 teaspoons mustard powder
2 tablespoons soft brown sugar
salt and black pepper

Blend well and pour over the salad.

*The*
*Cook's*
*Notes*

# Introduction

The pages that follow provide a framework on which to build an unforgettable culinary repertoire, whether you are a tentative beginner or a confident expert. Cooking is a creative art which gives deep satisfaction and is a constant challenge. The more you explore the enchanted gardens of herbs and spices the more you will enjoy bringing that little bit of garden to your table. The notes that follow can be changed, adapted and combined according to your personal preferences and taste. You are the master chef, and the blank pages that follow this section are for your notes as you explore, experiment and perfect.

You will notice thoughout this book that the emphasis is on health and only pure, fresh ingredients are used which are as close to natural as possible. A nation of health-conscious South Africans is the ultimate aim, and as the cook, part of the responsibility lies in your hands!

An edible tussie-mussi

# Seasoning

## SALT

No cook can be without salt and although it is a mineral, not a spice, it is the most important ingredient of all in cookery. Salt can be combined with herbs and spices to give variations in flavour and it is simple to make your own. Each is a wonderful (and easy) addition to savoury dishes. There are several types of salt: *sea salt* is healthy and has a fine flavour; *rock salt* is unrefined and often solid, so it needs to be broken down and crushed – it has a good flavour; *bay salt* is a coarse, impure salt made by evaporating sea salt in the sun, and is used only in pot-pourris and for preserving; and *table salt* is a refined, free-running salt because of the addition of magnesium carbonate, but it is so refined it lacks flavour.

## Seasoning Salt

Pound rock salt in a mortar and add to this one or two of the following dried herbs and spices, or a combination:

| | |
|---|---|
| *celery seeds* | *lovage seeds* |
| *fennel seeds* | *cumin* |
| *caraway* | *cassia* |
| *coriander* | *mustard seeds* |
| *dill seeds* | *dried thyme* |
| *marjoram* | *celery* |
| *rosemary* | *sage* |
| *bay* | *basil* |
| *dried and powdered garlic cloves* | |

My favourite combination comprises the following herbs pounded into 1 cup of sea salt.

| | |
|---|---|
| *1 tablespoon dried thyme* | *1 tablespoon dried basil* |
| *1 tablespoon dried lovage or celery* | *1 teaspoon dried garlic* |

I store this in a screw-top bottle with a metal lid in which I have pierced holes and keep it next to the stove for sprinkling on meat, fish and poultry before grilling.

# Spiced Salt

This spicy mixture is excellent with braais, and particularly good with fish. Also sprinkle it onto cheese and egg dishes and over salads.

Pound into 500 g sea salt or rock salt 1 tablespoon each of the following herbs:

*ground black peppercorns*        *ground coriander seeds*
*ground bay leaves*        *ground cloves*
*dried crumbled basil*        *dried crumbled marjoram*

Mix well and store in an airtight jar.

# Salt-free Seasoning

For health reasons many people are advised to go on a salt-free diet. Several herbs can replace salt and make a most delicious seasoning. I find dried herbs are most convenient and I mix a fairly large quantity so I always have some on hand.

*1 cup dried powdered celery leaves*    *1/2 cup dried summer savory*
*1 cup dried powdered marjoram*    *1/2 cup dried fennel seeds*
*1 cup dried thyme*    *1/2 cup dried celery seeds*

Either crush all of these together or use two or three, adjusting it until you find your favourite combination. All these herbs give a satisfying salty taste.

# PEPPER

Pepper is the most common of all spices and there are two types: *black pepper*, which is more pungent and aromatic, and *white pepper*, which is acrid and powerful. *Mignonette pepper* is a pungent combination of black and white pepper. Peppercorns should be ground just before you use them as they lose their flavour and strength when broken.

# Pepper Herbs

Nasturtium seeds, leaves and flowers, black and white mustard leaves, watercress and mustard lettuce all have a strong, peppery flavour and can be used fresh and chopped to replace pepper.

# SPICE MIXTURES

Spice mixtures give character to both sweet and savoury dishes and are an exciting seasoning. To draw out the flavour from spice mixtures gently heat the ingredients in a heavy, dry pan, stirring all the time, and then pound and grind the spices together in a mortar. Store in airtight bottles. Make small quantities, in order to keep the mixture as fresh as possible.

## Continental Spice Mixture

This is delicious in savoury tarts, pasta, breads and sauces.

1  tablespoon cloves
1  tablespoon nutmeg
1  tablespoon bayleaf

1  dessertspoon black pepper
1  teaspoon mace
1  teaspoon ginger

Grind all ingredients finely and mix well. Store in screw-top bottles.

## Garam Masala

This is a traditional curry flavouring which comes from India. Use it sparingly. Blend well 1 teaspoon each of the following, ground:

cardamom
cinnamon
cumin

nutmeg
cloves

Use in dressings, oil, and with stews and pasta dishes.

## Chinese Fine Spice Powder

Blend equal quantities of the following, finely ground:

star anise
pepper
fennel seed

cloves
cinnamon

This makes an unforgettable seasoning for meat, fish, egg and cheese dishes.

# Chilli Spice

This hot, peppery spice is Mexican in origin and is delicious in marinades and sauces or as a seasoning for grills.

1 tablespoon dried powdered capsicum
1 teaspoon cayenne
1 teaspoon cumin
1 teaspoon garlic

2 teaspoons paprika
1 tablespoon marjoram
1 teaspoon cloves

# Barbecue Spice Mixture

1 tablespoon cayenne
1 tablespoon paprika
1 teaspoon each cumin, cardamom,
    cloves, nutmeg, powdered garlic

3 tablespoons soft brown sugar

Pound together and use as a braai seasoning or for fish and poultry grills.

The following two mixtures give a glorious flavouring to cakes, biscuits, puddings and sweet tarts.

# Sweet Spice

Use equal quantities of the following, finely ground:

nutmeg
cinnamon
cloves
cardamom
ginger

cassia
aniseed
vanilla
allspice

Mix well and store.

# Basic Spice Mixture

1 tablespoon ground ginger
1 tablespoon ground nutmeg
1 tablespoon ground allspice
1 dessertspoon ground cinnamon

1 dessertspoon ground cloves
1 dessertspoon ground anise
1/2 teaspoon black pepper

# HERB MIXTURES

Here you can use either fresh or dried herbs and make your own combinations.

## Five Herbs

Use in omelettes, fish and cheese dishes. Mix together:

*1 tablespoon chopped marjoram*
*1 tablespoon chopped parsley*
*1 tablespoon chopped chervil*

*1 dessertspoon chopped tarragon*
*1 dessertspoon chopped chives*

## Bouquet Garni

There are many variations but this is a good basic recipe:

*½ cup parsley stalks*
*2 sprigs thyme*

*2 sprigs marjoram (about 15 cm long)*
*2 bay leaves*

Tie in a muslin bag and use in soups, casseroles and stews.

For fish dishes you can add a fennel stalk, a twist of pared lemon peel, and a sprig or two of lemon thyme or lemon verbena.

Vary your bouquet garni with a garlic clove, a twist of orange or naartjie peel paring, a sprig of winter savory, a celery stalk or a sprig of rosemary. The varieties and combinations are infinite, but do make a note of your most appetising combination, as one so easily forgets and an unrecorded taste can haunt you forever!

# MUSTARD

There are three types of mustard, black, white and brown, and in commercial brands these are usually blended.

Black mustard has the hottest, richest and most pungent taste, and contains much oil. Brown mustard often replaces black mustard, for although it does not have as strong a taste as black, it is easier to grow and harvest, so economically it is more viable. White mustard has a slightly bitter, acrid taste but has remarkable preserving qualities, so it is often included in pickling spice mixtures.

The best and most enjoyable way to get to know mustard is to grow one's own. Dried ground mustard powder can be stored indefinitely, for it is only when it is moistened that the hot, penetrating oil is formed. In the eighteenth century mustard was stored in the form of mustard balls and it is well worth experimenting with this method. Pounded, fresh seed was mixed with honey, vinegar and spices, formed into balls and stored in glass bottles. When needed, a mustard ball was taken out, pounded with a little vinegar and oil and used as a sauce or condiment.

# English Mustard

This is a standard combination of *dry black and white mustard seed* with *wheat flour* and *turmeric*. To make a paste, add *vinegar or cold water* just before serving. If you want to give it a different taste, herbs like *thyme, savory* or *oregano* can be added.

# Herb Mustard

This is a most delicious mustard and one which will give you endless pleasure. It imparts an unforgettable flavour to many dishes and is at its best with beef, pork, fish, egg and cheese dishes.

*1 cup mustard seeds, preferably half*
  *black half white*
*1 teaspoon salt*
*1 teaspoon black pepper*

*3 teaspoons dried powdered lemon peel*
*1 teaspoon turmeric*
*2 – 3 tablespoons honey*
*1 – 2 tablespoons herb vinegar*

Pound the mustard seeds and work in the salt, black pepper, dried powdered lemon peel and turmeric. Mix to a thick consistency with the honey and the herb vinegar. Blend well and store in a corked jar. Take out small quantities for use and blend in any one of the following herbs finely chopped:

*tarragon*
*oregano*
*marjoram*
*sage*
*rosemary*

*thyme*
*winter or summer savory*
*dill seeds*
*coriander seeds*
*myrtle seeds*

# Marinades

The principal ingredient in a marinade is either vinegar, wine, lemon juice or even yoghurt. These penetrate and break down the tough fibres of meat, fish or poultry. Oil carries the spices and herb flavourings and lubricates the meat. You can marinate a large piece of meat or fish for as long as five days in the refrigerator to get a strong flavour, or smaller pieces overnight, and minced meat and fish only need an hour or two. Once you have drained the marinade off whatever you are marinating, use it as a base for gravies and for basting, or as the basis for a sauce.

There are two types of marinade: a cooked one and a blended, uncooked one. Both are basic recipes and you can adjust the herbs and spices according to your taste. I have so enjoyed marinating that I have developed delicious vegetable roasts as well. Try sweet potatoes, kidney and butter beans, lentils, split peas, potatoes and pumpkin. For sweet potatoes, pumpkin and ordinary potatoes, I peel and slice thick slices and lay these in the marinade, turning them every couple of hours. I find 5 hours is fine as the flavour has penetrated at this stage. I then roast these in a baking dish, basting frequently with the marinade, and serve them with a roast or grill.

## Basic Cooked Marinade

2  cups red wine
2  sliced carrots
4  spring onions, chopped, or 1 small
    onion, chopped or sliced

3  bruised garlic cloves
few black peppercorns
2  teaspoons salt

Combine all the ingredients and add a thumb-length sprig of any of the following herbs to taste:

oregano
celery
marjoram
fennel
sage

thyme
lovage
rosemary
yarrow

Simmer in a covered pot for 15 minutes. Cool before pouring over the meat or fish.

# Basic Uncooked Marinade

This is excellent for all meats, fish and poultry. Mix well:

2 cups red wine
1 chopped onion
1 cup sunflower oil
1 teaspoon salt
¼ – ½ teaspoon black pepper
1 teaspoon crushed allspice berries

1 teaspoon crushed coriander seeds
1 tablespoon fresh herbs, e.g. parsley,
   thyme, marjoram, rosemary, sage,
   oregano, lovage, celery, nasturtium
   seeds or yarrow

# Yoghurt Marinade

This is particularly good with fish and chicken.

2 cups plain yoghurt
little salt and pepper
2 teaspoons soy sauce

1 cardamom pod, crushed
2 teaspoons crushed coriander seeds
3 tablespoons lemon juice

Combine all the ingredients and add a thumb-length sprig of any of the following herbs to taste:

tarragon
thyme
savory
salad burnet
yarrow

calendula
lemon balm
lemon grass
fennel
dill

# Herb Oils and Vinegars

Herb-flavoured oils and vinegars are the basis for dressings, sauces, gravies, soups, stews, mayonnaises and marinades and can be varied according to the individual taste of the cook. I find basting grills, braais and roasts with herbed oils gives a rich and exciting taste and I make 10 or 15 different sorts to stand on my kitchen shelf for constant variety and a ready supply. Try combining different herbs and spices for different dishes.

## Herb Oil

Choose an oil with an unpronounced taste such as sunflower, maize, or mild olive oil. Over the years I have found South African sunflower oil to be one of the best, so I use this one. You can use either fresh or dried herbs, and the procedure is simple.

Fill a jar with oil and push a bunch of herbs into the oil so that each sprig is well immersed. Cork the bottle or cover. Do not place directly in the sun, but in winter keep near the stove or on a warm window sill. You must avoid too hot a position or the herbs will cook and rot. In summer's intense heat I have found dried herbs seem to work best – I pick whole sprigs and dry them for 3 or 4 days before immersing them in the oil. Shake the jar at least once a day for 2 weeks, then strain out the herb and replace with a fresh batch. Repeat this procedure until the oil has a strong enough flavour. In my opinion doing this 3 times gives the perfect flavour, but some gourmets like it done 6 to 8 times for a really strong flavour.

## Herbs and Spices Suitable for Herb Oil

Either use the following herbs and spices singly or combine two or three:

| | | | |
|---|---|---|---|
| basil | chilli | lemon grass | onion |
| bay | chives | lemon verbena | rosemary |
| bergamot | dill | marjoram | sage |
| calendula | fennel | mint | savory |
| caraway | garlic | mustard | salad burnet |
| cassia | ginger | myrtle | shallots |
| coriander | horseradish | oregano | tarragon |
| celery | lovage | nasturtium | thyme |
| chicory | mace | nutmeg | yarrow |

# HERB VINEGAR

For herb vinegars choose a good quality grape or white wine vinegar. I always use fresh herbs as the vinegar preserves them and it is worthwhile making several varieties at the same time. The finished vinegars make an attractive kitchen decoration and will be conveniently at hand to give zest to your dishes.

Fill a bottle of vinegar with as much fresh herb as it will hold. (Pour out some of the vinegar first, and make a second bottle with it.) Be sure the herbs are properly immersed in the vinegar. Stand the bottles in the sun for 3 weeks. During that time – I find every 4 or 5 days is ideal – strain out the herb and replace with freshly picked herbs. When the taste is to your liking, bottle the vinegar in attractive bottles, push in an identifying fresh sprig of the herb, and label and date if so desired.

## Herbs and Spices Suitable for Herb Vinegar

Use the following herbs and spices singly or in combinations:

| | |
|---|---|
| anise | ginger |
| basil | horseradish |
| bay (use sparingly) | hyssop |
| bergamot | lemon balm |
| calendula | lemon grass |
| caraway | lemon verbena |
| cardamom | mace |
| cassia | mint |
| coriander | marjoram |
| cayenne (use the whole chilli) | mustard |
| celery | oregano |
| chervil | myrtle |
| capsicum (cut in strips) | nasturtium (leaves, flowers and seeds) |
| chives | pineapple sage |
| cloves | sage |
| coriander | rosemary |
| cumin | salad burnet |
| dill | savory |
| fennel | tarragon |
| fenugreek | thyme |
| garlic | yarrow |

# Flower Vinegar

Fresh flowers can be used in vinegar for a sweet, subtle flavour. My favourite is mint vinegar, with the flowers steeped in this. It makes a lovely salad dressing for a flower salad or for use in curries. Suitable flowers are:

*rose petals (cut off the white heel)*  *pinks*
*violets*  *elder flowers*
*calendula petals*  *lavender flowers*
*nasturtium flowers and seeds*  *myrtle flowers*
*clove carnations*  *jasmine flowers*

# Spiced Vinegar

I use this vinegar to pickle eggs, onions, cabbage and gherkins, or for giving flavour to chutneys and piccalilli. It is a good basic recipe and can easily be altered to suit your taste.

1  *litre good white grape vinegar*  1  *tablespoon celery seeds*
1  *cinnamon stick*  20  *peppercorns*
2  *bay leaves*  1  *tablespoon mustard seeds*
1  *piece root ginger*  2  *red chillis*
10  *allspice berries*  1  *tablespoon coriander*

Steep all the spices in a glass bottle of vinegar for 2 months. Shake every now and then. When the flavour is to your liking, strain and rebottle.

# Sauces, Dressings and Mayonnaises

Chopped herbs in sauces and dressings give a superb flavouring to ordinary dishes. Once again, you, the creative cook, will develop your own specialities and find combinations to suit each dish. I merely give the basics, which you dress!

## Butter Sauce

*100 g butter*
*3 tablespoons fresh herbs, finely chopped*
*    or minced*
*1 tablespoon thick cream*

*little salt*
*freshly ground black pepper*
*1 teaspoon finely minced lemon zest*

Melt the butter and stir in the other ingredients.

## Pesto Sauce

This is a basic basil sauce which can be stirred into pasta dishes, soups, like minestrone, or spread onto grills just before serving. It is one of the most exciting of all sauces and unusual dishes can be built around it.

*3 – 5 tablespoons fresh basil leaves*
*2 cloves garlic, peeled and finely chopped*
*salt and black pepper to taste*

*75 g grated Parmesan cheese*
*4 tablespoons sunflower or olive oil*

Finely chop and pound basil, garlic, salt and pepper. Work in the cheese. Add the oil a little at a time, stirring with a wooden spoon.

### Variations

Add 1 – 2 tablespoons herbs like tarragon, chervil, salad burnet, chives, borage, calendula, lemon balm or watercress, or add 2 tablespoons pine nuts, chopped walnuts or pecan nuts.

# White Sauce with Herbs

1 tablespoon butter
1 heaped tablespoon wholewheat flour
1 teaspoon mustard
1 cup milk

salt and pepper
2 – 3 tablespoons chopped herbs
1 tablespoon cream

Heat butter in a heavy-bottomed pan. Stir in flour and mustard. Add the milk a little at a time, stirring all the time to prevent lumps forming. Add cream, seasoning, and 2 – 3 tablespoons chopped herbs (e.g. parsley, tarragon, oregano, mint, savory, chives, basil, celery, or combinations). Serve over steamed vegetables, fish, pastas and grains. Use as a base for chicken or ham left-overs, or with hard-boiled eggs or mushrooms.

# Hot Herb Sauce

This is richly flavoured yet light and can be served as a gravy. It is particularly delicious with chicken, fish and veal.

1 tablespoon butter
1 tablespoon wholewheat flour
2 cups stock
½ cup chopped spring onion or chives
1 tablespoon either freshly chopped
    marjoram or oregano or rosemary

2 tablespoons parsley
1 tablespoon thyme
2 tablespoons chervil, lovage or celery
2 tablespoons tarragon
1 tablespoon lemon juice
salt and freshly ground pepper

Melt the butter and stir in the flour until it forms a smooth paste. Slowly add the stock, stirring to avoid lumps. Add the herbs and simmer gently until it thickens a little to form a gravy-like consistency (about 5 minutes). Add lemon juice, salt and pepper.

# Basic Vinaigrette Dressing

4 parts oil
2 parts vinegar or lemon juice
dash of mustard powder (optional)
little sugar (optional)
salt

pepper
chopped fresh herbs (e.g. tarragon,
    parsley, watercress, celery, thyme,
    marjoram, chives or garlic)

Place all the ingredients in a screw-top bottle and shake well. Use as a salad dressing or marinade.

# Mayonnaise

3  *egg yolks*
*pinch salt*

*300 – 450 ml oil*
*1  tablespoon lemon juice*

Beat the egg yolks and the pinch of salt, and add the oil drop by drop while beating constantly. When a quarter of the oil has been added, the rest can be slowly poured, while beating constantly. Once it has thickened and firmed, add a little juice and chopped herbs to your taste, e.g. tarragon, chervil, parsley, chives, nasturtium seeds, chillis, etc.

Herbs lend themselves to use in a vast range of sauces and vinegars

# Soups

Nothing is as warming on a winter evening as a hot bowl of soup and nothing is as refreshing on a summer evening as cold soup. Both the recipes below contain healthy ingredients that will sustain and nourish and both can be adapted to suit the vegetables in season.

## Basic Winter Soup                                                    Serves 8

1  cup chopped onions
2  cups chopped tomatoes
1  cup grated carrots
1  cup chopped celery
1  cup pearl barley or 1 cup brown rice,
    soaked overnight or for a few hours

2  litres stock or water
little oil
salt and pepper to taste
2  tablespoons debittered brewers yeast

Brown the onions in the butter, add tomatoes and carrots and stir well. Add all the other ingredients. Simmer covered for half an hour or until the barley or rice is tender. Add herbs, salt and pepper to taste. Sprinkle with parsley. Serve hot with croutons.

### Variations

Add butter or kidney beans, sugar and haricot beans that have been soaked overnight, chervil, borage, comfrey, salad burnet, lovage, sorrel, watercress, nettle, yarrow, tarragon or calendula.

# Summer Soup

This is a light, refreshing health soup which can be a complete lunch or supper dish.

1  *lettuce*
2  *peeled cucumbers, chopped*
1  *cup watercress*
2  *cups milk or chicken stock*
*salt and pepper to taste*
*little tahini or soy sauce*

2  *cups yoghurt*
*parsley*
*paprika*
1/2  *cup chives*
*twist lemon peel*

Put the lettuce, cucumber and watercress through the liquidiser with a little of the milk or stock. Avocado, tomato and mushrooms can also be added. Add other herbs, e.g. borage, salad burnet, comfrey, little oregano, tarragon or lemon balm. Add the rest of the milk, salt and pepper and a little tahini or soy sauce and the yoghurt. Blend well. Serve with a sprinkling of parsley, paprika and chives, and a twist of lemon peel.

# Salads

Salads are probably the most important part of our diets. Raw herbs and vegetables have been gathered and eaten by man since the earliest times and although they are perhaps not used to the same extent as they were previously, health-conscious people are acknowledging more and more the value of raw herbs and vegetables in our daily diets.

All cooks should have a knowledge of the medicinal properties of plants. The therapeutic food chart on pp. 248-58 will help you select the correct food for whatever condition ails you and many of those vegetables and fruits can be eaten in their healthiest form – raw. Experiment with your favourite combinations. I balance the milder-tasting plants and herbs like lettuce, borage, comfrey, chervil and salad burnet with the hotter ones like chives, mustard greens, celery, watercress and nasturtium and in this way get a delicious blend.

Below is a brief selection of salad ingredients and the herbs that best enhance them.

*Lettuce* – tarragon, parsley, chives, lovage, celery.

*Tomatoes* – basil, chervil, tarragon, watercress, savory.

*Cucumber* – fennel, dill, fenugreek, chicory, lovage, celery, bergamot.

*Avocado* – chives, basil, celery, lovage, rosemary, marjoram, thyme, sorrel.

*Beetroot (raw grated)* – sage, tarragon, chives, chervil, parsley, mint, rosemary.

*Cabbage (raw shredded)* – basil, bay, celery, marjoram, oregano, sorrel, salad burnet, tarragon, thyme, coriander, caraway.

*Radish* – borage, salad burnet, chervil, parsley, chives, comfrey, rosemary.

*Onion (raw sliced)* – borage, comfrey, salad burnet, tarragon, watercress, celery, parsley.

*Carrot (grated raw)* – tarragon, sage, oregano, marjoram, chives, salad burnet, lovage, celery, fennel, dill, watercress, yarrow.

# Weeds to Include in the Salad

The following weeds are wonderfully healthy and should be included daily in salad:

*fat hen* (Chenopodium album)
*chickweed* (Stellaria media)
*dandelion* (Taraxacum officinale)
*sow's thistle* (Sonchus alearceus)
*amaranthus* (Amaranthus caudatus)
*blackjack (young tender leaves only)*
  (Bidens pilosa)
*plantain* (Plantago lanceolata)
*purslane* (Portulaca oleracea)

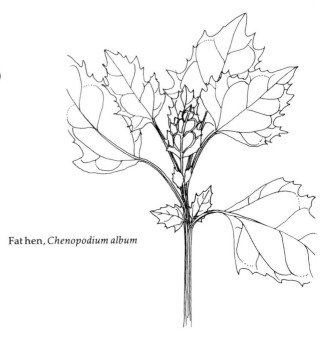

Fat hen, *Chenopodium album*

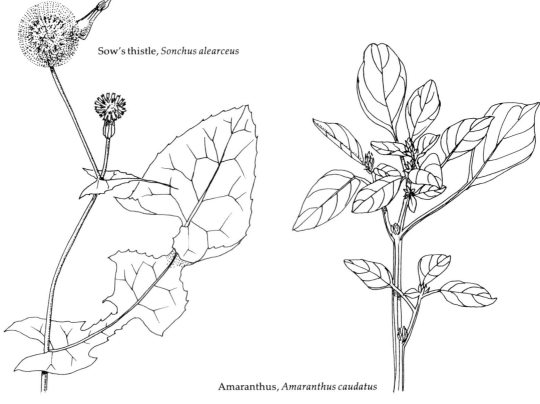

Sow's thistle, *Sonchus alearceus*

Amaranthus, *Amaranthus caudatus*

Plantain, *Plantago lanceolata*

Blackjack, *Bidens pilosa*

Chickweed, *Stellaria media*

Purslane, *Portulaca oleracea*

211

# SPROUTS

Sprouts are one of the most important of all foods and are an essential part of a healthy diet. They can be grown anywhere, anytime, by anyone. They are rich in enzymes, minerals, proteins and vitamins and will impart energy, strength and vitality in a mouthful. They are one of nature's rejuvenating tonics and are capable of correcting body malfunctions and imbalances, as they contain all the components of a mature plant in concentrated form.

## Quick Guide to Sprouting

Sprouters, tiers and trays are available from health food shops, but a quick sprouter can be made from a wide-mouthed glass jar covered with a square of cheese cloth tied on with a rubber band.

To grow sprouts, put your seeds (for example mung beans) into the jar, cover with water and leave them overnight. Next morning pour the beans into a sieve and rinse them under running water. Rinse out the bottle and return the beans to the damp bottle. Cover with the cheese cloth square and secure it with a rubber band. Tilt the jar and stand it on its head so that the excess water runs out, otherwise the beans will turn sour and rot. This washing procedure must be done every morning and evening and in 3 days the beans will be ready to eat. Start up the next bottle and keep a continuous supply going by making small quantities, or even invest in a tiered sprouter. You can do 3 or 4 batches at a time then, every 2 or 3 days.

Use your sprouts lavishly in salads. They are also delicious in stir fry cooking and sprinkled onto roasts, grills, soups and stews just before serving.

### SPROUTING CHART

| SEED | SOAKING TIME | READY TO EAT | LENGTH OF SHOOT | NOTES | MEDICINAL PROPERTIES |
|------|--------------|--------------|-----------------|-------|----------------------|
| Adukib beans | 15–20 hours | 4–6 days | 3,5 cm | Rather hard, excellent for stir frying. | Kidney cleanser; acts on hormones. |
| Chick peas | 15–20 hours | 4–6 days | 2,5 cm | Renew the water twice during soaking time and wash well. They are hard and easily turn sour unless well washed. | An excellent protein; body builder; muscle toner; builds stamina; good for underweight. |
| Lentils | 12–24 hours | 3–5 days | 2,5 cm | Use in breads and meat loaves. Brown lentils seem to sprout the best. Do not keep after 6 days. | Good protein; a staple food; excellent for bones and teeth. |
| Mung beans | 10–15 hours | 2–5 days | 1–5 cm | Probably the most popular sprout and the easiest of all to grow. Beans older than 5 days produce gas in the stomach, so eat them young. Use lavishly in salads. | Energy booster; regulates the bowel; a tonic and blood cleanser. |

| SEED | SOAKING TIME | READY TO EAT | LENGTH OF SHOOT | NOTES | MEDICINAL PROPERTIES |
|---|---|---|---|---|---|
| Soya beans | 12–24 hours | 4–6 days | 3,5 cm | Change the soaking water frequently. Very hard, not very palatable. Combine with other sprouts. Use in soups and stews. | One of the best sources of protein for stamina, energy and resistance to infection. |
| Sunflower | 10–15 hours | 2–3 days | 1 cm | Can be grown for the green leaves; leave the shoots to grow up to 10 cm, cut off the tops with scissors. | One of nature's richest enzyme and mineral plants; helps to stop smoking; excellent for eyesight and eye ailments. |
| Wheat | 12–20 hours | 3–4 days | 1 cm | Use in breads, soups, stews, salads and add to vegetable juice extracts. Drink the soaking water (called rejuvelac). Grow as a grass in a tray. | Full of vitamin B; rejuvenating. |
| Barley | 12–20 hours | 3–4 days | 1 cm | Use in soups, stews, drinks. Chop finely in salads. Excellent for stir frying. Can grow up to 10 cm. | Particularly good for fatigue, stress, anxiety; builds depleted bodies; gives valuable vitamins. |
| Oats | 12–20 hours | 3–5 days | 1 cm | Must use whole oats, change the soaking water frequently. Use in soups and broths. Can grow as a grass in a tray. | Cleansing and invigorating; good for stress and grief; helps convalescents and the aged to regain their strength. |
| Millet | 5–10 hours | 2–4 days | 1 cm or less | Buy from a health shop as it is often sprayed. Ferments easily so soak only briefly. Wash well through a fine sieve. | Full of vitamins; the only grain that is alkaline and a complete protein and easily assimilated. |
| Buckwheat | 24 hours | 5–8 days | 2,5 cm | Very tough outer shell. Change the soaking water frequently. Grow in a tray lined with wet cotton wool on a window sill. Cut off leaves for salads. | One of the few plants to contain rutin, which uplifts the spirits; excellent for hardening of the arteries, thread veins and for those who bruise easily. |
| Sesame | 6–8 hours | 1–2 days | 1 cm | Needs to be sprouted and quickly eaten otherwise very bitter. Sour in the stomach producing gas. | Contains vitamin E, oils, calcium and phosphorus; easily digestible. |
| Alfalfa (lucerne) | 6–8 hours | 2–4 days | 1 cm | Everyone's favourite! Easily sprouted. Use lavishly in salads. Also delicious mixed with mayonnaise as a sandwich filling. | Blood cleansing, toning, invigorating, energising, kidney cleanser, rejuvenating. Excellent for sportsmen and students as it is a brain food. |

| SEED | SOAKING TIME | READY TO EAT | LENGTH OF SHOOT | NOTES | MEDICINAL PROPERTIES |
|---|---|---|---|---|---|
| Fenugreek | 6–9 hours | 3–5 days | 1 cm | Very pungent curry flavour. Mix with other sprouts. Wash extra well as it inclines to sour. Do not eat after 6 days as it produces gas in the stomach. Use in curries and in vinegar salad dressings. | Detoxifier; eases stomach ache; rich in vitamins, nitrates and calcium; good for encouraging lactation in nursing mothers. |
| Mustard | 2 hours | 3–5 days | 2,5 cm | Grow on damp cotton wool or paper towels. In a week green leaves will cover the surface. Cut off with scissors. Eat on bread or in salads. | Tonic herb; excellent for aches and pains; blood toning, cleansing; energy giving; helps cramps and sore feet. |
| Cress | 2 hours | 3–5 days | 2,5 cm | Grow on damp cotton wool or paper towels. In a week green leaves will cover the surface. Cut off with scissors. Eat on bread or in salads. | Blood cleanser; tonic; rich in vitamins; aids depression, anxiety, weak eyesight and un-controllable tempers. |
| Radish | 6–8 hours | 4–5 days | 2,5 cm | Very hot and pungent. Delicious in salad dressings. Mix with other sprouts. Add to stews, soups, gravies just before serving. | Builds resistance to coughs and colds; antibiotic; relieves dyspepsia; increases the saliva flow; full of vitamin C. |

# Herb Butters and Cheeses

## HERB BUTTER

Herb butter is an easy and delicious way of bringing the flavour of herbs to vegetables, breads and pasta. All it comprises is finely chopped fresh herbs beaten into creamed butter together with seasonings like salt, freshly ground black or white pepper, lemon juice, onion or garlic juice. Spread sliced bread with the butter mixture, wrap in tin foil and place in the oven to warm through.

Suitable herbs are: chervil, parsley, tarragon, chives, garlic, basil, lovage, horseradish, coriander, dill, mint, oregano, marjoram, savory, thyme, lemon thyme.

## Herb Butter

*salt and pepper*
*squeeze lemon juice*
*1 tablespoon parsley*

*1 tablespoon chives*
*1 tablespoon sweet basil*

Blend salt, pepper and lemon juice into butter. Add herbs and beat in well. Shape into little loaves or press into shallow dishes and refrigerate.

# HERB CHEESE

This can be made with similar herbs to the butter and can include spices. Use cottage or cream cheese as a base, and use as a topping for pasta dishes, tarts, pies and breads.

## Savoury Cheese

1 cup cottage cheese
1 cup grated cheddar cheese
1 cup grated sweetmilk cheese
2 tablespoons spring onions or chives
2 tablespoons parsley

1 tablespoon chopped thyme or oregano
1 teaspoon caraway seeds
½ – 1 cup yoghurt (enough to bind)
1 tablespoon paprika
1 teaspoon allspice

Mix everything well. Press into a mould. Sprinkle with paprika. Also use as a spread on biscuits or toast, or on vegetables.

Herbs are wonderful mixed with, or as an accompaniment to, butter and cheese

# Eggs

Certain herbs lend themselves to eggs and can turn a plain omelette or hard-boiled egg into a gourmet's delight.

Boil eggs with sprigs of thyme or marjoram, lemon grass or oregano. The herb flavour will penetrate the shell and give a subtle and delicious taste. Herbs that go well with eggs are: tarragon, chervil, lemon balm, parsley, basil, bay, calendula, borage, cumin, capsicum, caraway, coriander, cayenne, celery, chives, dill, fennel, horseradish, lovage, lemon grass, lemon verbena, mustard, myrtle, nasturtium, oregano, paprika, pepper, sage, savory, sorrel, thyme, watercress, yarrow.

## Spiced Dressing for Hard-boiled Eggs                    Serves 6 – 8

This makes an excellent lunch dish, served with a salad of potatoes, lettuce and cucumber.

8  hard-boiled eggs, shelled and halved
1  tablespoon sunflower oil
pinch turmeric
½  teaspoon paprika
1  teaspoon ground coriander
1  teaspoon ground cumin
salt

black pepper
150 ml plain yoghurt
1  teaspoon mustard
1  tablespoon lemon juice
1  tablespoon chopped parsley or chervil
grated cheese, e.g. mozzarella or feta, for
    decoration (optional)

Warm the oil in a heavy-bottomed pan, add turmeric, paprika, coriander, cumin, salt and pepper, and simmer for 2 minutes. Remove from the stove. Stir in the yoghurt, mustard, lemon juice and chopped herbs (tarragon and marjoram are also delicious to replace the parsley or chervil). Pour over the eggs. Sprinkle with a little paprika and grated cheese, if liked.

# Vegetables

The healthiest way to eat vegetables apart from raw is steamed, and steamed vegetables lend themselves wonderfully well to herbs and spices. Try marinating vegetables like sweet potatoes and pumpkin, and even cabbage, cauliflower and broccoli, or try poaching them in a herb and spice dressing. Your own combinations will give you the most pleasure. Herb butters on steamed vegetables give a different texture and flavour and there are many exciting combinations.

## Vegetable Poach

In a heavy-bottomed pan gently poach a combination of summer vegetables until they are tender: e.g. thinly sliced carrots, leeks, courgettes, green beans, peas, cauliflower florets, egg plant, mealies cut off the cob (raw).

*1 teaspoon peppercorns*
*1 teaspoon coriander seeds*
*salt and freshly ground pepper*
*1 clove garlic*
*6 tablespoons sunflower oil*
*1 small glass white wine*

*juice of 2 lemons*
*½ – 1 cup water*
*1 tablespoon tarragon, chopped*
*1 tablespoon chives, chopped*
*2 bay leaves*

Crush the peppercorns, coriander and salt with the garlic clove. Warm the oil and stew the spices and garlic for 2 minutes. Add the wine, lemon juice, herbs and water. Stir well. Arrange the vegetables flat in the pan, cover, and gently simmer, stirring every now and then until the vegetables are tender. Serve with brown rice.

# Fish

Fish only tastes good with the addition of herbs and spices, and memorable dishes can be created with just a few combinations. From the day I tasted freshly caught Kabeljou grilled over a fire on the beach, and savoured the sweetness of the wild fennel that shrouded it, I have been hooked on herbed fish! Fennel grows wild in the Cape and can sometimes be found close to the sea, when it is at its best.

Fish combines beautifully with celery, parsley, chervil, dill, fennel, watercress, yarrow, sorrel, nasturtium, lovage, lemon thyme, chicory, cumin, bay, anise, cardamom, cassia, chives and horseradish.

Fish marinades are delicious and fish baked in an unglazed clay pot or in foil, wrapped in bundles of herbs with herb butter (see p. 215) or cream is a glorious meal. When frying fish add chopped herbs to the batter and fry in herbed oil (see p. 201). When grilling fish, brush with herbed oil or herb butter. When steaming fish wrap the fish completely in herbs, remove before serving and sprinkle with freshly chopped herbs.

## Baked Herbed Fish

*fish*
*herb butter or oil*
*chopped herbs, e.g. lovage and chervil*
*peppercorns, roughly crushed*
*coriander*
*garlic clove, peeled and crushed*
*salt*
*pepper*
*pat of butter*
*squeeze of lemon juice*

Brush the fish with herb butter or oil. Sprinkle the chopped herbs over it and the roughly crushed peppercorns and coriander. Make sure it is well coated with herbs. Tuck in the garlic clove, and add the salt, pepper, pat of butter and squeeze of lemon juice. Wrap the fish in either pastry, silver foil, greased, oiled paper or a greased paper bag.

Bake in a shallow tray in a medium oven for about 20 minutes to half an hour, or until the fish is tender. Serve with wedges of lemon and a green salad.

# Meat and Poultry

There are several ways of using herbs with meat and poultry.

- *As a marinade:* see p. 199.

- *As a paste:* chop herbs and spices and mix with a little oil and wheat germ to form a paste to spread onto meat before roasting or grilling.

- *Sprinkled on:* fresh or dried herbs.

- *As a sauce:* e.g. grated horseradish, vinegar and cream for pork or beef; chopped mint, vinegar, sugar and hot water for mutton; chopped onions, chives, savory, sweet basil and lemon juice for pork; chopped oregano and oil for mutton and veal.

- *As a stuffing:* chop herbs, e.g. sage, marjoram, lovage or thyme and mix with cream or yoghurt and breadcrumbs, onions and lemon juice.

- *As a baste:* Mix chopped tarragon or coriander or rosemary or mustard into oil and baste onto meat during roasting or grilling.

- *As a daub:* place pats of chopped herbs frozen into dripping or butter onto the grilling meat, e.g. chopped sage, caraway seeds and butter for pork; chopped mint, cardamom and bay for beef or mutton; chopped shallots, horseradish and paprika in dripping for beef or pork; chopped chervil, garlic and mustard in dripping for sausages; chopped sage, chives and cayenne in butter for pork; chopped rosemary and cloves in butter for lamb; chopped lemon thyme, caraway leaves and paprika in dripping for ham or bacon. Make pats or balls of these combinations and deep freeze them between sheets of greased paper.

## HERBS AND SPICES FOR BEEF

| | | | |
|---|---|---|---|
| allspice | cloves | mustard | salad burnet |
| basil | celery | myrtle | savory |
| bay | dill | nasturtium | shallot |
| cassia | fennel | onion | sorrel |
| coriander | garlic | oregano | tarragon |
| cayenne | ginger | paprika | thyme |
| chervil | horseradish | parsley | yarrow |
| chilli | lovage | pepper | watercress |
| chives | marjoram | poppy seed | |

# HERBS AND SPICES FOR MUTTON

| | | | |
|---|---|---|---|
| anise | dill | mustard | saffron |
| caraway | fenugreek | nasturtium | sage |
| cayenne | garlic | nutmeg | savory |
| cardamom | ginger | onion | shallot |
| chervil | lemon balm | paprika | sorrel |
| celery | lemon grass | parsley | tarragon |
| coriander | lemon thyme | poppy seed | turmeric |
| chives | mace | pepper | yarrow |
| cloves | mint | rosemary | watercress |

# HERBS AND SPICES FOR PORK

| | | | |
|---|---|---|---|
| allspice | cinnamon | marjoram | rosemary |
| basil | cloves | mint | sage |
| bay | dill | mustard | savory |
| caraway | fennel | myrtle | shallot |
| cassia | fenugreek | nutmeg | sorrel |
| cayenne | garlic | onion | tarragon |
| coriander | ginger | oregano | thyme |
| chervil | lemon grass | paprika | turmeric |
| chilli | lemon thyme | parsley | yarrow |
| chives | mace | pepper | watercress |

# POULTRY

The most delicious way of using herbs and spices with poultry are in a stuffing and by rolling pieces of raw chicken or duck in a spiced herb mixture such as a marinade or breadcrumb mixture. The most delicious herbs for poultry are:

| | |
|---|---|
| tarragon | celery |
| thyme | savory |
| sage | fennel |

Your own experiments with the other herbs and spices will give you exciting new tastes.

# Herb and Breadcrumb 'Blanket'

This batter coats each individual piece with a tasty 'blanket' for frying or braaing. It makes enough for a large chicken.

2  eggs, well beaten
1 – 1½ cups fine wholewheat
   breadcrumbs
½  cup chopped chervil or parsley

1  teaspoon crushed coriander
little cayenne, salt and black pepper
½  cup chopped tarragon
1  teaspoon powdered cumin

Beat everything together with a fork, coat the chicken pieces with the batter and fry or grill.

## Basic Poultry Stuffing

3  tablespoons finely chopped herb, e.g.
   tarragon, celery, lovage, chives, onion,
   watercress
½ – 1 tablespoon chopped sage, or
   marjoram, or oregano, or thyme, or
   savory, or combinations

2  tablespoons butter or thick cream
2  tablespoons wheat germ
1  tablespoon lemon juice
2  tablespoons yoghurt
salt, pepper or cayenne pepper

Mix well. Stuff the chicken, duck or turkey. Roast, or bake in an unglazed clay pot.

# Grains and Pulses

Grains and pulses form an important part of our diet, particularly for vegetarians. They are varied, nutritious, inexpensive and full of health-giving enzymes, vitamins, minerals, protein and carbohydrates. Many pulses can be soaked and eaten raw in salads or sprouted or ground for muesli, bread and porridge. All grains and pulses combine well with herbs and spices and there are so many combinations, tastes and textures that one need never be bored with experimenting. Here are a few basic recipes to get you started.

## Pilaf

This is perhaps the simplest way to cook grains such as rice, whole wheat, barley or millet.

1 *cup brown rice or whole wheat, etc.*
2 *tablespoons butter*
2 *cups stock or herb infusion*
1 *sprig thyme*
*salt*
1 *or 2 onions*

1 *garlic clove, finely chopped*
½ *cup almonds, well chopped*
½ *cup parsley or coriander leaves,*
  *or chervil or mint leaves*
*Parmesan cheese*
*paprika*

Fry the rice in the butter for 3 – 4 minutes, then add the stock, fresh thyme sprig and salt. Simmer until tender in a tightly closed pot until all the liquid is absorbed. Meanwhile fry the onions in oil with the finely chopped garlic clove, and add the almonds and the parsley or coriander leaves or chervil or mint leaves. Mix into the rice. Sprinkle with Parmesan cheese and paprika. Serve hot with a salad.

# Spiced Baked Beans

Any kind of bean can be used here and lentils, chick peas or dried peas can be added. This is very nourishing and a perfect meal in itself.

*500 g haricot beans, soaked overnight*
*2 bay leaves*
*1 piece lemon zest*
*1 small piece ginger root*
*4 cloves*
*3 – 4 thyme sprigs*
*1 tablespoon black peppercorns, crushed*
*2 tablespoons coriander seeds, crushed*

*2 large onions, finely chopped*
*3 tablespoons oil*
*4 cups tomato pulp*
*2 cloves garlic, finely chopped*
*2 tablespoons vinegar*
*1 cup honey*
*salt and pepper*
*paprika*

Cook the beans, in enough water to cover them, with the bay leaves, lemon zest, ginger root, cloves, thyme, peppercorns and coriander. Simmer until tender, drain, and reserve the liquid. Fry onions in the oil, stir in tomato pulp, garlic, vinegar and honey, and add a little stock from the beans (about 300 ml). Season with salt, pepper and paprika. Spoon beans into a casserole, pour over them the tomato and onion mixture and stir. Sprinkle with wheat germ or wholewheat bread crumbs. Bake in a slow oven at 150 °C/300 °F for about an hour. Serve with a salad.

For non-vegetarians add 500 g chopped bacon or 2 cups cooked ham to the onion and tomato.

# Spiced Mealie Meal Bread

For the mealie meal you can substitute wheat, rice, lentils or a combination. Again this is a basic recipe with which you can experiment by adding or substituting ingredients.

*3 beaten eggs*
*approx. 6 tablespoons soft butter*
*2 cups mealie meal or 1 cup cooked*
   *mealies*
*1 cup wholemeal flour*
*3 teaspoons crushed cumin or caraway*

*1 – 2 tablespoons chopped rosemary,*
   *or sage, or oregano*
*4 teaspoons baking powder*
*1 teaspoon salt*
*300 ml milk*

Beat the eggs and butter and add all the other ingredients. Pour into a greased baking dish about 20 cm x 30 cm. Bake at 200 °C/400 °F for about 20 minutes or until well risen and golden. Cut into thick slices and serve hot with bacon and eggs, sausages or savoury mince.

# Bread

One of the most satisfying things for any cook is baking a beautiful loaf of bread. So many people seem to think that baking bread is difficult, but these basic, easy recipes will soon change that! Have you ever eaten 'raw' bread that has been baked in the sun? It is surprisingly good, and filled with nourishment. Essene bread is a most unusual and nutritious bread which was made by the Essenes, an ascetic sect who lived on the shores of the Dead Sea during the time of Christ.

Herbs have been used to flavour breads since man first started to develop his daily loaf. Roots of herbs like angelica and lovage were used to make flour, as were the seeds of plants like amaranth, flax, fat hen and buckwheat. Dill and caraway still flavour loaves today and herbs like thyme and basil, marjoram and sage, chives and tarragon make appetising additions to a simple loaf. The modern cook has little time to knead dough and wait for yeast to rise, and this basic recipe will both cut that time and give you a nourishing and satisfying loaf. Vary it by adding raisins, sesame seed, poppy seed and herbs and bake it often.

## Essene Bread

Soak 2 cups whole wheat overnight, then sprout for 3 days. Mince the sprouts and make into a workable consistency with a little oil. If your dough is too wet, add wheat germ; if it is too dry, add a little more oil or water. You can also work in herbs like basil or tarragon or chives or watercress or thyme or rosemary. Pat or roll the bread on a board sprinkled with wheat germ to prevent it from sticking. Roll or press into a thin sheet, place in the sun or in front of a heater to allow the bread to 'bake' for 8 – 10 hours. Turn over with a spatula or cake lifter at half time.

*Variation:* To this you can add a little seasoning salt or herb dredge, grated carrots, celery, onions, parsley, raisins or sunflower seeds, and sprinkle with sesame seeds or chopped salted almonds.

# Health Bread

1  cake of yeast or 1 sachet dry yeast
1  litre luke-warm water
1  teaspoon sugar
1  tablespoon crushed wheat
1  kg wholewheat meal
15 ml salt

1  tablespoon sunflower seeds
1  tablespoon oats
1  cup seedless raisins or sultanas
15 ml honey
15 ml sunflower oil

Mix the yeast with the warm water and sugar. Stand in a warm place to rise (10 – 20 minutes). Grease 2 loaf pans with butter. Mix dry ingredients. Add honey, oil and herbs (if liked) and the frothy yeast. Mix to a fairly soft dough. Shake the crushed wheat into the buttered loaf tins and spoon in the dough. Sprinkle more crushed wheat over the loaf. Cover with a tea towel and leave in a warm place to prove, until it has risen level with the top of the loaf tin. Bake for 45 minutes at 350 °F/180 °C. (When it is ready a knock on the tin should sound hollow.) Remove from tins and keep well covered. Serve warm. Keep it in the fridge in summer, if there is any left over!

# Soft Herb Rolls                                        Yields about 12 rolls

These are easy to make and with the addition of a herb they make a most delicious bread.

15 g fresh yeast or 1 sachet dry yeast
1  teaspoon sugar
300 ml luke-warm water
450 g brown bread flour

salt
3  tablespoons chopped herb, e.g. chervil,
    chives, tarragon, marjoram or thyme
little finely minced garlic

Crumble yeast, blend with sugar and a little warm water and leave to stand until frothy. Mix the flour, salt and herbs with this and add the remaining water. Work into a ball. Place in a greased bowl, cover and allow to rise. Pull off pieces, form into rolls or balls, and lay in a cloth that has been sprinkled with flour. Cover and allow to rise for about 15 minutes. Grease a baking sheet and place the rolls on this, sprinkle with water and bake for 8 – 10 minutes at 240 °C/475 °F. Serve hot with herb butter.

# Cakes and Biscuits

The sweet herbs and spices come into their own in cakes and biscuits, and include scented geranium, anise, allspice, cinnamon, nutmeg, cloves, lemon mint, lemon grass, lemon verbena, vanilla, violet, rosemary, bergamot, calendula, cassia and ginger.

In combination or singly, each of these will change the flavour of your baking – all that is needed is your own creativity. These are basic recipes to which you can add your own flavour.

## Plain Cake

1 cup butter
1 cup brown sugar
1 teaspoon vanilla or 1 tablespoon herb
   e.g. lemon verbena, bergamot, etc.
3 eggs

2½ cups wholewheat flour
3 teaspoons baking powder
½ teaspoon salt
1 cup buttermilk or yoghurt

Preheat the oven to 350 °F/180 °C. Cream the butter and sugar, add the vanilla or herbs and the eggs and beat well. Combine the flour, baking powder and salt and add to the butter sugar mixture, alternating with the buttermilk. Turn into 2 well-greased loaf pans or round tins. Bake for 30 – 40 minutes.

*Variations*: Add sunflower seeds, sesame seeds, raisins, almonds, walnuts or pecan nuts.

# Fruit Crisp

These delicious crisps can be quickly and easily made and served. Vary the herbs and fruit to taste.

8 apples (or peaches, mangoes, quinces,
   nectarines, plums, bananas)
2 tablespoons sesame seeds
2 tablespoons wheat germ
herb to taste (e.g. lemon thyme)
juice of 1 lemon
3/4 cup raisins

2 tablespoons cinnamon
little apple juice or water
1 cup oats
4 tablespoons wholewheat flour
1 cup butter
1 cup brown sugar or 1/2 cup honey
1 teaspoon allspice

Preheat the oven to 375 °F/190 °C. Mix cored, peeled fruit with sesame seed, wheat germ, herb, lemon juice, raisins and cinnamon. Add enough water or apple juice to just cover. Mix oats, flour, butter, sugar or honey and allspice and press on top of the apples. Bake for about 25 minutes until brown and crisp.

## Digestive Biscuits

All the sweet herbs lend themselves to this recipe, and one never tires of these biscuits. Keep them in an airtight tin.

1 cup butter
1 cup sugar
2 cups wholemeal flour
herbs to taste, e.g. 1 tablespoon bergamot
   or lemon verbena or lemon thyme or
   lemon balm or rosemary or scented
   geranium

1/2 cup bran
1/2 cup wheat germ
2 teaspoons baking powder
salt
1/2 – 1 cup milk

Cream the butter and sugar and add the flour and herbs, bran, wheat germ, baking powder and salt alternately with the milk. Mix well. Pinch off pieces and flatten with a fork, or roll out and cut squares. Place on greased baking sheets and prick with a fork. Bake for 10 – 15 minutes or until they are golden brown.

# Savoury Biscuits

2  cups wholemeal flour
2  teaspoons dry mustard
1  teaspoon salt
2  tablespoons thyme, or marjoram, or
   oregano, or chives, or lovage or parsley
   or pinch cayenne

½  cup butter
1  cup grated cheddar cheese
½  cup Parmesan cheese
poppy seeds or sesame seeds or wheat
   germ

Combine the flour, mustard, salt and herbs. Rub in the butter and cheeses and add a little milk if it is too dry. Shape into little balls and roll in poppy or sesame seeds or wheat germ. Bake on a greased tray at 350 °F/180 °C for 12 – 15 minutes.

Sweet herbs and spices come into their own in cakes and biscuits

# Desserts

Spices, honey and herbs have been used as sweetening agents since the Middle Ages. The crusaders brought sugar cane from the Mediterranean and sugar became such a highly prized commodity that only well-to-do households enjoyed it. With sugar so easily available all over the world today, recipes for sweet things abound, and the consumption of sugar has reached alarmingly unhealthy proportions in the Western world. It is so much more sensible and healthy to use natural methods of sweetening, and sweet herbs and spices abound.

Sweet spices include angelica, cinnamon, anise, nutmeg, ginger, cardamom, allspice, cloves and vanilla. Sweet herbs include lemon verbena, lemon balm, lemon thyme, rosemary, bergamot, scented geranium, vetiver, rose, violet and myrtle. Fruit puddings, whips, creams and custards all become party treats with the inclusion of these herbs and spices.

A dessert that is always well received is fruit liquidised with a herb or spice or two and a little honey and milk, cream or yoghurt. Served in a tall glass with a long spoon and decorated with herbs, this is a sure favourite.

## Fruit Sorbet

You can vary this recipe with herbs and fruit in season. It is a most refreshing end to a summer meal.

1  cup grated apple
1  cup strawberries
2  cups yoghurt
little honey to taste
1  teaspoon cardamom

1  cup grated guava
1  cup seeded grapes
1  cup grenadilla pulp
2  tablespoons fresh bergamot leaves,
   finely chopped

Blend together all the ingredients in a liquidiser, pour into a glass bowl and freeze until nearly firm. Serve decorated with mint leaves, and violets or rose petals.

# Pancakes with Herbs and Flowers                Makes 10 – 12 pancakes

This is a quick and easy way to make a special dessert with just a few herbs or odd bits of fruit. The combinations are endless.

*1 cup wholemeal flour*
*2 large eggs*
*2 tablespoons sunflower oil*
*little salt*

*1¼ cups warm milk*
*2 tablespoons chopped herb*
*4 tablespoons flowers*

Combine the flour, eggs, oil, salt and milk. Lastly add the chopped herb, e.g. lemon verbena, elder flowers, bergamot, lemon thyme, scented geranium, violets or rose petals, and the flowers, e.g. violets, rose petals, borage flowers or elder flowers.

Lightly grease a frying pan. Drop spoonfuls of batter into the pan, flip when bubbly and cook so that both sides are golden. Add a little more oil, and continue to make the rest, keeping the pancakes warm. Dust with cinnamon and serve with lemon juice and fruit or cream.

# Syllabub

This is an unforgettable special treat and with a change of herbs and spices can be made into many different desserts. I add fruit like peaches, strawberries, litchis or sliced mangoes, and no one can ever get enough of it!

*600 ml thick cream*
*juice of 2 lemons*
*1 tablespoon honey*
*1 tablespoon herb, e.g. lemon balm,*
  *lemon verbena, lemon thyme or scented*
  *geranium*

*150 ml sweet white wine*
*finely grated zest of 2 lemons*
*nutmeg (for dusting)*

Whisk everything together until it thickens. Taste and add more honey if necessary. Leave for an hour or two to chill. Spoon into tall glasses. Dust with nutmeg and decorate with lemon balm leaves. Serve with a long spoon.

# Cheese Cake

Herbs and spices will turn this basic cheese cake into party fare. Add any of the sweet herbs and spices to it and experiment with sesame seeds, sunflower seeds, wheat germ, raisins, coconut and nuts.

*½ cup butter*
*1½ cup sifted wholemeal flour*

*1 egg yolk*
*1 tablespoon honey*

Rub the butter into the flour. Beat the eggs and honey and blend into the flour mixture. Press into a greased dish.

## Filling

*1 cup cottage cheese*
*1 cup cream cheese*
*3 eggs, separated*
*1 cup soft brown sugar*
*½ cup sesame seeds*

*½ cup wheat germ*
*juice and finely grated zest of 1 lemon*
*1 teaspoon herb, e.g. scented geranium or*
  *lemon verbena*
*little allspice*

Rub the cheese through a sieve. Whisk egg whites until stiff. Blend all the ingredients and fold in the egg whites. Pour filling into the case. Sprinkle with wheat germ and allspice. Bake at 350 °F/180 °C for 30 minutes. This cake keeps well in the refrigerator. Serve with lemon grass tea at tea time or as a dessert.

# Drinks and Teas

Hot winter warmers filled with the goodness of herbs are both medicinally beneficial and comforting. Summer cool drinks, iced herb teas and punches have similar properties and by experimenting with these as a base you will find your own favourites.

## Mulled Wine

*2 sticks cinnamon*
*2 sprigs rosemary*
*6 cloves*
*2 sprigs lemon verbena*
*twist of finely pared lemon peel*

*2 cups water*
*1 glass sherry*
*1 bottle red wine or port*
*3 – 6 tablespoons sugar*

Put the herbs, spices and peel into a pan. Boil up with the water. Simmer with the lid on for 20 minutes. Strain. Add sherry, wine and sugar. Warm to just under boiling point. Drink hot. This is excellent for colds and chills and will help you to sleep.

## Herb Wine

This is a simple way to flavour wine. Press one of the following herbs into a bottle of wine:

*clove carnation petals*
*lavender*
*lemon balm*

*mint*
*lemon verbena*
*bergamot*

A stick of cinnamon, or a piece of nutmeg, or 3 – 4 allspice berries or 2 – 3 cloves can also be added. Shake and leave for 2 or 3 days, well corked. Strain.

# Herb Tea

A standard infusion is ¼ *cup fresh herb* to *1 cup boiling water*. Stand, steep and strain. Drink sweetened with honey and a squeeze of lemon juice, or drink plain, hot or cold.

# Fruit Cup

This is the most popular of all drinks. I serve it every day in summer and everyone loves it. I give this recipe at every talk I give and it is a favourite with young and old alike. This is the basic recipe, which can be easily changed.

2  *litres boiling water*
4  *cups spearmint*
1  *cup lemon verbena leaves*

1  *litre fresh, unsweetened, unpreserved*
   *fruit juice*
*honey*

Pour the boiling water over the spearmint and lemon verbena. Steep overnight. Next day pour off through a strainer and add the fruit juice. Sweeten with honey. Refrigerate, decorate with mint sprigs, slices of lemon, etc.

### Other combinations that are refreshing

*bergamot* (tastes like Earl Grey tea) and *guava juice*
*lavender* and *apple juice*
*rosemary* and *orange juice*
*lemon grass* and *lemon juice*
*lemon verbena* and *grapefruit juice*
*pineapple sage* and *pineapple juice*
*lemon thyme* and *grape juice*

# Violet Liqueur

Here you can substitute carnation petals, rose petals, mint or lemon verbena for the violets.

*250 g violets*
*3  cloves*
*500 g soft brown sugar*
*3  allspice berries*
*1  litre cane spirit*

*1  stick cinnamon*
*600 ml water*
*1  nutmeg*
*1 – 3 pieces star anise*

Boil up flower petals with the sugar and spices. Stand, steep and cool. Add the cane spirit. Blend well. Sip as a liqueur or serve over ice-cream.

# Herb Syrup

This is a base for many cool drinks and all the sweet herbs are delicious in this recipe. Add iced water or soda water to this to taste.

2 *cups herb (or combinations), e.g.*
  *lavender, bergamot, mint, etc.*
2 *cups sugar*

3 *cups water*
1 *stick cinnamon*
*twist lemon peel*

Simmer gently for 10 – 15 minutes in a covered pot. Stand, steep, cool and strain. Bottle and then dilute ⅛ – ¼ glass syrup to 1 glass soda or cold water. Serve with ice, sprigs of mint and lemon slices.

# The Cook's Notes

# The Cook's Notes

# The Cook's Notes

# The Cook's Notes

# The Cook's Notes

# The Cook's Garden

# The Culinary Herb Garden

Over the years I have found that the only way to really get to know a herb is by growing it, having it near at hand, and being able to see it, smell it, taste it, propagate it and cook with it. No true cook or 'kitchen artist' can really manage without a few fresh herbs at hand, even if it is only a window box. Five or six herbs can easily be grown in a window box of approximately 90 cm – chives, parsley, marjoram, sage, creeping rosemary and thyme will give a wide range of flavouring. A tub of bay at the kitchen door is also well worth planting, as a fresh bay leaf is infinitely preferable to a dried one. Best of all, make a small herb garden. You will have endless hours of pleasure in it and it need only be a small bit of ground, in full sun. Most herbs need at least 7 hours of sunlight per day (although mints, chervil, lovage and angelica like partial shade) so the general rule is to choose a sunny site if you want your herbs to flourish – and as you will be picking daily they will need to flourish! A hedge of lavender, myrtle or rosemary could surround it, and lemon verbena and elder trees could be planted just outside it to give afternoon shade. Many herbs can be easily grown from seed or cuttings. Here is a list to get you started:

Angelica
Anise
Balm (lemon balm
  or melissa)
Basil
Bay
Bergamot
Borage
Calendula
Capsicum
Caraway
Coriander
Celery
Chervil
Chicory
Chilli
Chives
Comfrey
Dandelion

Dill
Elder
Fennel
Fenugreek
Garlic
Geranium (scented)
Ginger
Horseradish
Lemon grass
Lemon verbena
Lovage
Lucerne
Marjoram
Mint
Mustard
Nasturtium
Nettle
Onion
Oregano

Parsley
Peppermint
Pineapple sage
Rose
Sage
Salad burnet
Savory (summer
  and winter)
Shallot
Sorrel
Spearmint
Tansy
Thyme
Vetiver
Violet
Watercress
Yarrow

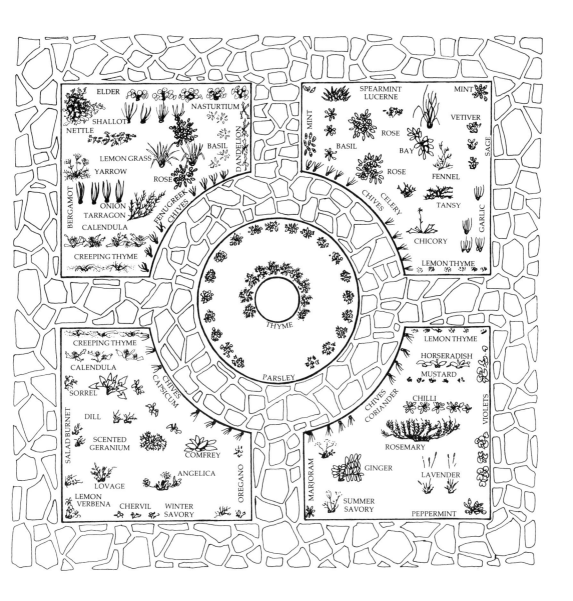

ELDER
NASTURTIUM
SHALLOT
NETTLE
LEMON GRASS
BASIL
YARROW
ROSE
BERGAMOT
ONION
TARRAGON
FENUGREEK
CHIVES
CALENDULA
CREEPING THYME
DANDELION

SPEARMINT
LUCERNE
MINT
MINT
VETIVER
ROSE
BASIL
BAY
ROSE
FENNEL
SAGE
CELERY
CHIVES
TANSY
CHICORY
GARLIC
LEMON THYME

THYME

PARSLEY

CREEPING THYME
CALENDULA
SORREL
CHIVES
CAPSICUM
SALAD BURNET
DILL
SCENTED
GERANIUM
COMFREY
LOVAGE
ANGELICA
LEMON
VERBENA
CHERVIL
WINTER
SAVORY
OREGANO

LEMON THYME
HORSERADISH
MUSTARD
CHIVES
CORIANDER
CHILLI
ROSEMARY
VIOLETS
MARJORAM
GINGER
LAVENDER
SUMMER
SAVORY
PEPPERMINT

243

The plan on p. 243 is the plan I have successfully used for the herb garden at my country kitchen cookery school. Every week students pick whatever herbs are needed for the classes and the size of the garden is perfect for all our needs – and it still looks good even after lavish picking. Adapt and change it to suit you; there are many sizes and shapes to fill each need. This one is my favourite and I have had much pleasure from it. I have edged the beds with rocks and paved the paths for easy maintenance. I have a sundial in the middle, but you might like a bird bath or a bay tree (remember bays grow to huge trees eventually!) or even an urn or pot planted with thyme or sage or a big clump of lemon grass.

Planning and planting a herb garden is the greatest joy and the pleasure you will get from it is endless.

# The Kitchen Garden

A kitchen garden is the next step for the cook, for once you have enjoyed the far superior taste and quality of your own home-grown vegetables and fresh herbs you will never again be satisfied with shop-bought ones. Vegetable growing is easy and with practice you will get to know your particular soil, climate and the seasonal plantings.

Robert Carrier's kitchen garden in England inspired my plan on p. 246 for a beautiful kitchen garden, which even looks good between plantings or in winter when summer's bounty doesn't fill all the spaces. I edge the beds with stones or bricks and gravel or pave the paths for easy maintenance and for dry feet when picking daily for the kitchen. I make full use of every bit of space and on the fence surrounding the garden I grow honeysuckle (which I use for garnishing fruit dishes and syrup), climbing Crimson Glory roses (for rose petal wine, jelly and syrup), runner beans, su-su squashes, grenadillas and jasmine (for teas). Arches can be raised over the paths, also for climbing plants, and neat rows of lettuces and cabbages can be interplanted with companionable herbs. This garden will give you unending delight and pleasure, and your greatest satisfaction will perhaps be derived from feeding your family and friends so economically. The plan is a basic one, and it can be adapted and changed to any size. My suggestions for planting, too, are merely intended to give you ideas – the rest is up to you. An important rule is to have enough paths for easy accessibility, and it is wise to remember that certain plants thrive in close proximity to others. You will notice that I interplant rather than have blocks of one sort of vegetable, for example celery planted near cabbage will help keep the cabbage moth away, and tomatoes interplanted with marigolds give a better yield of fruit. (See *Growing Herbs with Margaret Roberts* for more information on this aspect.)

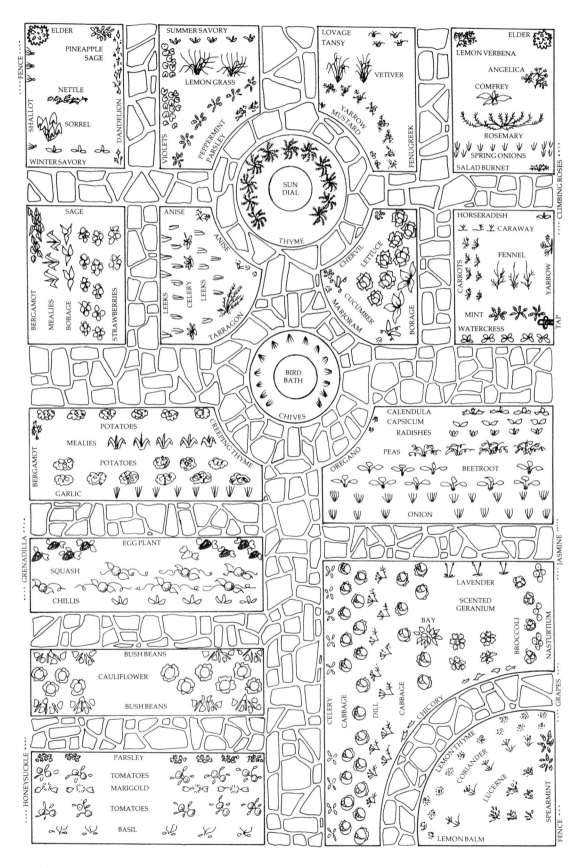

# Nature's
# Medicines

# Therapeutic Plants for Common Ailments

A healthy and balanced diet is one of the most important ways of preventing, alleviating and curing illness. It is simply not enough to treat a condition with a specific medicine or antidote – the inclusion in your diet during illness of soothing, healing and revitalising foods is of fundamental importance. The list below indicates what to include in your diet both during illness and as a preventative if you are prone to a particular ailment. However, be sure *always* before starting a home treatment to consult your doctor.

The more I work with students in my classes and answer the same questions repeatedly, the more I realise how easy it is to plunge into food or herb therapy to the exclusion of other foods. So my advice, which echoes that of my father as I stepped into the adult world is, 'Everything in moderation'. By all means include health-giving herbs, spices, fruit and vegetables in your diet but don't become fanatical. A healthy balance in living, eating and thinking is the only way to become a rounded human being. Always consult a doctor or homoeopathic doctor before trying home remedies, and always be sure of the identification of the herb you are using. This list is merely to encourage in your daily diet the use of nature's medicines and prophylactics.

A daily salad is of supreme importance in your diet, as is the exclusion of alcohol, strong tea and coffee, chocolates, sweets, refined flours and sugars, carbonated drinks, instant foods, pre-cooked packaged foods, fried food, preserved and tinned foods – in fact any food that is not natural. What you eat is of fundamental importance to your health and beauty. If South Africans would take advantage of the magnificent fruit, vegetables and herbs they have so abundantly at hand, we would have the makings of a beautiful, healthy nation – and that is the aim of this book!

## THERAPEUTIC PLANTS FOR COMMON AILMENTS CHART

ABDOMINAL PAIN:
mint, mushrooms, kale, peas, potatoes, rice, soybeans, tomatoes, oats.

ABSCESS:
figs, pumpkin, bergamot, potatoes.

ACIDOSIS:
Brussels sprouts, dandelion greens, endive, guavas, loquats, kale, parsley, peaches, pears, green pepper, quince.

| | |
|---|---|
| ACNE: | rhubarb, nasturtium, elder, comfrey, salad burnet. |
| ALCOHOLISM: | oranges, sunflower seeds, sprouts, lucerne. |
| ANAEMIA: | apples, beetroot, apricots, artichokes, barley, brazil nuts, broccoli, Brussels sprouts, cabbage, cauliflower, spinach, mealies, dandelion greens, figs, dates, kelp, endives, lemons, lettuce, mustard greens, guavas, grapefruit, horseradish, chicory, grapes, nettle, pumpkin, parsley, peas, pepper (cayenne), raisins, prunes, soybeans, tomatoes, watercress, pecan nuts. |
| ANTIBIOTIC: | garlic, grapes, nasturtium, radish, thyme. |
| ANTISEPTIC: | bay, garlic, lavender, myrtle, sage, thyme, quince. |
| APPETITE LOSS: | apricots, asparagus, beetroot, beans, cabbage, broccoli, carrots, mealies, lettuce, mustard greens, oranges, pawpaw, peas, sweet potatoes. |
| ARTERIES, hardening: | Brussels sprouts, garlic, cabbage, thyme, watercress, parsley. |
| ARTERIOSCLEROSIS: | spinach, watercress, celery, parsley, lovage, borage, comfrey, salad burnet, cabbage, mealies. |
| ARTHRITIS: | celery, comfrey, garlic, mustard, nettle, parsley, asparagus, beans, beetroot, melons, spanspek, carrots, cucumbers, green leafy vegetables, brown rice, popcorn, sunflower seeds, sesame seeds, pomegranate, pumpkin, turnips, quince, buck-wheat, mustard greens, sprouts. |
| ASTHMA: | apples, apricots, barley, cabbage, carrots, cauliflower, celery, figs, garlic, guavas, comfrey, ginger, horseradish, lemons, nectarines, peaches, peppers, raisins, turnips. |
| BACKACHE: | cabbage, corn, comfrey. |
| BAD BREATH: | barley, kale, mushrooms, peas, potatoes, rice, soybeans, tomatoes, mints, sage, rosemary, comfrey, parsley, turnip greens. |
| BALDNESS: | asparagus, barley, cabbage, figs, lettuce, oats, spinach, strawberries, tomatoes. |
| BILIOUSNESS: | mint, rosemary, cauliflower, endives, Jerusalem artichokes, lemon balm. |
| BLADDER AILMENTS: | cabbage, cauliflower, kale, melons, kohlrabi, celery, borage, parsley, mustard greens, nectarines, spinach, squash (summer), turnip greens, asparagus. |

| | |
|---|---|
| BLADDER STONES: | beets, celery, peaches, squash. |
| BLEEDING: | grapefruit, guavas, horseradish, kale, lemons, oranges, parsley, peppers, spinach, tomatoes, turnip greens, yarrow, watercress, comfrey. |
| BOILS: | bananas, nasturtium, pumpkin, onions. |
| BONES, weakness of: | currants, grapefruit, guavas, horseradish, kale, kohlrabi, lemons, oranges, parsley, peppers, rice, spinach, tomatoes, turnip greens, watercress, wheat. |
| BREATH, shortness of: | barley, brazil nuts, peas, pecan nuts, soybeans, |
| BRONCHITIS: | apricots, asparagus, beans, beet greens, broccoli, cabbage, carrots, corn, dandelion, dates, elderberry, endives, garlic, bergamot, kale, leeks, lettuce, comfrey, mustard greens, oranges, pawpaws, onions, parsley, pecan nuts, peaches, peas, pineapples, plums, potatoes, spanspek melons, honeydew melons, sweet potatoes, rhubarb, spinach, naartjies, turnip greens, watercress. |
| CANCER: | carrots, green vegetables, violets, grapes, almonds. |
| CARTILAGES, weak: | broccoli, Brussels sprouts, cauliflower, currants, grapefruit, guavas, horseradish, kale, lemons, oranges, parsley, peppers, spinach, tomatoes, turnip greens, watercress. |
| CATARACTS: | apples, beetroot, broccoli, cabbage, carrots, coconut, dandelion, grapefruit, lemons, lettuce, prunes, turnips, watercress. |
| CATARRH: | apples, apricots, Brussels sprouts, carrots, celery, cherries (fresh), endives, figs, garlic, ginger, gooseberries, grapefruit, guavas, Jerusalem artichokes, kumquats, lettuce, lucerne, parsley, pears, pineapples, naartjies, radishes, raisins, strawberries, sage, thyme. |
| CHOLESTROL, excessive: | olives, borage, parsley, peas, pineapples, tomatoes, sprouts, fresh mealies, mealiemeal. |
| CIRCULATION, poor: | dandelion greens, guavas, comfrey. |

| | |
|---|---|
| COLDS: | carrots, broccoli, Brussels sprouts, cauliflower, currants, dandelion greens, elderberries, garlic, grapefruit, guavas, horseradish, kale, lemons, onions, oranges, parsley, peppers, spinach, sage, rosemary, ginger, lucerne, mustard, winter savory, tomatoes, turnip greens, watercress. |
| COLITIS: | bananas, cabbage, carrots, dates, eggplant, figs, okra, parsnips, pears, persimmons, salsify, squash, tapioca, mealies. |
| COMPLEXION, poor: | celery, borage, watermelon, gooseberries, grapefruit, honeydew melon, green leafy vegetables, watermelon. |
| CONJUNCTIVITIS: | apples, apricots, asparagus, beans, broccoli, cabbage, carrots, coconuts, corn, dandelion greens, endives, grapefruit, kale, lemons, lettuce, mustard greens, oranges, pawpaws, parsley, peaches, peas, pecan nuts, potatoes, sweet potatoes, prunes, spinach, turnip greens, watercress, wheat germ. |
| CONSTIPATION: | apricots, asparagus, avocado, barley, beans, beetroot, broccoli, Brussels sprouts, cabbage, melons, cauliflower, celery, Swiss chard, cherries (fresh), coconut, currants, dandelion, dates, eggplant, endives, figs, gooseberries, grapes, Jerusalem artichokes, kale, lettuce, millet, mustard greens, oats, olives, onions, peaches, pears, peas, pecan nuts, peppers, persimmons, pineapples, plums, potatoes, prunes, pumpkin seeds, quince, radishes, raisins, fennel, sprouts, violets, rhubarb, sesame seeds, soybeans, spinach, squash (summer), strawberries, tomatoes, turnips, walnuts. |
| CONVULSIONS: | cabbage, mealies. |
| COUGH: | apricots, asparagus, beans, beet greens, broccoli, cabbage, carrots, dandelion greens, kale, endives, lettuce, mustard greens, melons, mealies, oranges, pawpaw, parsley, peaches, peas, pecan nuts, prunes, sweet potatoes, spinach, turnip greens, watercress, lemon balm, lovage, thyme. |
| CRAMPS: | barley, brazil nuts, walnuts, cherries (fresh), peas, pecan nuts, ginger, rosemary, soybeans. |

| | |
|---|---|
| DANDRUFF: | apples, beetroot, cabbage, carrots, coconut, dandelion, grapefruit, lemons, lettuce, prunes, turnips, watercress, cabbage, celery, dandelion greens, endives, olives, parsley, rosemary, soybeans, strawberries, apples, nettle, naartjies. |
| DEPRESSION: | barley, walnuts, brazil nuts, broccoli, cabbage, mealies, kale, mushrooms, peas, pecan nuts, potatoes, rice, soybeans, tomatoes, turnip greens, lemon balm, lavender, ginger. |
| DIARRHOEA: | bananas, barley, mealies, guavas, kale, peas, potatoes, sweet potatoes, rice, squash, tapioca, geranium (scented), quince, apples, ginger, yarrow. |
| DIGESTION, aid: | cayenne, garlic, grapefruit, horseradish, kelp, lemons, peaches, pears, mint, sage, strawberries, peppermint, ginger. |
| DIZZINESS: | barley, cabbage, kale, mushrooms, onion, peas, potatoes, rice, soybeans, tomatoes, turnip greens, rosemary, mint, lemon balm, mealies. |
| DYSENTERY: | apples, beetroot, coconut, scented geranium, ginger, quince. |
| DYSPEPSIA: | mint, gooseberries, parsley, pineapple. |
| EAR INFECTIONS: | carrots, dandelion greens, endives, kale, lettuce, mealies, mustard greens, pawpaw, parsley, peaches, peas, sweet potatoes, pecan nuts, prunes, spinach, turnip greens, watercress. |
| ECZEMA: | salad burnet, strawberries, calendula, cabbage, grapes, dandelion greens, lemons, mealies, nettle, soybeans. |
| EMACIATION: | avocado, beans, cashew nuts, chestnuts, mealies, dandelion greens, figs, hickory, kale, kelp, millet, olives, peanuts, pecan nuts, raisins, sesame seeds. |
| EMOTIONAL UPSETS: | raisins, sage, rosemary, apples, bananas, lemon balm, lavender. |
| ENERGY LOSS: | apricots, asparagus, barley, beans, beetroot, walnuts, brazil nuts, broccoli, Brussels sprouts, cabbage, carrots, cauliflower, mealies, currants, dandelion greens, endives, grapefruit, guavas, horseradish, kale, lemons, lettuce, mustard greens, oranges, pawpaw, parsley, peaches, peanuts, peas, pecan nuts, peppers, potatoes, sweet potatoes, rosemary, lucerne, prunes, soybeans, spinach, tomatoes, turnip greens, watercress, sunflower seeds. |

| | |
|---|---|
| EYESIGHT, poor: | acorns, apples, beetroot, broccoli, cabbage, carrots, coconut, dandelion, grapefruit, lemons, lettuce, onions, peanuts, prunes, turnips, borage, calendula, chicory, tansy, watercress, grapes, strawberries, nasturtium. |
| FAINTING: | barley, walnuts, brazil nuts, peas, pecans, soybeans, rosemary, lucerne, sunflower seeds. |
| FATIGUE: | barley, beans, cabbage, corn, oats, peas, rice, rye, wheat, lucerne, thyme, borage, watercress. |
| FERTILITY, improvement: | barley, beans, mealies, lettuce, peas, rice, rye, parsley, comfrey. |
| FEVER: | watermelon, spanspek, borage, garlic, strawberries, grapefruit, kumquats, mangoes, grapes, parsley, watercress. |
| GALLSTONES: | apples, apricots, celery, gooseberries, grapefruit, olives, parsley, radishes, squash, tomatoes. |
| GAS, abdominal: | beetroot, endives, garlic, angelica, anise, asparagus, mints, bergamot, lemon verbena, tarragon, olives, peaches, quince, figs, nectarines, plums, tomatoes, caraway, mustard, barley. |
| GENITO-URINARY SYSTEM AILMENTS: | apricots, asparagus, beans, beetroot, broccoli, cabbage, mealies, dandelion greens, endives, kale, lettuce, mustard greens, oranges, pawpaw, peaches, peas, pecan nuts, sweet potatoes, prunes, spinach, turnip greens, watercress, borage, parsley, tansy, celery, lucerne, nettle, ginger. |
| GLANDS, weak: | artichokes, broccoli, kelp, oats, rye. |
| GOITRE: | cabbage, carrots, celery, cucumbers, grapes, lettuce, mushrooms, oranges, pineapples, lucerne, thyme. |
| GONORRHOEA: | apples, beetroot, dandelion greens, onions, garlic. |
| GOUT: | beetroot, cabbage, cauliflower, cherries, endives, figs, grapes, kale, lettuce, parsnips, strawberries, tomatoes, turnip greens. |
| GUM AILMENTS: | broccoli, Brussels sprouts, cauliflower, grapefruit, guavas, horseradish, kale, lemons, oranges, parsley, peppers, spinach, tomatoes, turnip greens, watercress, sage, oregano, lucerne. |
| HAEMORRHOIDS: | bananas, beans, cabbage, parsnips, persimmons, plums, sweet potatoes, prunes, pumpkin, squash, mealies. |

| | |
|---|---|
| HAIR, improvement: | apples, apricots, asparagus, beetroot, rosemary, sage, broccoli, cabbage, carrots, coconut, grapefruit, lemons, lettuce, oats, onions, peanuts, prunes, radishes, rice, squash, turnips, watercress, nettles, sweet basil, bergamot, quince, rosemary. |
| HEADACHES: | barley, beans, beetroot, walnuts, brazil nuts, kale, lettuce, peas, rice, tomatoes, rosemary, violet, borage, lavender. |
| HEART, weak: | walnuts, brazil nuts, peas, pecan nuts, soybeans. |
| HIGH BLOOD PRESSURE: | barley, broccoli, carrots, cauliflower, celery, cucumbers, endives, garlic, guavas, kumquats, onions, nectarines, parsley, peaches, pears, peppers, pineapples, spinach, squash, straw-berries, naartjies, tomatoes, turnip greens, purslane. |
| HOARSENESS: | *see* Voice. |
| IMPOTENCE: | dates, kelp, barley, comfrey, lettuce. |
| INDIGESTION: | beans, beetroot, carrots, cucumbers, gooseberries, kale, peas, potatoes, pumpkin, rice, ginger, grenadilla, rosemary, mints, lavender, nasturtium, oregano, lemon verbena, lemon thyme, anise, angelica, chicory, coriander, fennel, dill, caraway, spinach, strawberries, tomatoes, turnips. |
| INFECTIONS: | broccoli, Brussels sprouts, cauliflower, currants, endives, grapefruit, guavas, horseradish, kale, chives, garlic, lemons, oranges, parsley, peppers, spinach, tomatoes, turnips, watercress, comfrey, mustard. |
| INFLUENZA: | sage, comfrey, mustard, leeks, lemons, onions, winter savory, lucerne, thyme, violets. |
| INSECT BITES: | borage, comfrey, lemons, mint. |
| INSOMNIA: | apples, avocado, barley, walnuts, brazil nuts, cabbage, carrots, celery, mealies, kale, leeks, lemon balm, lavender, lettuce, mushrooms, onions, parsnips, pecan nuts, peas, potatoes, rice, scented geranium, soybeans, spinach, tomatoes, turnip greens. |
| INTESTINE CLEANSER: | cabbage, apples, watermelon. |

| | |
|---|---|
| IRRITABILITY: | barley, beans, walnuts, brazil nuts, cabbage, mealies, kale, lettuce, mushrooms, peas, pecan nuts, potatoes, rice, soybeans, tomatoes, turnip greens, sunflower seeds, lucerne, watercress, borage, comfrey. |
| JAUNDICE: | oats, asparagus, elderberries, parsley, rosemary. |
| JOINT PAINS: | blackcurrants, broccoli, Brussels sprouts, cauliflower, grapefruit, guavas, horseradish, kale, lemons, oranges, parsley, peppers, spinach, tomatoes, turnip greens, watercress. |
| KIDNEY, improvement: | asparagus, avocado, beetroot, cabbage, spanspek, cauliflower, celery, dandelion greens, grapes, kohlrabi, mangoes, olives, parsnips, borage, celery, ginger, nettle, parsley, lucerne, radishes, spinach, squash, strawberries, watercress, watermelon. |
| KIDNEY STONES: | apples, parsley, peaches, thyme, squash. |
| LACTATION, improvement: | apricots, asparagus, beans, broccoli, cabbage, spanspek, carrots, corn, dandelion greens, endives, kale, lettuce, mustard greens, oranges, pawpaw, parsley, peaches, peas, pecan nuts, sweet potatoes, prunes, spinach, turnip greens, watercress. |
| LEGS, stiffness: | lucerne, cabbage, mealies. |
| LIMBS, swelling: | barley, walnuts, brazil nuts, peas, pecan nuts, soybeans. |
| LIPS, sores: | barley, kale, mushrooms, peas, potatoes, rice, soybeans, tomatoes, turnip greens, cornflour. |
| LIVER, improvement: | asparagus, beans, beetroot, broccoli, cabbage, carrots, cauliflower, mealies, cucumbers, dates, endives, gooseberries, lemons, lettuce, limes, onions, parsley, peaches, pomegranates, potatoes, watercress, comfrey, borage, spring onions, nasturtium, nettle, celery, quince, raisins, raspberries, sesame seeds, spinach, strawberries, tomatoes, turnip greens, walnuts. |
| LOW BLOOD PRESSURE: | barley, brazil nuts, brown rice, cucumber, celery, currants, dandelion greens, dates, leeks, onions, peas, pecan nuts, sweet potatoes, pumpkin, raisins, soybeans, walnuts. |
| LUMBAGO: | comfrey, beetroot, lucerne, cabbage. |

| | |
|---|---|
| LUNG AILMENTS: | beans, broccoli, cabbage, melon, comfrey, sage, thyme, celery, carrots, mealies, dandelion greens, lucerne, endives, kale, lettuce, mustard greens, oranges, pawpaws, peaches, peas, pecan nuts, spinach. |
| MAMMARY GLANDS, insufficient milk: | *See* Lactation. |
| MENSTRUATION, irregular: | barley, beans, beetroot, ginger, lettuce, parsley, peas, youngberries, rice, soybeans, yarrow, strawberries, celery. |
| MISCARRIAGE, prevention: | barley, beans, brazil nuts, lettuce, peas, rice, rye, mealies. |
| MUSCULAR pain: | barley, walnuts, brazil nuts, peanuts, peas, pecan nuts, soybeans, lucerne, comfrey, rosemary. |
| NAILS, improvement: | apples, beetroot, broccoli, cabbage, coconut, carrots, carrot tops, cucumber, dandelions, grapefruit, kohlrabi, lemons, lettuce, oats, onions, parsnips, prunes, radishes, rice, sunflower seeds. |
| NERVOUSNESS: | almonds, avocado, barley, beetroot, cabbage, maize oil, dates, eggplant, lemon balm, nasturtium, lavender, lettuce, mushrooms, peas, potatoes, rice, soybeans, tomatoes, turnip greens, scented geranium. |
| OBESITY: | apples, artichokes, beetroot, broccoli, Brussels sprouts, cabbage, melons, carrots, cauliflower, celery, chard, cherries, endives, gooseberries, grenadillas, grapefruit, guavas, honeydew melon, kumquat, lemons, lettuce, loquats, nectarines, okra, onions, oranges, parsley, peppers, pineapples, plums, pomegranates, radishes, raspberries, rhubarb, spinach, tomatoes, turnip greens, watercress, fennel, celery, asparagus, garlic, watermelon. |
| OSTEOPOROSIS: | celery, dates, figs, kale, mustard greens, raisins, sesame seeds, turnip greens, comfrey. |
| OVERWEIGHT: | apricots, asparagus, green beans, broccoli, beet greens, melon, cabbage, carrots, dandelion greens, endives, kale, lettuce, mustard greens, oranges, pawpaw, parsley, peaches, peas, spinach, turnip greens, watercress, watermelon, fennel. |
| PANCREAS, improvement: | cabbage, mealies, melons. |
| PERSPIRATION, lack of: | elderberries. |

256

| | |
|---|---|
| PIMPLES: | apple cider vinegar, beetroot, salad burnet, rhubarb, nasturtium, elder, comfrey, green leafy salads. |
| PLEURISY: | figs, okra, onions, persimmons, sweet potatoes, prunes, spinach, comfrey, violets. |
| PROSTATE: | pumpkin seeds, sunflower seeds, mealies. |
| RESTLESSNESS: | almonds, barley, beets, cherries, lemon balm, lavender, mealies, dandelions, prunes, raisins, spinach, walnuts. |
| RHEUMATISM: | artichokes, asparagus, watermelon, celery, cherries, cucumbers, dandelion greens, comfrey, endives, figs, grapes, honeydew melon, spanspek, kale, kelp, lettuce, mustard greens, nectarines, oranges, parsley, rhubarb, strawberries, tomatoes, watercress, garlic, nettle, yarrow. |
| SCALP, improvement: | apricots, asparagus, beans, beet greens, broccoli, cabbage, nettle, rosemary, sweet basil, bergamot, melons, carrots, mealies, dandelion greens, endives, kale, lettuce. |
| SINUS: | mints, horseradish, onions, tomatoes. |
| SKIN, improvement: | acorn, apples, beet greens, broccoli, cabbage, calendula, carrots, cauliflower, cherries, coconut, dandelion greens, figs, grapefruit, grapes, kale, lemons, lettuce, peaches, pears, prunes, turnip greens, watercress, melons, rhubarb, nasturtium, elder, comfrey, salad burnet, naartjies. |
| STERILITY: | almonds, apricots, asparagus, beans, beet greens, broccoli, cabbage, carrots, mealies, dandelion greens, endives, kale, lettuce, mustard greens, oranges, pawpaw, parsley, peaches, peas, pecan nuts, sweet potatoes, spinach, turnip greens, watercress. |
| STOMACH CRAMPS: | apples, beetroot, broccoli, mint, ginger, lemon balm, lemon verbena, cabbage, carrots, coconut, dandelion greens, lemons, lettuce, prunes, sage, fennel. |
| TEETH, saving enamel: | apricots, asparagus, beans, beetroot, broccoli, cabbage, melons, carrots, corn, dandelion greens, endives, kale, lettuce, mustard greens, oranges, pawpaw, parsley, peaches, peas, pecan nuts, sweet potatoes, prunes, spinach, turnip greens, watercress. |

| | |
|---|---|
| UNDERWEIGHT: | apples, beetroot, broccoli, cabbage, carrots, coconut, dandelion greens, prunes, lucerne, comfrey, nettle, elder, thyme. |
| URIC ACID, excessive: | grapes, fennel, watermelon. |
| URINATION, painful: | carrots, barley water, watermelon, asparagus, parsley, celery. |
| URINARY TRACT, diseases: | apples, lettuce, parsley, borage, salad burnet, asparagus, fennel, celery. |
| URINE, insufficient flow: | cucumbers, watermelon, spanspek, grapes, pawpaw, celery, asparagus. |
| VOICE, hoarseness: | apricots, asparagus, barley, beans, beetroot, walnuts, brazil nuts, broccoli, cabbage, carrots, mealies, dandelion greens, endives, kale, lettuce, mustard greens, oranges, pawpaw, parsley, peaches, peas, sweet potatoes, prunes, spinach, nasturtium, marjoram, sage, thyme, tarragon, rosemary, yarrow, bergamot. |
| VOMITING, prevention: | barley, mint, bergamot, ginger, lemon. |
| WORMS, removal: | apples, cherries, onions, peaches, peppers, pineapples, pomegranates, pumpkin seeds, sesame seeds, rosemary, sweet basil, garlic, nasturtium. |
| WOUNDS, to aid healing: | bergamot, calendula, comfrey, nasturtium, thyme, sage, elder, violet, sorrel. |

# Epilogue

Now that you have read these pages, my hope is that this book will create a new awareness, hope and excitement in those who have been needing a boost to their health, cooking and thinking. The lonely path I once walked in my quest for healing plants, nature's medicines, is no longer so and I now have many friends with whom to share my interest. My long years of study and research into these precious plants are daily being rewarded by those who search as I have. This book is intended to inspire you, the reader, to explore the wonders of natural medicine in the food we eat and in so doing develop into a healthy, happy and fulfilled human being. You are an heir to South Africa's green heritage and it is your responsibility to inspire in your children, your neighbours and your friends a concern for healthy and correct living.

Should you need help or advice, I would love to be of some assistance, and with so many years of cooking for health behind me, I like to think I could be. The Herbal Centre Country Kitchen Cookery School is at your service.

Herbal Centre Country Kitchen Cookery School
P O Box 41
De Wildt 0251
Transvaal
South Africa

# CULINARY HERB AND SPICE CHART

| | SOUPS | STOCKS, GRAVIES | SAUCES, STUFFINGS | SALADS | SALAD DRESSINGS | ROOT VEGETABLES | VEGETABLE DISHES | GARNISHING | SAVOURY RICE, PASTA | DAIRY FOODS | EGG DISHES | MEAT DISHES | FISH DISHES | POULTRY DISHES | SWEET DISHES, PUDDINGS | BAKING BREADS, BISCUITS, CAKES | JAMS, JELLIES, SYRUPS | VINEGARS, PICKLES, CHUTNEY | TEAS, COOLDRINKS | WINE, LIQUEURS, MEAD, ALE |
|---|---|---|---|---|---|---|---|---|---|---|---|---|---|---|---|---|---|---|---|---|
| ALLSPICE | ★ | | ★ | | | | ★ | | ★ | ★ | | | ★ | | ★ | ★ | ★ | | ★ | ★ |
| ANGELICA | | | | ★ | | | | ★ | | ★ | | | | | ★ | ★ | ★ | | ★ | |
| ANISE | | | ★ | | | ★ | ★ | | ★ | ★ | | | | | ★ | ★ | ★ | | ★ | ★ |
| BALM, LEMON, MELISSA | | | | ★ | | ★ | ★ | ★ | ★ | ★ | ★ | | ★ | | ★ | ★ | ★ | | ★ | ★ |
| BASIL | ★ | ★ | ★ | ★ | ★ | ★ | ★ | ★ | ★ | ★ | ★ | ★ | ★ | ★ | | ★ | | ★ | | |
| BAY | | ★ | ★ | | ★ | | | ★ | ★ | | ★ | ★ | ★ | ★ | | | | ★ | | |
| BERGAMOT | | | ★ | | | ★ | | | | ★ | | | | | ★ | ★ | | ★ | ★ | ★ |
| BORAGE | ★ | ★ | | ★ | | | ★ | ★ | ★ | | ★ | | ★ | ★ | ★ | | | ★ | ★ | ★ |
| CARAWAY | | ★ | ★ | | ★ | | ★ | ★ | ★ | ★ | ★ | ★ | ★ | ★ | ★ | ★ | | ★ | ★ | ★ |
| CARDAMOM | | | | | | | | | ★ | ★ | | | | ★ | ★ | ★ | ★ | ★ | ★ | ★ |
| CAYENNE | ★ | ★ | ★ | ★ | ★ | ★ | ★ | ★ | ★ | ★ | ★ | ★ | ★ | ★ | | | | ★ | | |
| CELERY | ★ | ★ | ★ | ★ | ★ | | | ★ | ★ | | ★ | ★ | ★ | ★ | | | | ★ | | |
| CHAMOMILE | | | | | | | | | | ★ | | | | | ★ | ★ | ★ | | ★ | ★ |
| CHERVIL | ★ | ★ | ★ | ★ | ★ | ★ | ★ | ★ | ★ | ★ | ★ | ★ | ★ | ★ | | | | ★ | ★ | |
| CHIVES | ★ | ★ | ★ | ★ | ★ | ★ | ★ | ★ | ★ | ★ | ★ | ★ | ★ | ★ | | | | ★ | | |
| CINNAMON | | | | | | ★ | | ★ | | ★ | | | | | ★ | ★ | ★ | ★ | ★ | ★ |
| CLOVES | | | | | | ★ | | | | ★ | | ★ | ★ | ★ | ★ | ★ | | ★ | ★ | ★ |
| CORIANDER | ★ | | ★ | | ★ | | ★ | | ★ | ★ | | ★ | | ★ | ★ | ★ | | ★ | | |
| CUMIN | | | ★ | | ★ | ★ | | | ★ | ★ | ★ | ★ | | ★ | ★ | ★ | ★ | ★ | ★ | ★ |
| DANDELION | ★ | | ★ | ★ | | | ★ | ★ | ★ | | ★ | ★ | ★ | ★ | | | | ★ | | |
| DILL | ★ | ★ | ★ | ★ | ★ | ★ | ★ | ★ | ★ | | ★ | ★ | ★ | ★ | | ★ | | ★ | ★ | ★ |
| ELDER FLOWER BERRY | | | | | | | | ★ | | ★ | | | | | ★ | ★ | ★ | | ★ | ★ |
| FENNEL | ★ | ★ | ★ | ★ | ★ | | ★ | ★ | ★ | ★ | ★ | ★ | ★ | ★ | | ★ | | ★ | ★ | |
| GARLIC | ★ | ★ | ★ | ★ | ★ | ★ | ★ | | ★ | ★ | ★ | ★ | ★ | ★ | ★ | | | ★ | | |
| GERANIUM, SCENTED | | | | | | | | ★ | | ★ | | | | | ★ | ★ | ★ | | ★ | ★ |
| GINGER | | | ★ | | | ★ | ★ | | ★ | ★ | | | ★ | | ★ | ★ | ★ | ★ | ★ | ★ |
| HORSERADISH | | ★ | ★ | | ★ | ★ | | | | ★ | ★ | ★ | ★ | ★ | | | | ★ | | |
| LAVENDER | | | | | | | | | | ★ | | ★ | | | ★ | ★ | ★ | | ★ | ★ |
| LEMON VERBENA | | | | | | | | | | | | | | | ★ | ★ | ★ | | ★ | ★ |

| | SOUPS | STOCKS, GRAVIES | SAUCES, STUFFINGS | SALADS | SALAD DRESSINGS | ROOT VEGETABLES | VEGETABLE DISHES | GARNISHING | SAVOURY RICE, PASTA | DAIRY FOODS | EGG DISHES | MEAT DISHES | FISH DISHES | POULTRY DISHES | SWEET DISHES, PUDDINGS | BAKING BREADS, BISCUITS, CAKES | JAMS, JELLIES, SYRUPS | VINEGARS, PICKLES, CHUTNEY | TEAS, COOLDRINKS | WINE, LIQUEURS, MEAD, ALE |
|---|---|---|---|---|---|---|---|---|---|---|---|---|---|---|---|---|---|---|---|---|
| LOVAGE | ★ | ★ | ★ | ★ | ★ | ★ | ★ | ★ | ★ | ★ | ★ | ★ | ★ | ★ | | | | ★ | | |
| MACE | | | ★ | | ★ | ★ | | | ★ | ★ | ★ | | ★ | | ★ | ★ | ★ | ★ | ★ | |
| MARJORAM | ★ | ★ | ★ | ★ | ★ | ★ | ★ | ★ | ★ | ★ | ★ | ★ | ★ | ★ | | | | ★ | | |
| MINT VARIETIES | | | ★ | ★ | ★ | ★ | ★ | ★ | ★ | ★ | | ★ | | | ★ | ★ | ★ | ★ | ★ | ★ |
| MUSTARD | | ★ | ★ | | ★ | | | | ★ | ★ | ★ | ★ | ★ | ★ | | | | ★ | | |
| NASTURTIUM | ★ | | ★ | ★ | ★ | | ★ | ★ | ★ | | ★ | | ★ | ★ | | | | ★ | | |
| NETTLE | ★ | ★ | ★ | | | | ★ | | ★ | | | ★ | ★ | | | | | ★ | ★ | ★ |
| NUTMEG | | | ★ | | ★ | ★ | ★ | ★ | ★ | ★ | ★ | | ★ | ★ | ★ | ★ | ★ | ★ | ★ | ★ |
| OREGANO | ★ | ★ | ★ | | ★ | ★ | | ★ | ★ | ★ | ★ | ★ | ★ | ★ | | | | ★ | | |
| PAPRIKA | ★ | ★ | ★ | | ★ | ★ | ★ | | ★ | | ★ | ★ | ★ | ★ | | | | ★ | | |
| PARSLEY | ★ | ★ | ★ | ★ | ★ | ★ | ★ | ★ | ★ | ★ | ★ | ★ | ★ | ★ | | | | ★ | | |
| PEPPER, GREEN | ★ | ★ | ★ | ★ | ★ | | ★ | ★ | ★ | | ★ | ★ | ★ | ★ | | | | ★ | | |
| PEPPER, GROUND | ★ | ★ | ★ | ★ | ★ | ★ | ★ | | ★ | ★ | ★ | ★ | ★ | ★ | | | | ★ | | |
| ROSE PETALS | | | ★ | | | | ★ | | ★ | | | | | | ★ | ★ | ★ | | ★ | ★ |
| ROSEMARY | | ★ | ★ | | ★ | ★ | ★ | ★ | ★ | ★ | ★ | ★ | ★ | ★ | ★ | ★ | ★ | ★ | ★ | ★ |
| SAFFRON | | | ★ | | ★ | | | | ★ | ★ | ★ | | ★ | ★ | ★ | | | | | ★ |
| SAGE | | ★ | ★ | | ★ | | | | ★ | ★ | ★ | ★ | ★ | ★ | | | | ★ | ★ | ★ |
| SALAD BURNET | ★ | ★ | | ★ | ★ | | ★ | ★ | | | ★ | ★ | | ★ | | | | ★ | | |
| WINTER & SUMMER SAVORY | ★ | ★ | ★ | ★ | ★ | | ★ | ★ | ★ | ★ | ★ | ★ | ★ | ★ | | | ★ | ★ | | |
| SESAME SEED | | | | | ★ | ★ | ★ | | ★ | ★ | | | | | ★ | ★ | | | | |
| SORREL | ★ | ★ | ★ | ★ | ★ | ★ | ★ | ★ | ★ | | | ★ | ★ | ★ | | | | ★ | ★ | |
| SPRING ONIONS | ★ | ★ | ★ | ★ | ★ | ★ | ★ | ★ | ★ | ★ | ★ | ★ | ★ | ★ | | | | ★ | | |
| TANSY | | | | | | | | | ★ | ★ | | ★ | ★ | | ★ | ★ | ★ | ★ | | ★ |
| TARRAGON | ★ | ★ | ★ | ★ | ★ | ★ | ★ | ★ | ★ | | ★ | ★ | ★ | ★ | | | | ★ | | |
| THYME | | ★ | ★ | ★ | ★ | ★ | ★ | ★ | ★ | ★ | ★ | ★ | ★ | ★ | | | | ★ | | |
| THYME, LEMON | | | ★ | | ★ | | | | ★ | ★ | ★ | | ★ | | ★ | ★ | ★ | | ★ | ★ |
| TURMERIC | ★ | ★ | ★ | | | | | | ★ | ★ | ★ | ★ | ★ | ★ | | | | ★ | | |
| VANILLA | | | | | | | | | | | | | | | ★ | ★ | ★ | | ★ | ★ |
| VIOLET | | | | ★ | | | ★ | | ★ | | | | | | ★ | ★ | ★ | | ★ | ★ |
| WATERCRESS | ★ | ★ | ★ | ★ | ★ | ★ | ★ | ★ | ★ | ★ | ★ | ★ | ★ | ★ | | | | ★ | | |
| YARROW | ★ | ★ | ★ | | ★ | | | ★ | ★ | | ★ | ★ | ★ | ★ | | | | | | |

# Index